Product Marketing Wisdom

Real World Lessons on Market Research, Competitive Analysis, Go-To-Market, Storytelling, Sales Enablement, KPIs, and more

Nitin Kartik

Global Top-50 Product Marketing Creator

Karibu Press

PRODUCT MARKETING WISDOM

Karibu Press

Copyright © 2025 by Nitin Kartik

All rights reserved, including the right to reproduce this book or portions thereof in any form whatsoever.
For information, please email info@karibupress.com

First Karibu Press edition January 2025

ISBN 979-8-9920931-0-0 (Paperback)

ISBN 979-8-9920931-1-7 (Hardcover)

ISBN 979-8-9920931-2-4 (eBook)

CONTENTS

- CONTENTS 3
- INTRODUCTION 11
  - Purpose of This Book 11
  - How to Use This Book 12
  - Inspiration and Growth 13
- WISDOM ON THE FOUNDATIONS 15
  - The Definition of Product Marketing 15
  - Core Principles of Product Marketing 16
  - Differentiating Product Marketing from Other Disciplines .. 20
  - Essential Skill: Market & Competitive Research 26
  - Essential Skill: Positioning & Messaging 28
  - Essential Skill: Go-To-Market (GTM) Strategy 30
  - Essential Skill: Storytelling & Content Strategy 32
  - Essential Skill: Sales Enablement & Training 34
  - Essential Skill: Cross-Functional Collaboration 36
  - Essential Skill: Key Performance Indicators 38
  - Essential Skill: Personal Development 40
  - Essential Skill: AI & Technology 42
  - Career Pathways and Evolving Roles 44
- GLOBAL WISDOM WITH HILA LAUTERBACH 53
  - Success in International Product Marketing 53
  - Universal Truths in Product Marketing 54
  - The Ever-Evolving PMM Role 54
  - Regional Flavors of Product Marketing 55
  - Looking Forward 58

WISDOM ON MARKET AND COMPETITIVE RESEARCH............61

Anastasia Albert (Berlin, Germany)....................................... 62
Carolyne Mweberi (Nairobi, Kenya).................................... 64
David Lim (New York, NY, USA) 66
Jan-Eike Rosenthal (Hamburg, Germany) 68
Mason Yu (Chicago, IL, USA) 70
Nida Ateeq (Toronto, ON, Canada) 72
Olena Bomko (Ukraine) 74
Olivier Josefowitz (Israel) 76
Priyanka Mandhyan (San Diego, CA, USA)........................ 78
Randi-Sue Deckard (Dallas Area, TX, USA)....................... 80
Surbhee Mishra (Bengaluru, Karnataka, India).................... 82
Zach Roberts (California, USA)... 84

WISDOM ON POSITIONING AND MESSAGING 87

Aleksi Lehtola (Mexico City Area, Mexico)........................ 88
David LaCombe (New York City, NY, USA) 90
Dom Einhorn (Los Angeles, CA, USA)............................... 92
Liudmila Kiseleva (Washington, DC, USA)........................ 94
Paul Terrasson Duvernon (France & Sweden)..................... 96
Rob Kaminski (Austin, TX, USA) 98
Roger Lanctot (Herndon, VA, USA).................................. 100
Ryan Sorley (Wayland, MA, USA).................................... 102
Shoshana Kordova (Israel) 104
Sid Khaitan (Chicago, IL, USA) 106
Thiago Neres (Ontario, Canada)... 108

WISDOM ON GO-TO-MARKET STRATEGY 111

Akshaya Chandramouli (USA) 112

Archita Fritz (Dusseldorf, Germany)...... 114

Björn W. Schäfer (Zurich, Switzerland)...... 116

Jonathan Pipek (Illinois, USA)...... 118

Kirsten Jepson (Florida, USA)...... 120

Lesia Polivod (Elk Grove Village, IL, USA)...... 122

Mark Assini (Ontario, Canada)...... 124

Meenal Relekar (San Francisco, CA, USA)...... 126

Norman Rohr (Munich, Germany)...... 128

Partho Ghosh (Vancouver, BC, Canada)...... 130

Stuti Dutt (Canada)...... 132

Tzufit Herling (Lisbon, Portugal)...... 134

Yuliya Andreyuk (Portugal)...... 136

WISDOM ON STORYTELLING AND CONTENT STRATEGY...... 139

Andrew Wood (Montreal, Quebec, Canada)...... 140

John Cook (Milton, WI, USA)...... 142

Jordan Rahtz (Denver Area, CO, USA)...... 144

Laura Hall (Germany)...... 146

Lauren Parker (Oakland, CA, USA)...... 148

Madhav Bhandari (San Francisco, CA, USA)...... 150

Nora Stark (Israel)...... 152

Omprakash Karuppanan (Bengaluru, India)...... 154

Oren Blank (Israel)...... 156

Puru Mehta (San Francisco Bay Area, CA, USA)...... 158

Ran Blayer (Tel Aviv-Yafo, Israel)...... 160

Tarun Kishnani (New York, NY, USA)...... 162

WISDOM ON SALES ENABLEMENT AND TRAINING...... 165

Ashley Herbert Popa (Amsterdam, Netherlands)...... 166

Catie Ivey (Atlanta, GA, USA) 168

Deon Jamy Joseph (Milpitas, CA, USA) 170

Dillon McDermott (Boston, MA, USA) 172

Jaren Krchnavi (Munich, Germany) 174

Joe Parlett (Danville, CA, USA) 176

Josh Britton (Harrogate, England, UK) 178

Nitya Kirat (Los Angeles, CA, USA) 180

Russ Somers (Pflugerville, TX, USA) 182

Yitzy Tannenbaum (Israel) 184

WISDOM ON CROSS FUNCTIONAL COLLABORATION 187

Abby Rodrigues (Toronto, ON, Canada) 188

Alexandra "Sasha" Mitroshkina (Turkey) 190

Andrew Hatfield (Brisbane, Australia) 192

Elan Keshen (Toronto, ON, Canada) 194

Hila Lauterbach (California, USA) 196

Leonard Burger (United Kingdom) 198

Mary Lim (Austin, TX, USA) 200

Nicky Dibben (Cambridge, England, UK) 202

Rice Tong (London, United Kingdom) 204

Shobhit Bhutani (San Francisco Area, CA, USA) 206

Stefan Gladbach (Seattle, WA, USA) 208

Tanwistha Gope (Bangalore, India) 210

Vanisha Mittal (Boston, MA, USA) 212

Yael Kahn (Germany) 214

WISDOM ON KEY PERFORMANCE INDICATORS 217

Aaftab Ahluwalia (Toronto, ON, Canada) 218

Aditi Salke (USA) 220

Akshaya Ravi (USA) 222
Alexandre Contador (The Randstad, Netherlands) 224
Ankita Chaturvedi (Gurugram, Haryana, India) 226
Deepika Tripathee (USA) 228
Div Manickam (California, USA) 230
Gab Bujold (Quebec, Canada) 232
Megan Pratt (Salt Lake City Area, UT, USA) 234

WISDOM ON PERSONAL DEVELOPMENT 237
Anna Borbotko (Amsterdam, Netherlands) 238
Bianca Stanescu (Bucharest, Romania) 240
Emily Pick (Bend, OR, USA) 242
Eric Lindroos (Ocean Shores, WA, USA) 244
Esther Akinsola (Lagos, Nigeria) 246
Julian Dawkins (United Kingdom) 248
Michal Lasman (Germany) 250
Natália Tóth (Budapest, Hungary) 252
Nevine Ismael (Toulouse, France) 254
Prashanth Shankara (Ann Arbor, MI, USA) 256
Shirin Shahin (Massachusetts, USA) 258
Shruti Verma (Greater Toronto, ON, Canada) 260
Shuja Hasan (Delhi, India) 262
Stephanie Schwab (Barcelona, Spain) 264
Zach Hoskins (Springfield, MO, USA) 266

WISDOM ON AI AND TECHNOLOGY 269
Akshita Kanumury (Dubai, UAE) 270
Chandrakumar "CK" Pillai (Brussels, Belgium) 272
Dalit Heldenberg (Israel) 274

    Emmanuel Umoh (Oshawa, ON, Canada) 276

    Luka Kankaras (Vienna, Austria) 278

    Spyros Tsoukalas (Athens, Greece) 280

THE FUTURE OF PRODUCT MARKETING 283

    AI and Automation in Product Marketing 283

    The Shift to Customer-Centric Marketing 285

    Cross-Functional Collaboration in a Hybrid Workforce 287

    The Future of Data-Driven Decision Making 289

    The Future of Sustainability and Ethical Marketing 291

    The Future is Fractional 293

    The Best is Yet to Come 295

ACKNOWLEDGEMENTS 297

BY NITIN KARTIK

"Wisdom is not a product of schooling but of the lifelong attempt to acquire it."
- Albert Einstein

INTRODUCTION

INTRODUCTION

Welcome to Product Marketing Wisdom, a curated collection of insights and strategies from over 100 thought leaders in the product marketing community. This book is your companion at every stage of your career—whether you're just starting out or striving to master the craft—offering valuable knowledge to help you thrive in this ever-evolving field.

Purpose of This Book

In today's fast-paced marketplace, product marketing has never been more essential. From startups seeking product-market fit to sales leaders unlocking new markets and corporate strategists exploring acquisitions, the skills of a product marketer are critical. This book serves as a guide to help you navigate these complexities through the wisdom and experiences of industry leaders.

The purpose of this book is threefold, as explained herein.

To Inspire:

Discover the journeys and successes of accomplished product marketers. Each chapter features unique stories and lessons that showcase the potential for growth, creativity, and strategic thinking in the field.

To Educate:

Gain practical insights and actionable takeaways. From sharpening core skills to mastering advanced techniques, this book is packed with knowledge to help you make a lasting impact.

To Empower:

Embrace change and seize new opportunities. By applying proven frameworks, methodologies, and strategies shared by experienced practitioners, you'll be equipped to face challenges head-on and achieve your professional goals.

More than a collection of advice, this book is a call to action. It invites you to embrace your role as a leader, challenge conventional thinking, and drive meaningful impact within your organization.

How to Use This Book

This book is designed to support you at every step of your product marketing journey. Drawing from interviews with over 100 industry experts, it covers key areas of the discipline that directly drive business success. Whether you're sharpening existing skills, exploring new trends, or solving pressing challenges, Product Marketing Wisdom offers the guidance you need to grow.

The following sections share how you can get the most out of this book.

Structured Learning:

The book is organized to take you from foundational concepts to advanced applications. You'll begin with essential skills like Market Research, Positioning, Go-To-Market (GTM) Strategy, Messaging, Sales Enablement, and Key Performance Indicator (KPI) Measurement. Each topic builds on the last, providing you with a solid foundation for growth.

Real-World Insights:

The heart of the book lies in its practical guidance from experienced product marketers. Through case studies, lessons learned, and behind-the-scenes strategies, you'll see how successful professionals tackle real-world challenges.

Navigate with Purpose:

Use the Table of Contents to jump directly to topics that matter most to you. Want to master Positioning? Need help with Go-To-Market strategy?

Looking for inspiration from a specific industry leader? Start where your needs are greatest.

Inspiration and Growth

This book isn't just a resource—it's a roadmap for continuous development. Whether you're navigating a career transition, tackling new challenges, or refining your expertise, the wisdom shared here will support you on your journey. Real-world stories are paired with actionable advice to keep you motivated and focused.

With this introduction complete, let's begin with the foundations of Product Marketing—the essential skills that will set you up for success.

WISDOM ON THE FOUNDATIONS

WISDOM ON THE FOUNDATIONS

Product marketing is a pivotal function within companies, responsible for shaping how products are perceived and adopted by customers. It intersects product development, marketing, and sales to align on positioning, launch, and promotion strategies. The discipline is geared towards answering one essential question: **How can a product best address the needs of its target audience while standing out in the marketplace?** A product marketer not only identifies a product's unique value but communicates it effectively to both customers and internal teams to drive adoption, retention, and revenue.

This section explores the essential definition of product marketing and the core principles that guide its practice, demonstrating its relevance in today's customer-centric market.

The Definition of Product Marketing

At its core, product marketing connects product potential with market needs. It is the practice of bridging the gap between a product's capabilities and the demands of its intended market, ensuring a product not only meets market needs but is also well positioned to achieve success. A strong product marketer develops a deep understanding of the target customer, assesses competitive offerings, crafts clear and resonant positioning and messaging, and supports effective go-to-market (GTM) strategies.

Product marketing roles vary by company size, industry, and maturity. In some organizations, product marketers work closely with product development teams, guiding product features and improvements based on customer feedback. In others, they may focus more on the GTM strategy, supporting sales teams, crafting product narratives, and creating demand generation campaigns. A successful product marketer must be both analytical and creative, understanding data and trends while shaping compelling stories around a product's value.

Core Principles of Product Marketing

To effectively understand Product Marketing, we must become familiar with the following core principles of the field.

Customer-Centricity

The primary principle of product marketing is a relentless focus on the customer. Product marketers prioritize understanding who the customer is, what challenges they face, and how a product can address those pain points. This customer-centric approach starts with market research, which may involve surveys, interviews, and behavioral analysis to gather both quantitative and qualitative insights.

With these insights, product marketers can create detailed personas that capture not only demographics but also the specific problems customers are trying to solve. This empathy-driven approach ensures that all messaging, positioning, and marketing efforts resonate with the target audience. **A customer-centric product marketing strategy builds trust, loyalty, and long-term customer relationships** by showing customers they are heard and understood.

Differentiation and Positioning

In a crowded market, successful product marketing requires clear differentiation. Product marketers must answer why a customer should choose their product over competing alternatives. This process begins with a thorough analysis of the competitive landscape, identifying what differentiates a product in terms of features, price, quality, or brand perception.

Positioning is the foundation of differentiation. A well-defined positioning statement captures the product's unique value and explains why it matters to the target audience. This statement serves as a guide for all marketing and communication efforts, ensuring that customers understand what sets the product apart. For example, Apple's positioning of the iPhone as a premium, user-friendly, and innovative product appeals to customers who prioritize design and usability over price. By clarifying and communicating differentiation, product marketing creates a compelling narrative that resonates with customers and strengthens brand identity.

Cross-Functional Collaboration

Product marketing does not operate in isolation; it thrives on collaboration across departments, from product development and sales to customer success and engineering. Each team brings a unique perspective and set of insights that enriches the product marketing process. Product teams provide technical insights, sales teams offer feedback from prospects, and customer success teams understand pain points in user experience.

Collaboration is especially critical during a product launch. Product marketers work with product managers to finalize features, coordinate with sales to build enablement materials, and partner with marketing to develop promotional campaigns. Regular cross-functional meetings, alignment on KPIs, and open lines of communication are essential for ensuring that all teams work towards a unified goal: the product's success in the market.

Storytelling

In product marketing, storytelling is the art of translating complex product information into compelling narratives that resonate with customers. An effective product marketer crafts a story that not only explains what the product does but also shows why it matters and how it can improve the customer's life. **Storytelling brings the product to life, making it relatable and memorable.**

Storytelling in product marketing involves understanding the customer's journey, from awareness to consideration and decision. Each stage presents an opportunity to address different aspects of the product, from its problem-solving capabilities to its unique benefits. By crafting narratives that connect on an emotional level, product marketers can influence buying decisions and foster brand loyalty.

Data-Driven Decision-Making

Data is fundamental to modern product marketing, guiding every decision from market analysis to campaign optimization. A data-driven approach enables product marketers to validate assumptions, measure success, and make informed adjustments. Key metrics might include customer acquisition cost (CAC), lifetime value (LTV), retention rates, and net promoter scores (NPS). These metrics help product marketers understand what's working and where improvements are needed.

A successful product marketer continuously tests and refines strategies based on data. For instance, analyzing the performance of a product's messaging might reveal that certain phrases resonate more with the target audience, prompting a shift in messaging for future campaigns. Data-driven decision-making not only improves marketing effectiveness but also aligns product marketing efforts with broader business objectives.

Adaptability and Agility

In today's fast-paced business environment, agility is a crucial principle for product marketing success. Market conditions, customer preferences, and competitive landscapes can change rapidly. Product marketers must stay attuned to these shifts and adapt their strategies accordingly. Agile product marketing involves iterative processes, where campaigns are frequently tested, analyzed, and refined based on real-time feedback.

Agility also extends to product development. Product marketers often collaborate with product managers to test new features or pivot strategies based on emerging customer needs. An adaptable product marketing approach ensures that the product remains relevant and competitive, even as market dynamics evolve.

Customer Advocacy

Product marketers play a significant role in fostering customer advocacy, turning satisfied customers into brand ambassadors. By listening to customers, addressing their feedback, and creating value that exceeds expectations, product marketing builds customer loyalty and encourages positive word-of-mouth. Customer advocacy can also be enhanced through user-generated content, testimonials, and case studies, which highlight actual stories of how customers have benefitted from the product.

In many organizations, product marketers manage customer feedback channels, such as NPS surveys or online reviews. **By actively engaging with customers and amplifying their voices, product marketing not only builds trust but also enhances the brand's reputation and credibility.**

Bringing it Together

Product marketing is an essential function that connects product capabilities with customer needs, creating value for both the company and its customers. Defined by its focus on the customer and driven by key principles—customer-centricity, differentiation, cross-functional collaboration, storytelling, data-driven decision-making, adaptability, and customer advocacy—product marketing plays a vital role in achieving product success.

By mastering these principles, product marketers create compelling product experiences, develop strong market positions, and drive sustained growth. The strategic impact of product marketing extends beyond mere sales and revenue; it shapes a brand's relationship with its customers, fosters loyalty, and positions the brand for long-term success. In an increasingly competitive market, organizations that prioritize strong product marketing practices are better equipped to deliver products that not only meet customer needs but also inspire and resonate with them on a deeper level.

Differentiating Product Marketing from Other Disciplines

Product marketing is often mistaken for—or intertwined with—other marketing and product functions, such as brand marketing, content marketing, and product management. While each of these roles shares some common ground, they differ significantly in purpose, responsibilities, and impact within an organization. Product marketing sits at the intersection of product development, marketing, and sales, working to define and communicate a product's value proposition and to drive adoption and engagement. This section explores the distinctive role of product marketing by comparing it with related disciplines and highlighting what sets it apart.

What Product Marketing is and What it is Not

Product marketing takes a product from development to market, driving customer engagement, adoption, and long-term success. Product marketers identify a product's unique value and develop strategies to communicate that value effectively to the intended audience. Unlike other marketing functions that may focus on branding, demand generation, or content creation, product marketing encompasses market research, competitive analysis, customer insights, positioning, messaging, sales enablement, and go-to-market (GTM) strategies. **In short, product marketing's mission is to ensure that the right product reaches the right customer with a message that resonates and encourages action.**

Product Marketing vs. Product Management

Product management and product marketing often work in close collaboration, but they have distinct responsibilities and objectives. Product management focuses on building the right product by defining its features, capabilities, and roadmaps based on market needs and customer feedback. Product managers oversee the product lifecycle from ideation through development and launch, prioritizing features, and coordinating with engineering and design teams to ensure the product aligns with the overall business strategy.

On the other hand, product marketing takes ownership of how the product is positioned and communicated to the market. While a product manager's role revolves around what the product is and how it works, a product marketer is responsible for why the product matters to customers and who it serves best. The two roles can be thought of as complementary halves of a whole, with product management focused on building a product that meets specific needs and product marketing ensuring the product's story resonates with the intended audience.

To illustrate this distinction, imagine a team developing new project management software. The product manager would be responsible for defining features, like task tracking and collaboration tools, based on user feedback. They would prioritize these features and work closely with developers to build them. The product marketer, in contrast, would focus on how to position this software in a crowded market, identifying what differentiates it from competitors, crafting messaging that highlights these differentiators, and working with sales and marketing teams to communicate its value effectively.

Product Marketing vs. Brand Marketing

Brand marketing and product marketing both play essential roles in shaping a company's reputation and driving customer engagement, but their focus and objectives are different. Brand marketing aims to build and maintain a strong, recognizable brand identity that resonates with customers on an emotional level. It encompasses brand strategy, storytelling, and the development of a cohesive brand voice and visual identity. The goal of brand marketing is to create a lasting impression that differentiates the company, fostering trust, loyalty, and long-term relationships with customers.

In contrast, **product marketing centers on a specific product or line of products, focusing on how to bring it to market and promote its unique value to drive adoption**. While brand marketing works at a higher level to shape how people perceive the company, product marketing zeroes in on how to communicate a product's specific benefits, features, and relevance to customer needs.

For instance, a company like Nike invests heavily in brand marketing to cultivate a global identity associated with empowerment, athleticism, and innovation. At the same time, product marketing teams work on promoting specific product lines—such as the latest running shoe—by highlighting unique features like advanced cushioning, responsiveness, and durability. In this way, brand marketing builds an overarching identity and emotional connection, while product marketing drives immediate interest and adoption of specific products.

Product Marketing vs. Content Marketing

Content marketing and product marketing intersect frequently, particularly in creating customer-facing materials that drive awareness and engagement. However, the two functions differ in their strategic aims. Content marketing focuses on generating and distributing valuable content to attract and retain a specific audience, usually with a long-term view toward building brand awareness, trust, and engagement. Content marketers create blog posts, articles, videos, social media posts, and more, designed to inform, entertain, or inspire the target audience.

Product marketing, however, is more targeted in its approach. While content marketing aims broadly to attract and engage potential customers, **product marketing's focus is on driving product adoption and retention**. Product marketing content often includes specific messaging that addresses a product's unique value, aligns with a customer's pain points, and helps to move prospects through the sales funnel. While content marketing is largely educational and relationship-building, product marketing content is focused on directly converting readers or viewers into product users.

Consider a tech company launching a new CRM tool. Content marketing might create a series of blog posts on "best practices in customer relationship management" to drive traffic and build credibility. The product marketing team, in turn, might create case studies, whitepapers, and demo videos specifically designed to showcase the CRM tool's unique features, targeting potential buyers who are further along in the decision-making process.

Product Marketing vs. Demand Generation

Demand generation and product marketing share a goal of driving revenue, but they operate at distinct stages of the buyer's journey and with different objectives. Demand generation focuses on creating interest and leads for the company's offerings, often through a combination of inbound and outbound tactics like webinars, email campaigns, and paid advertising. Its goal is to fill the top of the sales funnel with qualified leads who may eventually convert to customers.

Product marketing, in contrast, is responsible for positioning the product and guiding these leads through the funnel by ensuring the product's value proposition is clear and compelling. While demand generation works to attract potential customers, product marketing equips these prospects with the information they need to make an informed decision. Product marketers often create sales enablement materials, case studies, and testimonials that demand generation teams can use to nurture leads and facilitate conversions.

As an example, consider a B2B SaaS company. The demand generation team might create a lead-generation campaign promoting an eBook on improving business efficiency with digital tools, attracting interest from a range of prospective buyers. The product marketing team would then take over, providing targeted messaging and case studies on how the SaaS product specifically addresses the pain points discussed in the eBook, thereby moving the leads closer to conversion.

Product Marketing vs. Customer Success

While customer success and product marketing both focus on customer engagement and retention, they do so from different perspectives. Customer success teams work to ensure customers are satisfied with the product after purchase, helping them achieve their desired outcomes and resolving any issues that arise. Their role is hands on, focusing on building long-term relationships, managing accounts, and reducing churn through continuous support.

Product marketing, however, is more proactive in its approach to customer engagement. Product marketers anticipate customer needs and provide educational content, user guides, and other resources to ease the onboarding process and increase satisfaction. They may work closely with customer success teams to identify common pain points or areas of confusion and develop targeted campaigns or content to address these challenges.

For instance, if a customer success team identifies a frequent issue with a feature, product marketing might create a video tutorial or FAQ that explains the feature's functionality more clearly. In this way, product marketing supports customer success by helping to prevent issues before they arise, contributing to a smoother customer experience and enhancing overall satisfaction.

The Distinct Value of Product Marketing

Product marketing holds a unique and vital position within an organization, acting as the bridge between product development, sales, and broader marketing efforts. It plays a pivotal role in translating complex technical features into customer-focused benefits, ensuring that the product not only meets market needs but also resonates deeply with target audiences. While other marketing disciplines, such as brand marketing or content marketing, contribute significantly to a company's overall growth, **product marketing's specific blend of market insights, customer understanding, and strategic messaging offers a distinct and critical advantage in driving product adoption and customer loyalty**.

At its core, product marketing ensures that a product fulfills both the technical requirements of the development team and the practical, emotional needs of the customer. While the development team focuses on functionality and innovation, and the sales team is concerned with conversion and closing deals, product marketing's role is to ensure the product speaks directly to the customer. It does this by crafting clear, compelling narratives that not only highlight the product's technical capabilities but also position it in a way that speaks to the customer's pain points, desires, and goals.

For example, a product might be technologically advanced and feature-rich, but if it fails to communicate how these features translate into tangible value for the customer, it may struggle to gain traction in the market. Product marketers take these features and translate them into customer benefits, positioning the product as the solution to specific challenges, ensuring it stands out in a crowded market.

Furthermore, product marketing is essential in aligning the product's messaging with customer expectations. This goes beyond simply understanding what customers need. This deeper level of insight allows product marketers to craft messaging that resonates on an emotional level, leading to stronger brand affinity and more enduring customer relationships. It's this connection that often drives customer loyalty and advocacy long after the initial sale.

The value of product marketing also lies in its ability to integrate feedback loops from the market, the sales team, and customers into future product iterations and marketing strategies. By closely monitoring customers and competitors, product marketers help ensure relevancy and competitiveness over time.

By recognizing the distinct value of product marketing and understanding how it differs from related functions like brand or content marketing, organizations can leverage each discipline's strengths.

Now that we have distinguished Product Marketing from other marketing disciplines, we are ready to discuss some of the essential skills in Product Marketing.

Essential Skill: Market & Competitive Research

Market and competitive research are cornerstone skills for product marketers, serving as the foundation for making informed decisions and crafting impactful strategies. By understanding the market landscape and competitive environment, product marketers can identify opportunities, navigate challenges, and drive product success in a crowded and ever-evolving marketplace.

Market research provides a deep understanding of the industry landscape, including trends, customer behaviors, and emerging opportunities. This insight helps product marketers identify target segments, assess demand, and align products with customer needs. **Knowing the size of the market and its growth potential allows marketers to prioritize efforts effectively, ensuring resources are allocated to the most promising opportunities.** In an increasingly competitive environment, understanding where the market is headed is critical for staying ahead of trends and not being caught off guard by changes in customer preferences or technological advancements.

Additionally, market research enables product marketers to uncover customer pain points, preferences, and unmet needs. These insights are essential for crafting messaging that resonates with the audience and for developing products that address those specific needs. Understanding customers deeply ensures that product marketers can position their solutions as indispensable to their target audience. Without this level of understanding, even the most innovative products may fail to gain traction, as they may not be aligned with the actual needs or desires of the market.

Competitive research is equally critical, as it equips product marketers with the knowledge needed to differentiate their offerings from others in the market. Understanding competitors' strengths, weaknesses, strategies, and product positioning enables marketers to craft strategies that stand out. Competitive research can highlight gaps in competitors' offerings, presenting opportunities for differentiation. For example, if a competitor's product lacks a certain feature or has usability issues, product marketers can position their own product as a superior alternative.

Moreover, competitive research can uncover risks and challenges, such as price wars or shifting customer loyalty. By recognizing these threats, product marketers can proactively address them by adjusting product features, pricing strategies, or messaging. This proactive approach helps mitigate the impact of potential challenges before they arise.

Competitive research extends beyond product offerings to include branding, marketing campaigns, and sales strategies. By analyzing these elements, product marketers can learn what resonates with their target audience and adopt best practices while avoiding potential pitfalls. For example, if a competitor's campaign highlights customer success stories, product marketers may choose to adopt a similar approach while tailoring it to their own brand's voice and positioning.

Armed with insights from both market and competitive research, product marketers can craft precise positioning and messaging. Effective positioning highlights a product's unique value and relevance to the target audience, while messaging communicates this value clearly across all touchpoints. These elements are grounded in data and real customer insights, making them resonate deeply with customers.

Finally, market and competitive research play a crucial role in stakeholder alignment. Sharing insights with product teams, sales, and leadership fosters a unified vision, ensuring that everyone is working toward the same goals and driving cohesive go-to-market strategies.

In a rapidly changing business environment, market and competitive research empower product marketers to anticipate trends, outmaneuver competitors, and maintain relevance. This skill is not just valuable—it's indispensable for achieving sustained product success in today's competitive and fast-moving market landscape.

Essential Skill: Positioning & Messaging

After market and customer research, positioning and messaging are the next fundamentals to the success of any product marketing strategy. These skills enable product marketers to define a product's unique value in the market and communicate it effectively to target audiences. In a crowded and competitive business landscape, strong positioning and messaging are critical to cutting through the noise, driving demand, and fostering customer loyalty.

At its core, positioning answers the question: Why should a customer choose your product over competitors? It involves identifying the product's unique value proposition and mapping it to customer needs and preferences. Proper positioning clarifies a product's relevance, value, and place in the market.

Positioning is vital because it creates a foundation for all subsequent marketing efforts. It helps product marketers establish clarity on key questions like:

- Who is the product for?
- What problem does it solve?
- How does it differ from competitors?
- What value does it deliver?

For example, a SaaS product designed for small businesses will be positioned differently than one targeting enterprise clients. The features, benefits, and communication style will reflect the specific needs of each audience. Without strong positioning, marketing campaigns lack focus, sales teams struggle to articulate value, and customers remain uncertain about a product's relevance to their needs.

Messaging is the art of telling the story behind the product's positioning. Where positioning defines the what and why, messaging defines the how—how the product's value is communicated to customers.

Effective messaging boils down complex ideas into clear, compelling, and relatable narratives. It involves creating tailored messages that resonate with specific audiences, align with their pain points, and inspire action.

Messaging is applied across various touchpoints, including websites, social media, email campaigns, sales decks, and more.

For instance, if a product's positioning highlights its speed and efficiency, the messaging must reinforce those attributes with proof points such as customer testimonials, measurable metrics, or use cases. By doing so, messaging ensures the positioning feels authentic and credible.

Positioning and messaging work hand in hand. **Strong positioning without clear messaging can leave a product underappreciated, while strong messaging without a differentiated position can lead to a generic narrative that fails to engage.** Together, they ensure a product is not only relevant but also compelling to the target audience.

Positioning and messaging don't just impact external communications; they also drive internal alignment. A clear positioning document ensures product, sales, customer success, and marketing teams all understand and articulate the product's value consistently. This alignment is essential for cohesive go-to-market strategies and for enabling sales teams to succeed in their efforts.

The ability to adapt positioning and messaging to market changes is another critical aspect. Customer needs, competitive landscapes, and industry trends evolve over time. Product marketers must continuously refine their approach to remain relevant and competitive, ensuring that their product always speaks directly to the needs of its audience.

Positioning and messaging are indispensable skills for product marketers. They define how a product stands out in the market and ensure its value is communicated effectively. When executed well, they empower product marketers to drive demand, build customer trust, and establish a strong market presence, paving the way for product success.

Essential Skill: Go-To-Market (GTM) Strategy

Go-to-market (GTM) strategy is yet another critical skill for a product marketer to master. It serves as the roadmap for successfully introducing a product to the market, aligning stakeholders, and driving measurable business outcomes. A well-crafted GTM strategy ensures that all elements of a product's launch and ongoing adoption are meticulously planned and executed, reducing risks and maximizing the chances of success.

A GTM strategy outlines how a company will deliver its product to its target audience. It encompasses market analysis, audience segmentation, messaging, sales enablement, pricing, and distribution channels. Product marketers orchestrate these components to ensure the product's value is clearly communicated and effectively delivered to the right customers at the right time.

Why is GTM Strategy Essential?

- **Aligning Cross-Functional Teams**: Product marketers act as the central hub between product, sales, customer success, and marketing teams. A solid GTM strategy aligns these stakeholders with a unified vision, ensuring consistency in messaging, positioning, and execution. A GTM strategy creates alignment, minimizing miscommunication and operational silos.

- **Targeting the Right Audience**: An effective GTM strategy starts with a deep understanding of the target market. By segmenting audiences based on demographics, behavior, and pain points, product marketers ensure efforts are focused on the most promising customer groups. Focus optimizes resources and boosts ROI.

- **Competitive Differentiation**: A GTM strategy positions a product distinctively against competitors. Product marketers leverage competitive research to highlight unique value propositions and craft messaging that resonates with customer needs. Without a strategic GTM approach, a product risks blending into the noise of similar offerings in the market.

- **Driving Revenue Growth**: The goal of a GTM strategy is to generate revenue. By determining optimal pricing models, distribution channels, and promotional tactics, product marketers ensure the product reaches its intended audience efficiently - whether through direct sales, partnerships, or digital marketing campaigns.

- **Mitigating Risks**: Launching a product without a GTM strategy is like setting sail without a compass. Product marketers leverage the GTM framework to identify and address potential pitfalls, such as market saturation, misaligned messaging, or inadequate sales training. This proactive approach minimizes risks and prevents costly missteps.

A product marketer is not only responsible for crafting the GTM strategy but also for its execution. This involves:

- **Market Readiness**: Ensuring the product is tailored to customer needs.
- **Sales Enablement**: Providing sales teams with tools and training.
- **Campaign Management**: Collaborating with demand generation teams to launch campaigns that build awareness and demand.
- **Metrics and Iteration**: Monitoring key performance indicators.

In today's rapidly evolving market landscape, GTM strategies are not static. Product marketers must adapt their approach based on customer feedback, competitor moves and shifting market conditions.

Go-to-market strategy is one of the cornerstones of product marketing. It enables product marketers to align teams, target the right audience, differentiate effectively, and drive revenue. By mastering this skill, product marketers become indispensable in translating product potential into tangible business success.

Essential Skill: Storytelling & Content Strategy

In the competitive realm of product marketing, connecting with customers requires more than highlighting features and benefits. It demands compelling narratives that resonate emotionally and intellectually, making storytelling and content strategy vital skills. Together, they allow marketers to craft messages that inspire trust, build loyalty, and drive engagement throughout the customer journey.

The Power of Storytelling in Product Marketing

Storytelling transforms products into relatable solutions with purpose and value. Customers don't just buy products—they buy the stories that align with their needs and aspirations. Key benefits of storytelling include:

- **Creating Emotional Connections**: Stories evoke emotions that drive decision-making. A fitness app marketed through personal success stories is far more engaging than a list of technical specifications.

- **Simplifying Complexity**: For intricate products, especially in technology, storytelling breaks down complex ideas into relatable scenarios. This clarity enhances understanding and eases adoption.

- **Reinforcing Brand Identity**: Storytelling communicates a brand's mission and values, building trust and loyalty. A consistent narrative across touchpoints strengthens brand perception and makes it memorable.

Content Strategy as the Vehicle for Storytelling

While storytelling provides the emotional framework, content strategy ensures delivery of the right message at the right time to the right audience. A robust content strategy involves crafting, curating, and distributing content that meets customer needs and aligns with business goals.

- **Driving Engagement Across Channels**: Content brings stories to life through blog posts, videos, webinars, and social media. A well-planned strategy ensures these assets support the buyer's journey, guiding prospects from awareness to conversion.

- **Positioning Thought Leadership**: Educational and insightful content positions a brand as an authority in its field. By addressing industry challenges and sharing solutions, marketers elevate the brand's credibility.

- **Enabling Personalization**: Modern buyers expect tailored experiences. Data-driven content strategy allows product marketers to deliver personalized messages for specific personas, industries, or segments, increasing relevance and conversions.

Synergy of Storytelling and Content Strategy

These skills must work together seamlessly. Marketers craft a control narrative that captures the product's value and relevance, then develop a content strategy to distribute this narrative consistently across formats and channels.

For example, if a software company's story focuses on empowering small businesses, its content might include case studies, educational blogs, and testimonial-driven social campaigns. Each asset reinforces the narrative while addressing audience needs at various touchpoints.

In Sum

Storytelling and content strategy aren't just complementary skills—they are foundational for driving engagement, differentiation, and loyalty. Together, they transform products into compelling solutions, brands into trusted partners, and customers into advocates. These skills define modern product marketing success.

Essential Skill: Sales Enablement & Training

In the dynamic world of product marketing, success hinges on more than just creating compelling campaigns or crafting persuasive messaging. Product marketers act as a bridge between product development and sales, ensuring that customer-facing teams are equipped with the knowledge, tools, and resources to effectively communicate value to prospects and customers. This makes sales enablement and training essential skills for product marketers.

Driving Alignment Between Marketing and Sales: Product marketers play a pivotal role in aligning the marketing vision with sales execution. Through sales enablement, they ensure that sales teams fully understand the product's value proposition, competitive differentiators, and target audience. This alignment fosters consistency across messaging and enhances credibility during customer interactions.

When marketers collaborate closely with sales, they gain valuable frontline insights. These insights shape messaging and product positioning, ensuring both are responsive to market realities and buyer pain points. The result is a seamless experience for prospects that builds trust and drives conversions.

Delivering Effective Training Programs: Sales teams need to be fluent in a product's benefits, features, and use cases to sell effectively. Product marketers provide the foundational training necessary to build this fluency. Comprehensive training programs might include:

- **Product Knowledge Sessions**: Sales reps must understand the product deeply—its features, benefits, and technical details—so they can confidently address customer questions and objections.

- **Persona and Use Case Education**: By teaching sales teams about buyer personas and relevant use cases, product marketers help reps tailor their messaging to resonate with specific customer needs.

- **Competitive Insights**: Product marketers empower sales teams with insights into competitors' offerings, enabling them to position the product effectively and highlight unique advantages.

- **Objection Handling**: Anticipating and preparing for customer objections ensures sales reps are equipped to navigate challenging conversations.

Empowering Through Sales Enablement Tools: Beyond training, product marketers develop and maintain enablement tools that streamline the sales process. These tools include:

- **Playbooks** with scripts, value propositions, and objection-handling.
- **One-pagers and decks** with product benefits for quick reference.
- **Case studies and testimonials** that showcase real-world impact.

When delivered effectively, these assets allow sales teams to focus on relationship-building and closing deals instead of struggling to find or create materials.

Enhancing Performance Through Feedback Loops: Sales enablement is not a one-time effort; it requires ongoing collaboration. Product marketers gather feedback from sales teams to refine messaging, tools, and training programs. This iterative process ensures continuous improvement and alignment with evolving market undercurrents.

In Sum: Sales enablement and training are vital skills that elevate product marketers from storytellers to revenue enablers. By equipping sales teams with the knowledge, confidence, and tools they need, product marketers ensure their efforts translate into measurable business outcomes, driving growth and success.

Essential Skill: Cross-Functional Collaboration

Product marketers operate at the intersection of multiple departments, acting as a linchpin that connects product, sales, marketing, and customer success. To achieve organizational goals and deliver value to customers, cross-functional collaboration is not just beneficial—it's essential. The ability to work seamlessly across teams ensures that product marketers align strategies, enhance efficiency, and drive business success.

Aligning Goals Across Teams

At its core, cross-functional collaboration ensures alignment between teams with diverse objectives. For example, while product teams focus on building innovative solutions, sales teams prioritize closing deals, and marketing aims to increase brand visibility and lead generation.

By working collaboratively, product marketers gather insights from each department to craft messaging that resonates with the target audience, refine product positioning, and develop go-to-market strategies that align with business priorities. This alignment creates a unified approach that reduces silos and fosters a culture of teamwork.

Enhancing Product Launch Success

Launching a product is a high-stakes endeavor requiring input from various teams. Product marketers lead this charge, ensuring contributions from engineering, design, sales, and customer support are coordinated.

- **With Product Teams**: Collaborating with product managers and engineers allows product marketers to deeply understand the product's features and benefits. This understanding forms the foundation for crafting compelling messaging and positioning.

- **With Sales Teams**: Sales teams provide frontline insights into customer pain points and objections. Product marketers use these insights to equip sales teams with enablement materials, like playbooks, to address those challenges effectively.

- **With Customer Success**: Input from customer success teams ensures that post-purchase messaging aligns with user needs, driving satisfaction and retention.

Through these collaborative efforts, product marketers ensure that every aspect of the launch is cohesive and impactful.

Driving Innovation Through Diverse Perspectives

Cross-functional collaboration fosters innovation by bringing together diverse perspectives. Marketing teams might identify emerging trends, sales teams highlight buyer feedback, and customer success teams uncover challenges faced by existing users. Product marketers synthesize these inputs to refine product roadmaps and messaging strategies.

This feedback loop not only ensures the product stays relevant but also allows the organization to stay competitive in dynamic markets.

Building Organizational Trust

Effective collaboration requires trust and communication. Product marketers serve as communicators who break down silos, ensuring every stakeholder feels heard and valued. By facilitating open dialogue and resolving conflicts, product marketers build trust across teams, which enhances productivity and morale.

In Sum

Cross-functional collaboration is a cornerstone of successful product marketing. By uniting diverse teams, product marketers ensure alignment, drive innovation, and deliver cohesive strategies that propel organizational growth. This skill enables product marketers to transform potential conflicts into opportunities for shared success.

Essential Skill: Key Performance Indicators

Key Performance Indicators (KPIs) are the compass that guides product marketers toward achieving strategic goals. By setting, monitoring, and analyzing KPIs, product marketers can evaluate the effectiveness of their initiatives, justify investments, and make informed decisions. Managing KPIs is an essential skill for product marketers, as it bridges the gap between strategic intent and measurable outcomes.

Driving Strategic Alignment

KPIs provide clarity and focus by aligning product marketing efforts with broader organizational objectives. Whether the goal is increasing market share, improving customer retention, or driving revenue growth, KPIs ensure that product marketers remain on track.

For example, if a company is focused on expanding its customer base, a product marketer might track KPIs such as the number of qualified leads generated through campaigns, conversion rates, or customer acquisition cost (CAC). These metrics highlight the progress toward achieving growth targets and keep the team aligned on measurable results.

Measuring Campaign Effectiveness

Product marketers often execute campaigns to promote new features, drive adoption, or support sales teams. Without KPIs, assessing the success of these efforts becomes guesswork. Metrics such as website traffic, click-through rates (CTR), lead-to-customer conversion rates, and customer engagement scores provide tangible evidence of a campaign's impact.

Tracking KPIs also helps uncover what works and what doesn't. For example, if a campaign generates high traffic but low conversions, it may indicate a mismatch between the message and the target audience. This data-driven insight enables product marketers to adjust their strategies in real time, optimizing performance.

Supporting Data-Driven Decision Making

In an era where intuition is no longer enough, product marketers must rely on data to inform decisions. Managing KPIs equips them with the ability to pinpoint areas of success and identify gaps in their approach.

For instance, tracking metrics such as Net Promoter Score (NPS) or churn rate can reveal whether a product meets customer expectations. If the NPS is low, it signals dissatisfaction and prompts marketers to refine messaging or collaborate with product teams to address user pain points.

Demonstrating Value and Accountability

KPIs serve as proof of the value that product marketers bring to the organization. By presenting data-backed results, such as how a product launch contributed to increased revenue or how a marketing campaign boosted lead generation, product marketers can demonstrate their impact.

Moreover, KPIs instill accountability, as they create benchmarks for success. Regularly reporting on these metrics fosters transparency and trust across teams.

In Sum

Managing KPIs is an indispensable skill for product marketers. It empowers us to align strategies with goals, evaluate the effectiveness of their initiatives, and adapt based on real-time insights. In doing so, KPIs transform product marketing from an intuitive art into a measurable, results-driven discipline.

Essential Skill: Personal Development

In the fast-evolving world of product marketing, personal development is not just a professional asset—it is a critical skill that defines success. By committing to ongoing self-improvement, product marketers can sharpen their expertise, adapt to industry changes, and drive impactful results. Personal development empowers marketers to remain competitive, innovative, and effective in an ever-changing landscape.

Staying Ahead of Industry Trends: Product marketing is shaped by constant innovation, from emerging technologies to shifting consumer behaviors. Personal development ensures that marketers stay informed about the latest trends, tools, and methodologies. Whether it's mastering AI-driven analytics, understanding the nuances of behavioral psychology, or staying updated on competitor strategies, continuous learning enables product marketers to maintain their relevance and effectiveness.

For example, as AI tools revolutionize campaign automation and personalization, product marketers who proactively develop their skills in AI-powered platforms can lead more efficient and targeted initiatives. This forward-thinking approach positions them as strategic assets within their organizations.

Adapting to Changing Roles: Product marketing roles often expand to encompass cross-functional collaboration, stakeholder management, and strategic decision-making. Personal development equips marketers to excel in these evolving responsibilities. Skills like communication, negotiation, and project management become crucial as marketers coordinate with sales, product, and executive teams.

Through personal development, product marketers can also build leadership capabilities, preparing them for senior roles where their influence extends beyond individual campaigns to shaping organizational strategy.

Building Emotional Intelligence: Personal development fosters emotional intelligence (EQ), which is vital for product marketers navigating complex team dynamics and customer relationships. High EQ helps marketers empathize with customers, understand their needs, and craft more resonant messaging. It also strengthens relationships with colleagues, enabling smoother collaboration and conflict resolution.

For instance, a marketer who invests in developing active listening skills can better address customer feedback and work constructively with cross-functional teams to refine products or strategies.

Driving Innovation Through Self-Reflection: Personal development encourages self-reflection, helping product marketers identify their strengths and areas for improvement. By understanding their own biases, habits, and blind spots, marketers can adopt innovative approaches to problem-solving and decision-making.

For example, a marketer who acknowledges a gap in data analysis skills might invest in learning analytics tools. This self-awareness not only enhances their performance but also brings fresh perspectives to their work.

Boosting Confidence and Resilience: The dynamic nature of product marketing often involves navigating uncertainty, managing high expectations, and learning from failures. Personal development builds resilience and confidence, enabling marketers to handle challenges with a growth mindset.

Whether it's enrolling in mentorship programs, attending industry conferences, or pursuing certifications, personal development empowers product marketers to take charge of their careers and excel.

In Sum: Personal development is an essential skill for product marketers, fostering continuous growth, adaptability, and innovation. By prioritizing self-improvement, marketers enhance their ability to lead, collaborate, and deliver impactful results in a competitive industry.

Essential Skill: AI & Technology

In today's data-driven business environment, mastering artificial intelligence (AI) and technology has become indispensable for product marketers. These tools are not just enablers—they are transformative forces that redefine how marketers understand audiences, optimize campaigns, and demonstrate value. Product marketers who develop AI and technology expertise gain a strategic edge, ensuring they remain relevant and impactful in an increasingly competitive market.

Leveraging Data for Precision Marketing: AI and technology empower product marketers to make data-driven decisions, transforming raw data into actionable insights. Advanced analytics tools can predict customer behavior, identify trends, and reveal patterns that inform positioning, messaging, and targeting strategies.

For example, AI-powered tools like predictive analytics enable marketers to anticipate customer needs and tailor campaigns that resonate on a deeper level. Machine learning algorithms can analyze customer behavior and segment audiences with remarkable accuracy, ensuring that marketing efforts are both precise and effective.

Enhancing Customer Personalization: Today's customers expect hyper-personalized experiences, and AI is at the forefront of meeting this demand. AI-driven personalization tools analyze vast amounts of customer data to deliver targeted content, offers, and messaging.

For instance, a product marketer leveraging AI can create dynamic email campaigns that adapt to individual user preferences, boosting engagement and conversions. AI-powered chatbots and recommendation engines further enhance customer interactions, driving satisfaction and loyalty.

Streamlining Campaign Execution: AI and technology streamline marketing workflows, enabling product marketers to focus on strategy and creativity. Automation tools handle repetitive tasks such as scheduling social media posts, sending follow-up emails, and generating reports.

AI also enhances A/B testing, allowing marketers to test multiple campaign variables simultaneously and identify the most effective combinations in real-time. This not only saves time but also ensures higher accuracy in optimizing campaigns.

Improving Competitive Analysis: AI tools are revolutionizing competitive intelligence, providing real-time insights into market trends, competitor positioning, and customer sentiment. Marketers can use these insights to craft differentiated strategies and identify opportunities for innovation.

For instance, natural language processing (NLP) tools can analyze customer reviews, social media chatter, and competitor content to extract key themes, enabling product marketers to adjust their messaging and value propositions effectively.

Driving Innovation and Agility: AI fosters innovation by enabling marketers to experiment with emerging trends such as generative AI for content creation, augmented reality (AR) for immersive product demos, and voice search optimization. These technologies allow marketers to engage customers in novel ways and stay ahead of the curve.

In Sum: The integration of AI and technology into product marketing is no longer optional—it is essential. By mastering these tools, product marketers can deliver personalized, data-driven strategies that drive customer engagement, optimize operations, and maintain competitive advantage. Embracing AI and technology equips marketers to lead in a rapidly evolving landscape, ensuring success in both current and future markets.

Career Pathways and Evolving Roles

The product marketing landscape is rapidly evolving, driven by advances in technology, shifts in consumer behavior, and changing business expectations. As companies recognize the strategic value of product marketing, the career pathways within this field are expanding, offering professionals a range of specialized roles, leadership opportunities, and skills-building avenues.

This section explores the typical career trajectories in product marketing, emerging roles within the discipline, and how product marketers can thrive in an environment that demands continuous learning and adaptability.

The Typical Product Marketing Career Pathway

The traditional career pathway in product marketing typically begins with entry-level roles, advancing through mid-level positions, and culminating in senior leadership. Here's a breakdown of the key stages:

Entry-Level Roles: Product Marketing Associate or Specialist

At the start of their career, a product marketer often takes on a role as an associate or specialist. In this capacity, their responsibilities generally focus on supporting go-to-market (GTM) strategies, conducting market research, assisting with sales enablement materials, and collaborating with other marketing teams.

Key skills developed at this level include:

- Foundational market research and customer persona development
- Assisting in crafting messaging and positioning frameworks
- Learning to align with product management and sales teams

Mid-Level Roles: Product Marketing Manager (PMM)

As product marketers gain experience, they typically advance to the role of Product Marketing Manager (PMM). Here, they begin to take on ownership of specific product lines or segments and play a critical role in driving GTM strategy. PMMs are often responsible for shaping positioning, conducting competitive analysis, enabling the sales team, and tracking product success metrics.

In a PMM role, product marketers deepen their skills in:

- Developing and implementing comprehensive GTM plans
- Owning the positioning and messaging for a product or feature set
- Analyzing customer insights and adapting strategies to meet their needs

Senior Roles: Senior Product Marketing Manager, Head of Product Marketing

The next step up is often Senior Product Marketing Manager, where product marketers refine their strategic skills, handle more complex product lines, and play a stronger role in cross-functional leadership. They may also mentor junior team members and collaborate closely with senior stakeholders across product and sales departments.

In these roles, product marketers gain experience in:

- Leading cross-functional teams and coordinating large product launches
- Handling budgeting and resource allocation for product marketing initiatives
- Using advanced data analytics to measure performance and optimize strategy

Leadership Roles: Director, VP of Product Marketing, or Chief Marketing Officer (CMO)

For product marketers who aspire to leadership, director, VP, or even CMO roles offer the opportunity to shape product marketing strategy at an organizational level. At this stage, product marketers are often responsible for aligning the company's vision, mission, and overall GTM strategy across all products. They also play a key role in setting budgets, defining key performance indicators (KPIs), and driving team development.

Leadership roles demand robust skills in:

- Strategic planning and organizational alignment
- Team leadership, mentorship, and talent development
- Collaborating with C-suite executives and influencing company direction

Emerging and Specialized Roles in Product Marketing

As product marketing evolves, new roles are emerging to address specialized needs within the discipline. These roles allow product marketers to home in on specific aspects of product marketing or cater to distinct markets, thereby opening diverse career pathways.

Growth Product Marketing Manager

The Growth Product Marketing Manager is a specialized role focused on customer acquisition, retention, and overall revenue growth. Unlike traditional PMMs, growth PMMs often work closely with growth marketing teams to optimize conversion rates, identify up-sell and cross-sell opportunities, and refine customer segments.

Growth PMMs bring skills in:

- Conversion rate optimization and funnel analysis
- Data-driven decision-making for revenue growth
- Experimentation with growth channels and tactics

Technical Product Marketing Manager (TPMM)

For product marketers with a technical background, the role of Technical Product Marketing Manager (TPMM) offers a blend of marketing and technical expertise. TPMMs work closely with engineering teams to understand complex technical features and translate them into customer-friendly language. They often focus on technical audiences, such as developers or IT professionals, and create highly detailed technical content, demos, and training materials.

Technical PMMs specialize in:

- Translating complex technical information into accessible messaging
- Creating content for highly technical audiences
- Collaborating with engineering to understand and showcase technical differentiators

Customer Marketing Manager

Customer Marketing Managers focus on post-purchase engagement, working to build brand loyalty and drive advocacy among existing customers. Their responsibilities often include managing customer reference programs, creating case studies, gathering testimonials, and driving customer satisfaction metrics. This role is particularly valuable in SaaS and subscription-based industries, where customer retention is critical to business success.

Customer Marketing Managers bring skills in:

- Building and managing customer advocacy programs
- Creating content to highlight customer success stories
- Using feedback to improve the customer experience and inform product decisions

Field Product Marketing Manager

Field Product Marketing Managers focus on regional or industry-specific needs. They may tailor the messaging and positioning to a specific market or collaborate closely with local sales teams to drive targeted campaigns. Field PMMs often attend industry events and customer meetings to gain firsthand insights and align closely with regional sales goals.

Field PMMs bring skills in:

- Regional or industry-specific marketing
- Direct customer engagement and relationship building
- Aligning with local sales teams to meet regional targets

The Evolving Role of Product Marketing

Product marketing is not a static discipline, and as technology, consumer expectations, and business needs shift, the role of product marketing continues to evolve. There are several key trends shaping the future of product marketing:

Increased Focus on Data and Analytics

With the advent of advanced analytics and big data, product marketers are now expected to be data-savvy and able to interpret complex metrics. Modern product marketers leverage customer data, product usage data, and sales data to gain insights that inform product strategy, customer segmentation, and campaign optimization.

Product marketers of the future will need strong analytical skills, including familiarity with tools like Google Analytics, Tableau, and customer data platforms (CDPs). Being able to make data-driven decisions allows product marketers to create more personalized customer experiences and demonstrate the ROI of their initiatives.

Product Marketing as a Strategic Partner

As the role of product marketing grows in importance, product marketers are increasingly viewed as strategic partners to the product management and executive teams. Rather than simply supporting product launches, product marketers now play a role in shaping the product roadmap, defining competitive strategies, and driving revenue growth.

This shift means product marketers must develop skills in strategic planning, business acumen, and executive communication. By aligning more closely with organizational goals, product marketers can influence key business decisions and strengthen their position within the company.

Greater Emphasis on Customer-Centric Marketing

Today's consumers expect brands to understand and anticipate their needs, which has led to a stronger emphasis on customer-centric marketing. Product marketers are increasingly focused on gaining a deep understanding of their customers, personalizing messaging, and creating experiences that build trust and loyalty.

This trend toward customer-centricity requires product marketers to be proficient in customer research, persona development, and journey mapping. By centering the customer in all marketing efforts, product marketers can create more effective campaigns that foster long-term customer relationships.

Rise of Digital and Self-Service Models

As more companies embrace digital and self-service models, product marketers are adapting their strategies to cater to these customer preferences. Digital-native products, such as SaaS solutions, often allow customers to explore, trial, and purchase products without direct interaction with sales representatives.

For product marketers, this means designing digital touchpoints and crafting content that educates and guides customers through the self-service experience. A strong understanding of digital marketing channels, including social media, SEO, and content marketing, is critical in this evolving landscape.

Building a Product Marketing Career for the Future

Given the ongoing evolution in product marketing, professionals looking to build a successful career in this field should prioritize continuous learning and adaptability. Here are a few key strategies for staying competitive in the product marketing field:

Invest in Continuous Learning

The rapid pace of change in product marketing means that skills and knowledge must be continuously refreshed. Product marketers should seek ongoing education through professional courses, certifications, and industry conferences. Engaging in learning opportunities related to data analysis, digital marketing, and customer experience can enhance one's ability to adapt to new challenges.

Build a Strong Professional Network

Networking with peers, mentors, and industry thought leaders is invaluable for career growth. Joining professional communities, attending industry events, and engaging on platforms like LinkedIn can help product marketers stay connected with new trends and open career advancement opportunities.

Stay Agile and Embrace Change

Adaptability is essential to a career that involves both strategic and tactical responsibilities. Product marketers who are willing to test new ideas, adopt emerging tools, and pivot their strategies based on market shifts are better equipped to stay relevant and effective.

Bringing it Together

The evolution of product marketing has opened a wealth of specialized career opportunities, allowing professionals to carve out unique paths in the field. From entry-level roles to senior leadership positions, product marketers are continuously developing new skills to stay relevant and impactful. As new positions such as Growth Product Marketing Manager, Technical Product Marketing Manager, and Customer Marketing Manager emerge, professionals can specialize in areas that best align with their expertise and passions.

In addition, the role of product marketing is shifting from a tactical function to a more strategic, data-driven discipline. Today's product marketers are expected to be not only experts in customer insights and market research but also savvy in analytics, enabling them to make data-informed decisions. As the discipline grows, there is an increasing emphasis on customer-centricity, as businesses realize the importance of deeply understanding their customers and creating personalized experiences.

Furthermore, product marketers are now seen as strategic partners, working closely with product management and leadership teams to shape product roadmaps, define competitive strategies, and drive revenue growth. This shift in responsibilities means product marketers must develop skills in executive communication, strategic planning, and cross-functional collaboration to truly influence business decisions.

To thrive in this evolving landscape, product marketers must prioritize continuous learning, stay agile in their approach, and build strong networks. By embracing change and proactively acquiring new skills, product marketers can position themselves for long-term success, driving both personal and organizational growth in a rapidly changing marketplace.

Having covered the foundations, let's take a trip around the world to discover global perspectives on Product Marketing from a top expert in the field.

GLOBAL WISDOM WITH HILA LAUTERBACH

GLOBAL WISDOM WITH HILA LAUTERBACH

Hila Lauterbach is a VP of Product Marketing with 15 years of experience leading high-performing GTM teams in global tech startups and enterprises. She has managed and overseen marketing, product marketing, and sales teams throughout her career while building multiple product marketing organizations from scratch. A three-time startup founder, she has established strategic partnerships with FAANG companies. Her expertise spans building PMM and Competitive Intelligence teams, leading dozens of B2B SaaS product launches, and driving growth across multiple industries in the US and EMEA. Based in Silicon Valley, she serves on advisory boards of innovative companies and is recognized as a Top PMM Influencer and accomplished keynote speaker.

In the following sections, Hila shares her global perspectives on Product Marketing – **in her own words**.

Success in International Product Marketing

Product marketing has been my passion and profession for fifteen years, leading me through a fascinating journey across three continents.

I consider Product Marketing Managers (PMMs) at all seniority levels to be akin to General Managers, possessing both a bird's-eye view and a detailed understanding of their business units' gaps and opportunities. This dual approach requires a leadership mindset, strong ownership of products, solutions, and sales motions, and the ambition to connect the dots to ensure a significant impact on the company. A successful PMM should seamlessly transition between these perspectives—from strategic planning to day-to-day tactical activities—while keeping bottom-of-the-

funnel (BoFu) objectives as the North Star of driving revenue, reducing churn, increasing retention, and promoting upsells.

Success in international product marketing demands more than understanding regional differences—it requires developing true cultural intelligence, which goes far beyond surface-level adaptations.

What strikes me the most about the cultural and geographical differences worldwide isn't just how PMM practices and core functions vary by geography–but how deeply market context, business culture, and technological advancement shape them. Whether building a start-up in Tel Aviv or managing global enterprise initiatives from Berlin to San Francisco, I've learned that these variations are critical in shaping how we structure, execute, and measure product marketing success globally.

Universal Truths in Product Marketing

While implementation varies, certain fundamentals remain constant across markets. Strategic positioning, clear value articulation, and effective go-to-market execution form the backbone of product marketing globally. However, prioritizing and executing these elements varies significantly based on market maturity, organizational structure, and regional business practices.

The Ever-Evolving PMM Role

Before diving into regional differences, I've discovered that two principal factors dramatically impact how we practice product marketing: company size and go-to-market philosophy. In my journey from start-up founder to enterprise leader, I've experienced both extremes.

Company Size and Structure Impact

In start-ups, PMMs own everything from positioning to demand generation, GTM motions, content, local events, and even customer marketing plans across the entire product portfolio globally. At large multinational corporations, specific teams focus solely on specific products or regions, such as Europe, Middle East and Africa (EMEA), collaborating with specialized PMMs worldwide with laser-focused expertise (from GTM to competitive enablement, Vertical Solutions, Sales enablement, and even BI and research).

Go-to-Market Philosophy

The distinction between sales-led and product-led organizations typically shapes the PMM function.

In sales-led companies, I found myself deeply embedded with sales teams, focusing on enablement, training, discovery and proposal materials, win-loss analysis, and messaging refinement consistency. I also ensured field teams were equipped with the right strategies and tactics to improve velocity and win rates. This required more sales-oriented specific roles within the PMM team, which is typically built with professionals from sales and marketing backgrounds.

In product-led environments, the focus shifts to product usage and engagement, improvement cycles including conversion optimization and user testing, and stickiness increase, and requires a lot of MVP work. PMMs typically come from product management backgrounds with a highly technical mindset and maintain a closer ratio with product managers (ideally 1:2, though reality often stretches to 1:4+ in start-ups).

Regional Flavors of Product Marketing

The Middle East: Speed and Innovation

The Israeli tech ecosystem, known as Start-Up Nation, taught me my first crucial lessons about product marketing. Here, the market demands PMMs who can move quickly from strategy to execution and are unfazed by high levels of uncertainty. PMMs often work in lean, fast-moving environments where role boundaries are fluid, and decisions are made on the fly. The emphasis on rapid iteration and immediate results shapes everything from customer research and quick insights implementation to product launches and ad hoc processes.

When I was on the founding team of HRTech start-ups, our team secured 30 major clients before launching and having an MVP through sheer determination and guerrilla execution, generating a solid revenue stream in the first year of operation.

The Israeli work style—direct communication, resilience, intense pace, and a winning mentality that prioritizes quick results over a meticulously defined process—initially challenged many global teammates. While American and European professionals often favor diplomatic, indirect approaches, especially around feedback, the direct Israeli communication style creates complex dynamics. I've seen teams across cultures come to appreciate and even adopt these traits once they understand the intent behind them.

In the Israeli tech scene, high-achieving PMMs quickly learn to proactively over-communicate to prevent potential friction and achieve alignment. It is also standard to work 12+ hours a day, which requires thoughtful conversations and expectation setting with global teams, leading to very fruitful and insightful discussions about work perception and career development.

Europe: Complex Market Dynamics & Process Excellence

In Europe, success demands navigating not just cultural differences but fundamentally different business philosophies. Sales cycles run longer than in other regions, and brand credibility and trust-building play crucial roles.

European product marketing represents a fascinating contrast in approaches, management styles, objectives, and priorities, even among European nations. Some leaders focus intensely on new business acquisition and sales enablement, while others prioritize customer retention, directly impacting PMM focus and organizational support. This diversity extends to technology adoption - European markets often show stronger resistance to process changes and digital transformation.

GTM strategies require careful adaptation for each market. Beyond mere translation, PMMs must understand the deep cultural context and intent behind messaging. The competitive landscape shifts significantly by country, demonstrating the importance of local market knowledge. This 'home field advantage' factor demands nuanced competitive approaches that account for global brand presence and regional market dynamics. This also results in different positioning strategies, tactics, and marketing channel selection. Our paid social media strategy varied by country; for example, LinkedIn campaigns that effectively drove event attendance in the US and many European countries required complete adaptation, utilizing different local social media channels to engage German audiences.

European product marketing also emphasizes structured processes and comprehensive planning. The region's complex regulatory environment, particularly GDPR, has led to the development of robust frameworks for market research, customer data management, and campaign execution.

During my experience launching AWS cloud products in Europe, I observed how PMMs must balance innovation with compliance. This often results in more thorough pre-launch planning phases and structured go-to-market processes. I created detailed frameworks for the launch that accounted for regional variations in data privacy requirements, marketing regulations, and business practices across European markets.

North America: Scale and Sophistication

The US market represents the most mature product marketing practices, where specialization and process refinement reach their peak. Building the product marketing department at SpotOn and later at Scorpion, I implemented distinct teams for Products, GTM, market segments and verticals, competitive intelligence, BI, and sales enablement. This structure would seem overly rigid in Tel Aviv, but perfectly matched US market needs and scale.

American product marketing emphasizes data-driven decision-making within clear organizational structures. What constitutes compelling evidence varies significantly across cultures. While specific metrics and methodologies might convince Silicon Valley teams, the same data points often need different contexts and presentations to resonate with European or Middle Eastern stakeholders.

The relatively consistent workplace culture across regions in the US allows for more standardized approaches, though market segmentation remains crucial. Resource optimization and efficiency drive many decisions, with clear metrics and ROI expectations shaping strategy. In the US, you can expect formal processes for product launches and go-to-market execution, sophisticated market research combining quantitative and qualitative methodologies, and comprehensive competitive enablement programs (including sales enablement, win-loss analysis, and competitive intelligence).

The relationship between regional teams (in Europe and the Middle East) and US headquarters adds another layer of complexity. Regional PMMs must advocate for the "voice of the market" as they apply and localize global materials in their marketing activities. While the headquarters PMM balances global strategy and consistency with regional flexibility, they create original materials distributed globally and collaborate more closely with the product and marketing teams. As technology drives market globalization, product marketers must adapt to bridge regional differences while honoring local nuances. Representing the market voice while maintaining global standards becomes an essential skill.

Looking Forward

As our profession continues evolving and markets continue to globalize, successful product marketers must master both global standards and local needs nuances. The future belongs to those who can adapt their strategies based on organizational context, market dynamics, and company go-to-market approach and consistently balance regional requirements with headquarters while maintaining core PMM excellence.

We're increasingly required to think like CEOs and demonstrate strategic impact and direct revenue contribution. As PMM leaders in the global community, we have the responsibility to educate and demonstrate proof *of concept of the breadth and depth PMM can add to business strategy and growth.*

The stories that follow in this book will dive deeper into regional perspectives. As you read them, remember that while product marketing fundamentals remain constant, success lies in understanding how to adapt them across different contexts–whether those differences stem from geography, company size, go-to-market approach, organizational structure, or market dynamics.

This journey has taught me that product marketing is both art and science, requiring us to be strategic thinkers and cultural chameleons. It's a challenging balance, but mastering it makes our profession fascinating and rewarding.

Having seen a global perspective on Product Marketing, let's dive into the first essential Product Marketing skill — that of Market and Competitive Research.

WISDOM ON MARKET AND COMPETITIVE RESEARCH

WISDOM ON MARKET AND COMPETITIVE RESEARCH

Research on market and competitive dynamics is a cornerstone of product marketing, providing the insights needed to shape strategies, refine messaging, and outmaneuver competitors. While books and courses offer valuable frameworks, real-world insights from experienced professionals bring the practice to life, offering a perspective shaped by hands-on experience and industry nuances.

Professionals with real-world expertise share stories that uncover the hidden intricacies of market landscapes. They illustrate how to read between the lines of customer data, track competitors' moves and identify unmet needs in the market. Learning from their successes—and failures—helps marketers avoid common pitfalls while gaining actionable strategies that are grounded.

For instance, an experienced product marketer might explain how they combined qualitative customer interviews with quantitative market data to validate a product pivot. Another could share how they analyzed a competitor's product roadmap to anticipate and counter a disruptive launch. These first-hand accounts go beyond theory, teaching the nuances of collecting, interpreting, and applying insights effectively.

Engaging with real-world professionals through interviews, case studies, or mentorship fosters a practical understanding of market and competitive research. It equips product marketers to adapt research techniques to changing environments, ensuring strategies are both insightful and impactful in real-world scenarios.

In the subsequent sections, we pick the minds of rising stars and industry titans to better understand these ideas in the real world.

Anastasia Albert (Berlin, Germany)

Bio

Anastasia Albert is an experienced Go-To-Market and Demand Generation expert for B2B tech, with a dynamic 12-year career spanning major roles across Europe's tech scene. She has led high-impact growth initiatives at companies like Xentral and Project A Ventures, contributing to the success of two unicorns and two exits, including Coresystems (acquired by SAP) and Mila (acquired by Swisscom). In 2023, she founded B2B Practitioners, an advisory specializing in growth and GTM strategies. An LSE alumna, Anastasia actively shares her insights at conferences like OMKB and d3Con and supports Women in SaaS and 2hearts communities.

Anastasia Albert on Market & Competitive Research

In my interview with Anastasia Albert, she shares valuable insights into the importance of getting product marketing fundamentals right, especially for B2B software founders. Anastasia emphasizes that many founders make the mistake of launching marketing efforts without first establishing a solid product marketing foundation. According to her, the key to success lies in thoroughly understanding and applying the basics of product marketing before scaling your marketing engine.

Anastasia explains that the product marketing fundamentals include clearly defining your Ideal Customer Profile (ICP) and personas, understanding their buying decision process, positioning your product effectively, and crafting strong messaging. Without getting these elements right, everything else in the marketing process falls apart. For example, if you don't define your ICP and personas, you risk trying to appeal to everyone and reaching no one. If your messaging lacks clarity and focuses too much on features rather than the value your product provides, your sales efforts will be ineffective, and you won't create the urgency needed in your sales process.

She stresses that many marketers in the B2B space often fail to go deep enough into understanding the industry they are marketing to. Anastasia advises that product marketers should invest time in immersing themselves in the industry through customer interviews, expert discussions, and talking to internal stakeholders. This research allows marketers to better understand customer pain points and industry trends. Additionally, she recommends reading analyst reports and staying informed about competitors to ensure a comprehensive understanding of the market landscape.

Anastasia also underscores the importance of being curious and not taking things at face value. By digging deeper into the industry and market dynamics, product marketers can develop more nuanced and effective strategies that truly resonate with target audiences. She highlights that product marketing is not just about positioning the product; it's about deeply understanding the market and its needs to drive better product development, messaging, and ultimately, sales success.

In summary, Anastasia's advice revolves around the importance of mastering the core principles of product marketing and taking the time to dive deep into understanding your target market. By focusing on the fundamentals and continuously immersing yourself in the industry, you'll be better equipped to craft compelling messages, create urgency, and ensure your product resonates with the right customers.

Carolyne Mweberi (Nairobi, Kenya)

Bio

Carolyne Mweberi is a certified Senior Product Marketing Manager, and a recognized Top 100 Product Marketer based in Kenya. With expertise in positioning and scaling technologies in frontier and emerging markets in Africa, she excels at connecting tech product strategies to marketing initiatives driving customer adoption, engagement, usage, loyalty, and advocacy. Currently, she leads product marketing at Qhala, where she analyzes market trends and competitors to identify opportunities for growth and differentiation. Carolyne has successfully developed go-to-market strategies that leverage market insights to drive data-informed business decisions, enhancing customer experience. Having worked in the digital transformation and innovation management space in Africa for close to 5 years, Carolyne has been able to engage various stakeholders and partners in harnessing opportunities in the digital economy as a driver for growth and innovation. She's passionate about transforming economies in Africa through digital innovation. An active ambassador for the Product Marketing Alliance, she also hosts the podcast SCALE, focusing on product marketing in Sub-Saharan Africa.

Carolyne Mweberi on Market & Competitive Research

In her interview with me, Carolyne stresses the critical importance of understanding the ecosystem in which a product operates. She explains that successful product marketing goes beyond the product itself; it involves understanding how the product fits into the broader market environment. This understanding directly impacts key aspects of product marketing—such as positioning, messaging, and storytelling—and ultimately influences conversion rates and overall brand success.

Carolyne shares her experience working with Qhala, a company focused on catalyzing Africa's digital future. At the heart of Qhala's mission is driving digital transformation in Africa, with the goal of positioning the continent as a global leader in innovation and technology. Carolyne emphasizes that achieving this ambitious vision requires a deep understanding of the local and regional ecosystem. For her team, this knowledge is not just theoretical; it is actively applied in their daily work, enabling them to connect with key stakeholders, including policymakers, thought leaders, governments, and regulators, who often have a comprehensive understanding of market dynamics and trends.

By engaging with these influential groups, Carolyne and her team gain invaluable insights into how external factors—such as government policies, regulatory changes, and regional economic drivers—affect the market and shape the needs and expectations of customers. This understanding allows them to refine their product positioning to ensure that it aligns with the broader goals of digital transformation and economic growth in Africa. Additionally, this insight informs their messaging and storytelling, making it more relevant, compelling, and tailored to stakeholders in the digital transformation space.

Carolyne underscores that understanding the ecosystem is not a one-time task but an ongoing process. It requires continuous engagement with the market and its key players to stay informed about shifting landscapes and emerging trends. Without this level of understanding, marketers risk misaligning their products with market needs, which can ultimately undermine their efforts and lead to missed opportunities. Carolyne advises product marketers to move beyond traditional market research and take a proactive approach by connecting with policymakers, thought leaders, and regulators who can provide valuable insights into the ecosystem.

Her key takeaway is clear: product marketers must understand the environment in which their product exists to position it effectively, communicate its value convincingly, and drive meaningful results. For Carolyne, a deep understanding of the ecosystem is the foundation for crafting successful, impactful product marketing strategies. It allows product marketers to anticipate market shifts, respond to customer needs, and ultimately drive the success of their products.

David Lim (New York, NY, USA)

Bio

David Lim is a seasoned product marketing leader known for simplifying complex ideas and delivering clear, impactful messaging. With 10+ years of experience spanning tech giants like Google and emerging B2B companies, he specializes in product launches, growth strategies, and strategic partnerships. As a Senior Product Marketing Manager at Brivo and former Director of Product Marketing at RentSpree, David has a proven track record in consumer insight, analytics, and content creation, recognized by industry awards like "Best of CES 2013." Based in New York, David is a Certified Product Marketing Manager committed to straightforward, compelling communication.

Market & Competitive Research Insights from David Lim

In his interview with me, David Lim emphasizes the importance of staying close to customers and deeply understanding them to drive successful product marketing. His approach to market and competitive research is grounded in learning not only about how customers use a product but also about their personal goals, preferences, and behaviors. By developing a comprehensive understanding of customers, product marketers can position their products more effectively and create a go-to-market strategy that resonates with the target audience.

David advocates for engaging directly with customers through calls and other forms of interaction. This enables product marketers to gather valuable insights about how customers perceive the product, the benefits they derive from it, and the challenges they face. However, he stresses that understanding customers goes beyond just learning about product usage. It's critical to understand who the customers are as individuals—what drives them, what their personal objectives are, and where they go for information. These insights, according to David, can be crucial for shaping the marketing strategy and messaging.

One key component of this customer-centric research involves identifying where customers go to learn and consume information. David highlights the example of security professionals in the multifamily space who often read publications like BizNow or Multifamily Insider. By knowing which influencers or publications are trusted by their customers, product marketers can tailor their outreach, refine content strategies, and better align messaging with what their audience values. This level of insight helps in identifying effective channels for customer engagement and establishing trust in the target market.

Furthermore, David notes that competitive research plays a significant role in understanding the broader market landscape. By analyzing competitors' messaging, their market positioning, and the channels they use to communicate with customers, product marketers can identify gaps and opportunities. Understanding where competitors are succeeding or failing can provide valuable insights into differentiating your product in the market.

In sum, David stresses that the more a product marketer learns about their customers, the more effective they will be in crafting strategies that resonate with the market. By focusing on understanding the customer's personal goals, their information consumption habits, and staying attuned to market trends and competitors, product marketers can ensure they are well-equipped to drive successful product positioning and go-to-market initiatives.

Jan-Eike Rosenthal (Hamburg, Germany)

Bio

Jan-Eike Rosenthal is an accomplished product marketing professional and Product Marketing Alliance ambassador with over a decade of digital marketing experience. As the Product Marketing Team Lead at Haiilo, Jan-Eike combines strategic insights with hands-on execution, guiding product positioning, messaging, and go-to-market strategies. He has a robust background in B2B marketing, having worked closely with cross-functional teams to streamline product communications and foster competitive intelligence frameworks. Known for his curiosity and technical fluency, Jan-Eike is dedicated to driving value and innovation in product marketing while staying at the forefront of industry trends. Based in Hamburg, he's passionate about continuous learning and community engagement.

Jan-Eike Rosenthal on Market & Competitive Research

In his interview with me, Jan-Eike Rosenthal shares key insights into how Haiilo leverages its client community to enhance market and competitive research. He explains how building a client community has transformed their approach from one-way communication to two-way interactions, which significantly improves Haiilo's ability to gather meaningful client insights. By engaging directly with customers in a dedicated client community, Haiilo gains immediate feedback on product updates, hears client preferences and needs, and accesses valuable best practices, all of which strengthen their competitive edge.

Streamlining Feedback: Shift to a Community-Driven Model

Previously, Haiilo relied on traditional methods like newsletters or one-off surveys to gather customer input, a process that was often slow and limited in scope. Now, with a structured client community, the feedback process is streamlined and organic, allowing Haiilo to observe user engagement, collect feedback on specific product features, and understand how clients are responding to updates or changes in real time. This community-driven model removes barriers to customer input, making it easier for product marketers to access high-quality data that reflects current client sentiment and usage patterns.

Personalized Outreach: Targeted Communication Strategy

A key aspect of Haiilo's strategy is the shift from mass communication to targeted outreach within the community. Rather than relying on general communications, Haiilo's marketing team can now create tailored messages based on the information that clients voluntarily share in their profiles. This personalized approach not only improves the relevance of their messages but also allows Haiilo to engage clients with content that speaks directly to their specific needs and use cases. This refined targeting approach provides insights into what clients prioritize, enabling Haiilo to sharpen its value proposition and differentiate itself from competitors more effectively.

The Magic of Client Communities

Jan-Eike's approach underscores the strategic value of a robust client community for market research and competitive intelligence. By transitioning from one-way to two-way communication, Haiilo gains direct access to actionable insights that fuel competitive strategy. The community model not only provides real-time feedback on product updates but also allows Haiilo to tailor communications, deepen customer relationships, and stay agile in response to market trends. Ultimately, Haiilo's client community exemplifies how product marketers can tap into the voices of users to strengthen competitive positioning and build products that resonate deeply with the target audience.

Jan-Eike Rosenthal (Hamburg, Germany)

Mason Yu (Chicago, IL, USA)

Bio

Mason Yu is a seasoned Growth Marketing Lead based in Chicago, adept at revitalizing B2B marketing strategies through a systems-first approach. Holding an MBA from Chicago Booth and an MS in Computer Science, he integrates engineering principles with marketing expertise, leveraging programmatic advertising and AI to drive substantial revenue growth. As a co-founder of the Omer Quartet and Arete Media, Mason blends creativity with analytical thinking, achieving impressive results such as a 160% increase in organic traffic and building scalable marketing functions. With a passion for teaching, he also shares his knowledge as a guest lecturer at The Juilliard School.

Mason Yu on Market & Competitive Research

In his interview with me, Mason Yu shares valuable insights into the ever-changing landscape of marketing and emphasizes the need for market and competitive research to stay ahead in this dynamic environment. His primary lesson revolves around the realization that there is no universal marketing playbook that guarantees long-term success. Marketing tactics and strategies often yield significant results early on, but as competitors quickly adopt similar approaches, the initial advantages diminish, and the market becomes saturated. Once a marketing channel or tactic is overrun, its returns often plateau, as the enormous effort required to maintain the same level of success becomes less effective.

Mason's perspective underscores a key aspect of marketing: its inherently competitive and ever-evolving nature. Marketing strategies are subject to constant change, and as new methods emerge, older tactics often become commonplace. This fast-paced evolution, fueled by technological advancements such as AI, causes once-innovative strategies to quickly lose their effectiveness as they are replicated and adapted by other marketers. The rapid pace of change in marketing makes it both an exciting and stressful industry, where marketers must continuously innovate and refine their strategies to remain relevant. For some, this fast pace can be overwhelming, but for Mason, it represents one of the more exciting aspects of the field.

To navigate this turbulent landscape, Mason advocates for returning to "first principles" in marketing. The foundation of successful marketing lies in deeply understanding customer needs, pains, and behaviors. By engaging directly with customers and immersing oneself in their journey, marketers can gain critical insights into what their audience truly values. This customer-centric approach enables marketers to identify which aspects of their product align best with their target market, allowing them to refine their product-market fit. Once a solid product-market fit is identified, Mason stresses the importance of consistently and clearly communicating this fit in the market. The goal is to create a strong association between the product and the customer's needs, ensuring that when the customer is ready to purchase, the product is top-of-mind.

Additionally, Mason highlights the importance of balancing short-term and long-term marketing strategies. In a constantly shifting market, it is crucial to achieve immediate results while also investing in building long-term brand recognition and loyalty. This balance allows marketers to take calculated risks in emerging areas while maintaining a focus on sustainable growth. By blending both short-term agility and long-term vision, marketers can position themselves for success amid a competitive and rapidly evolving marketplace.

In summary, Mason's insights stress the significance of market and competitive research in maintaining relevance in a fast-changing environment. By focusing on understanding customer needs, establishing a strong product-market fit, and balancing both short-term and long-term strategies, marketers can navigate the challenges of the marketing world and continue to drive business success.

Nida Ateeq (Toronto, ON, Canada)

Bio

Nida Ateeq is a growth-focused marketing strategist with a rich background in engineering and B2B marketing, spanning agency, in-house, and consultancy roles. She specializes in data-driven SaaS and B2B strategies that enhance growth and pipeline impact through digital, product, and performance marketing. A founder of Anagar Media and currently leading global growth and lifecycle marketing at ABC Fitness, Nida is celebrated for her technical precision and creative storytelling that resonates with audiences. With experience as a reverse mentor and shadow board member, she has collaborated with visionary firms like Mahindra to drive impactful, holistic marketing strategies.

Nida Ateeq on Market & Competitive Research

In her interview with me, Nida Ateeq shares invaluable advice for immigrant professionals and entrepreneurs moving to North America, particularly when it comes to navigating market dynamics and understanding the local business landscape. From a market and competitive research perspective, her tips focus on how newcomers can successfully enter a new environment, leveraging knowledge and strategic relationships to position themselves effectively.

The first piece of advice Nida offers is the importance of in-depth research. She emphasizes newcomers must take the time to understand their new market thoroughly. This includes researching industry trends, understanding customer behavior, and especially, recognizing cultural differences. These nuances are crucial when adapting products, services, and marketing strategies to align with local preferences. According to Nida, the job market and customer expectations in North America are often vastly different from those in other regions like India, and this shift requires a well-informed approach to succeed. By gathering data, analyzing competitors, and learning about local consumer preferences, newcomers can better position themselves in this new market landscape.

BY NITIN KARTIK

The second piece of advice Nida shares is the importance of networking. She highlights that joining communities and attending in-person events is a critical way to build connections and get familiar with the local business ecosystem. Networking not only helps in making professional connections but also aids in gaining insights into the market from people who have navigated similar challenges. This approach can prove particularly helpful when entering a new industry or launching a business, as it provides access to both knowledge and potential partnerships. Networking, she suggests, can create opportunities and help newcomers stay informed about market trends, which is vital when trying to stay ahead of the competition.

Last, Nida advises everyone to find a mentor. She notes the significant benefits of having someone to guide you, particularly when navigating unfamiliar territories. Mentors who have walked similar paths can offer critical insights, advice on market entry strategies, and emotional support during challenging times. By seeking mentors who understand both the immigrant experience and the nuances of the local business environment, newcomers can gain an edge in understanding how to maneuver effectively within the market. According to Nida, mentors can act as trusted advisors who help in refining strategies based on market realities, providing invaluable competitive intelligence along the way.

In sum, Nida's tips focus on leveraging thorough research, building meaningful networks, and seeking mentorship to better understand market conditions and competition. By utilizing these strategies, newcomers can equip themselves with the tools necessary to successfully compete in North American markets and navigate the challenges of being an immigrant entrepreneur.

Olena Bomko (Ukraine)

Bio

Olena Bomko is a skilled Product Marketing and Go-To-Market strategist based in Ukraine, specializing in assisting tech startups with effective product marketing and launches. With a strong background in creative writing and social media marketing, she leverages her expertise to craft compelling messaging that resonates with target audiences. Olena's approach includes fractional marketing roles, consultation, and project-based support, making her an asset for growth-focused companies. A graduate with honors, she combines her technical knowledge with strategic insights to drive successful go-to-market strategies, helping clients increase visibility and achieve their business goals.

Olena Bomko on Market & Competitive Intelligence

In her compelling interview with me, Olena Bomko shares a powerful lesson on the role of Market and Competitive Intelligence in driving effective product marketing strategies. Drawing from her extensive experience, Olena emphasizes the importance of immersing yourself in the environments where your customers and potential customers naturally operate. This approach enables a deeper understanding of their behaviors, needs, and challenges, which is critical for staying ahead in competitive markets.

Olena uses a vivid analogy to drive her point home: just as talented actors immerse themselves in the real-world settings of their characters to prepare for roles, marketers must embed themselves in the lives of their customers. Borrowing wisdom from bestselling author Martin Lindsrtrom, Olena explains, "If you want to discover how animals live, you don't go to the zoo—you go to the jungle." For product marketers, this means stepping outside the comfort of internal assumptions and actively engaging with customers in their natural environments.

She stresses the importance of continuously surrounding yourself with customers, whether through social platforms like LinkedIn, niche communities, conferences, or industry-specific podcasts. This engagement is not a one-time effort but an ongoing marathon that helps marketers stay attuned to evolving customer needs and industry trends. Olena's personal connection to her customers, rooted in her seven years of studying computer engineering and being immersed in the tech community, reinforces the value of genuine familiarity with the audience.

Olena also highlights the significance of goal-oriented research in market and competitive intelligence. She advises marketers to approach research projects with a clear objective and to immediately translate insights into actionable strategies. By doing so, marketers can ensure their efforts yield tangible results, such as better messaging, more targeted campaigns, or refined go-to-market strategies.

The underlying theme of Olena's advice is the necessity of being proactive and authentic in understanding your customers. She warns against limiting customer interaction to launch days or product testing phases. Instead, she advocates for continuous engagement as the foundation for developing products and strategies that truly resonate with the market.

In summary, Olena's approach to Market and Competitive Intelligence centers on active customer immersion and purposeful research. By going beyond superficial observations and engaging deeply with their audience, marketers can uncover actionable insights that give them a competitive edge. Her advice serves as a reminder that great marketing starts with a commitment to understanding and serving the customer in their own "jungle."

Olivier Josefowitz (Israel)

Bio

Olivier Josefowitz is a seasoned Product Marketing and Education Team Lead at Nayax with extensive experience across tech and FinTech. Based in Israel, he spearheads product marketing for retail, hospitality, and payment products, focusing on GTM strategies, persona-driven messaging, and sales enablement. Known for his strategic thinking, collaborative approach, and ability to simplify complex concepts, Olivier brings a strong analytical mindset and attention to detail. His previous roles at RISCO Group and IBM involved diverse responsibilities in product positioning, customer training, and global HR, showcasing his versatility and depth across product marketing, sales, and HR functions.

Olivier Josefowitz on Market & Competitive Research

In his insightful interview with me, Olivier Josefowitz shares two crucial lessons on competitive analysis that go beyond the conventional approach. Olivier emphasizes the importance of examining not just direct competitors but also alternative options that buyers might consider, as well as combining digital research with hands-on field observations to gain a full understanding of the competitive landscape.

Olivier begins by explaining his first key lesson: look at competitors through the lens of buyer alternatives. He uses a simple but effective analogy from the food industry, where someone deciding between two ketchup brands may also consider mustard as an alternative, even though it's not a direct ketchup competitor. Translating this to the tech world, he points out that analyzing competitors for a product like Monday.com shouldn't only include similar project management tools like Asana or Trello but should also consider broader solutions such as Adobe or Microsoft, which also offer collaboration capabilities. By broadening the scope to include alternative solutions, product marketers can better understand the range of options a customer might explore, allowing them to position their product more strategically in the market.

The second lesson Olivier shares is the need for both top-down and bottom-up approaches in competitive research. While AI tools and online resources provide an abundance of valuable insights about competitors' strategies, pricing, and product features, Olivier stresses that digital information alone can miss important details. He recommends supplementing these insights with field research and direct user interviews. In the retail technology space, for example, observing what businesses are using in real-world settings and gathering competitive intelligence from sales representatives offer unique perspectives that online data may not capture. He highlights the value of leveraging insights from sales reps through CRM tools like Salesforce, where reps can record competitive information based on direct interactions with clients, competitors, and end users.

According to Olivier, combining these top-down and bottom-up approaches creates a more nuanced and complete competitive landscape, which can then guide more informed marketing and product positioning strategies. He believes this dual approach is particularly crucial in sectors like retail and hospitality, where rapidly evolving technologies require marketers to stay agile and connected to what's happening on the ground.

Olivier's advice challenges product marketers to expand their perspective on competition and to balance digital research with practical, real-world observations. His approach to competitor analysis encourages marketers to think holistically and strategically, keeping in mind both the buyer's alternatives and the dynamic realities of the field. This comprehensive method provides a solid foundation for more effective and adaptive product marketing strategies.

Priyanka Mandhyan (San Diego, CA, USA)

Bio

Priyanka Mandhyan is a Product Marketing Manager and USC Marshall MBA with a passion for driving success in B2B SaaS. Known for her ability to enhance GTM strategies, stakeholder alignment, and customer insights, Priyanka has made significant contributions in previous roles, including as a fractional product marketer and ex-VMware intern. Her expertise spans persona creation, channel strategy, and competitive intelligence, with a record of achievements like increasing organic leads on her previous company's website by 500% resulting from go-to-market campaigns. She has recently scored the chance to be the first marketing hire at a B2B SaaS AI company. As the first hire, she is getting to work on so many amazing product marketing projects such as defining the very first positioning and messaging, choosing top customer segments to go after, and conducting customer interviews and analyzing them for patterns. Priyanka is bilingual in English and Hindi, with limited proficiency in French and Sindhi, and holds multiple marketing certifications, including a CPMM.

Priyanka Mandhyan on Market & Competitive Research

In her interview with me, Priyanka Mandhyan shares a powerful insight on conducting market and competitive research, emphasizing the importance of sourcing high-quality, unbiased data. Through a relatable anecdote, she illustrates how authentic customer insights can shape better-informed strategies.

Priyanka recounts a personal experience deciding between two Mediterranean restaurants. While both seemed appealing, the deciding factor was customer reviews. One restaurant boasted a 4.8-star rating, while the other had 4.2 stars. As she read the reviews, she noticed polarizing opinions—some praised specific dishes, while others criticized the service or value for money. This experience sparked a realization: reviews often represent the extremes of customer sentiment, with people sharing only when they're either highly satisfied or deeply disappointed.

BY NITIN KARTIK

She draws a parallel to product marketing, highlighting how relying solely on review sites can result in biased insights. This underscores the need to identify more balanced and objective data sources when conducting secondary research.

Priyanka stresses the critical role of channel selection in market and competitive research. While review sites provide a starting point, they often lack the nuance necessary for comprehensive analysis. To counter this, she advocates exploring alternative sources such as community forums, Slack groups, Discord channels, and LinkedIn communities. These platforms host organic conversations, where customers freely discuss their likes, dislikes, challenges, and frustrations.

According to Priyanka, these community-driven dialogues offer "gold nuggets" of information—unfiltered insights that reflect genuine user experiences. By tapping into these conversations, marketers can gain a holistic understanding of their product's reception and its position in the competitive landscape.

For Priyanka, the key to effective market research lies in balancing diverse perspectives. She recommends combining traditional sources like reviews with emerging platforms that foster direct customer interaction. Engaging in forums or groups not only provides insights but also helps marketers uncover gaps in product adoption, refine messaging, and understand competitive dynamics.

Additionally, Priyanka encourages product marketers to remain curious and adaptive. By exploring unconventional data sources and engaging directly with customers, they can identify emerging trends and respond to market needs.

Priyanka's approach to market and competitive research is rooted in finding authentic customer voices. By venturing beyond the confines of review sites and into community spaces, she demonstrates how marketers can access richer, more objective data. This method empowers teams to craft strategies informed by real customer experiences, ensuring products resonate in evolving markets.

Priyanka Mandhyan (San Diego, CA, USA)

Randi-Sue Deckard (Dallas Area, TX, USA)

Bio

Randi-Sue Deckard is an accomplished Senior Vice President of Strategy, Sales, Marketing, and Customer Success with extensive expertise in B2B healthcare and AI. A Dallas-based leader and Pavilion DFW Co-Chair, Randi excels at creating growth strategies that drive sustainable revenue through customer-centered approaches. With a background in clinical science, she brings a research-based mindset to building resilient, high-performing teams and cross-functional collaborations. Known for her skill in simplifying complex data for actionable insights, Randi is also a sought-after advisor, thought leader, and future author, recognized for her proficiency in GTM strategies and commitment to enhancing customer experience.

Randi Deckard on Market & Competitive Research: Building a 360-Degree Customer View

In her interview with me, Randi Deckard emphasizes the transformative power of adopting a holistic, 360-degree approach to customer research. She advocates for a nuanced understanding of customers that goes beyond surface-level insights, incorporating both external customer behavior and internal team dynamics to craft a winning market and competitive strategy.

Randi frames customer obsession as the cornerstone of effective market and competitive research. However, she points out that many organizations only pursue this halfway. Traditional methods often center on external customers, seeking to understand their usage patterns and how they articulate the value of a product. While valuable, this focus can be limiting. True customer obsession requires walking in their shoes—understanding not only their needs but also their language and emotional connection to the product. This level of empathy enables product marketers to align messaging and positioning with how customers naturally perceive value.

Randi introduces an often-neglected aspect of customer research: internal customers, such as sales and marketing teams. These teams serve as crucial conduits between the external customer and the organization. How well internal teams digest customer insights and translate them into meaningful conversations often dictates the success of a product's market positioning. Randi stresses organizations must pay equal attention to how sales and marketing teams interpret and communicate customer feedback. Misalignment here can result in mixed messaging, fragmented strategies, and missed opportunities.

A 360-degree customer view integrates external and internal perspectives to deliver a comprehensive understanding of the market. For external customers, it involves gathering qualitative and quantitative insights about their challenges, goals, and experiences with the product. For internal teams, it means understanding how they leverage this feedback in their strategies, messaging, and interactions with potential buyers. By bridging the gap between these two dimensions, organizations can ensure consistency and clarity in their go-to-market efforts.

Key Takeaways for Product Marketers

- **Expand Research Focus**: Go beyond studying external customers to analyze how internal teams process and utilize customer insights.
- **Foster Alignment**: Create mechanisms to ensure that internal teams are aligned with the customer's language and needs, promoting consistent messaging.
- **Adopt a 360-Degree Approach**: Integrate both external and internal customer perspectives to inform competitive and market strategies.

Randi's insights underline the importance of viewing customer research as a holistic practice. By taking the time to understand both the customer's voice and how internal teams interpret it, product marketers can craft strategies that resonate more deeply, differentiate effectively, and drive sustained success in competitive markets.

Surbhee Mishra (Bengaluru, Karnataka, India)

Bio

Surbhee Mishra is an accomplished Global Marketing Manager specializing in B2B technology, product marketing, and partner marketing across EMEA, APAC, and North America. With over seven years of experience, she has driven multi-channel demand generation campaigns that yielded 500+ leads and over $20M in business, improving marketing efficiency by 30%. Surbhee has deep expertise in account-based marketing, field marketing, and event management, having led over 15 ABM campaigns and 12 international events. Known for her strategic approach and strong cross-functional collaboration, she also hosts management webinars and podcasts, engaging audiences and driving thought leadership in B2B marketing.

Surbhee Mishra on Market & Competitive Research

In my interview with Surbhee Mishra, she shares a powerful insight into the importance of understanding the customer and collaborating effectively across teams. Surbhee's core message emphasizes the need to "know your customer well," which she describes as an essential foundation in creating an ideal customer profile. This process, she explains, is not just about identifying surface-level traits but involves a deep dive into what drives the customer—what truly "makes them tick."

Surbhee highlights the collaborative nature of product marketing, likening the role to an "Avengers" team effort where product marketers join forces with sales, product, and project management teams. For Surbhee, successful product marketing cannot happen in isolation; it's the synergy between different departments that drives results. She points out that working closely with cross-functional teams enables product marketers to deliver campaigns that resonate strongly with target audiences. This collaboration allows the team to create a message that goes beyond the typical, boring corporate pitch and instead demonstrates unique value that speaks directly to the customer's needs and aspirations.

Campaigns that intrigue audiences and "hit home" are essential, according to Surbhee. She believes the goal is not just to catch the customer's attention, but to engage them with messaging that shows the company offers something truly beneficial to their enterprise. For her, crafting a message that is relevant, engaging, and tailored to customer pain points is the essence of impactful product marketing. This type of messaging ultimately reinforces the company's value proposition and helps it stand out in a crowded B2B market.

Surbhee also emphasizes the necessity of data-driven strategies, particularly in the process of fine-tuning customer profiles and assessing campaign success. She notes that "crunching numbers" is a crucial responsibility for product marketers, as it enables them to ensure a high return on investment for their marketing budgets. Analyzing data helps the marketing team refine their understanding of the ideal customer, optimize campaigns, and allocate resources effectively. By leveraging metrics and insights, product marketers can continuously improve their strategies, adapt to changing customer preferences, and maximize impact.

The essence of Surbhee's advice lies in teamwork, deep customer understanding, and data-driven insights. She encourages product marketers to embrace their "Avengers" roles, using both creativity and analytical rigor to deliver value to customers. Her message is a reminder that great product marketing requires a holistic approach—one that involves connecting with customers on a meaningful level, collaborating across departments, and grounding decisions in data. Her insights reinforce the idea that product marketers are not just storytellers, but strategic partners capable of driving growth and innovation.

Zach Roberts (California, USA)

Bio

Zach Roberts is a seasoned product marketer with a unique blend of sales and marketing expertise, specializing in B2B SaaS. With five years of experience in B2B sales before transitioning to product marketing in 2020, he leverages his deep understanding of buyers to create personalized, relatable messaging that resonates. As the founder of Break into Product Marketing, Zach helps SaaS marketing leaders bridge the gap with sales teams through tailored enablement strategies. He also co-hosts the podcast "We're Not Marketers," which provides valuable insights for product marketers navigating internal challenges. Zach's diverse background includes prior roles at Dropbox, Klarity, and Faire.

Zach Roberts on Market & Competitive Research

In his interview with me, Zach Roberts emphasizes the importance of being action-oriented in product marketing, advocating for a focus on the immediate next steps that drive momentum. He stresses that while it's easy to get caught up in lofty goals, it's the smaller, actionable steps that lead to successful outcomes. By continuously assessing the next move and its impact, product marketers can avoid skipping crucial stages that may hinder the overall customer experience and understanding of the product. This practical approach allows for a more seamless and effective marketing strategy.

Zach provides an insightful example from his work on the podcast We're Not Marketers, which he co-hosts with Gab Bujold and Eric Holland. In treating the podcast as a product, the goal is to convert casual listeners into regular followers. Instead of aiming for broad, overwhelming objectives like massive listenership or widespread recognition, the team focuses on the specific action they want their audience to take at every stage of the journey. The key question they always ask is: "What is the immediate next step we need to keep momentum going?" This mindset helps them prioritize the actions that lead to growth without jumping ahead too quickly.

One notable example involves their strategy for converting someone who encounters the podcast on LinkedIn into a listener. Rather than directly asking potential listeners to commit to a full episode, they break the process down into smaller steps. The immediate next step is getting these individuals to engage with their company page or visit their website. To facilitate this, they create a teaser—a brief and engaging snippet from an episode that highlights a conversation directly relevant to their audience's interests and challenges. This teaser serves as a hook, sparking curiosity and leading potential listeners to take the next logical step in exploring the full episode.

Zach highlights that understanding the ideal customer profile (ICP) is essential when creating these teasers. By aligning the content with the target audience's needs, pain points, and aspirations, they ensure the snippet resonates deeply, prompting action. This approach, according to Zach, has been a significant factor in the podcast's growth and engagement.

For Zach, the key takeaway is that being action-oriented isn't just about executing a marketing plan, but about breaking down larger objectives into smaller, manageable actions that create a path for customers to follow. In product marketing, focusing on these incremental next steps allows for a more organic, sustainable approach to growth. By consistently refining and optimizing these steps based on audience behavior and feedback, marketers can build stronger relationships with their customers, ultimately driving long-term success and brand loyalty. This mindset not only accelerates conversions but also ensures the product resonates more deeply with the intended audience.

Having mastered Market and Competitive Research, we are ready to tackle the next essential Product Marketing skill: Positioning and Messaging.

WISDOM ON POSITIONING AND MESSAGING

WISDOM ON POSITIONING AND MESSAGING

P ositioning and messaging are pivotal in differentiating products and connecting with target audiences. While theoretical models offer essential frameworks, real-world professionals provide invaluable insights into how these concepts translate into effective strategies in competitive and dynamic markets.

Experienced marketers bring practical knowledge gained from crafting and refining positioning statements and messages for diverse industries. They share stories of what worked—and what didn't—when aligning products to customer needs, market trends, and competitive landscapes. Learning directly from these professionals reveals the subtle art of tailoring a message to resonate emotionally while remaining rooted in value propositions.

For example, a product marketer might recount how they shifted a product's positioning to appeal to a previously untapped audience, unlocking additional revenue streams. Another might explain how they developed messaging that clarified a complex product's benefits, overcoming customer confusion and boosting adoption rates. These insights demonstrate the iterative nature of positioning and messaging in real-world scenarios.

By engaging with seasoned professionals through interviews, case studies, or workshops, product marketers can gain a deeper understanding of the nuances behind creating compelling narratives. This hands-on wisdom equips them to develop positioning and messaging strategies that not only stand out but also drive measurable business impact.

In the following sections, we dive into the minds of industry titans as well as rising stars to better understand these concepts and their practical applications.

Aleksi Lehtola (Mexico City Area, Mexico)

Bio

Aleksi Lehtola is a technology-focused entrepreneur, investor, and CEO of SSO Agency, SmartAlly.io, and Platamoon.mx. Based in Mexico City, he brings over a decade of expertise in artificial intelligence, SaaS, and go-to-market strategies to lead high-growth tech companies. Aleksi is passionate about building scalable sales and marketing systems that align with his "people-first" philosophy, creating a collaborative, top-performing work culture. A certified trainer, speaker, and mentor, he has a diverse portfolio across North America and Europe and champions sustainable growth through digital innovation, smart processes, and automation within the HubSpot ecosystem.

Positioning & Messaging Insights from Aleksi Lehtola

In his interview with me, Aleksi Lehtola offers a deep perspective on positioning and messaging, stressing the importance of customer-centricity in crafting effective go-to-market strategies. Drawing on his extensive experience in marketing, sales, and product, Aleksi believes that the core principle of successful positioning lies in understanding and aligning with the customer's journey, not merely pushing a product.

Aleksi's approach begins with creating detailed customer personas, a fundamental step in the positioning process. These personas allow businesses to truly understand the target audience and, more importantly, map out their journey. He emphasizes the need for a customer journey map, an often-overlooked exercise that helps businesses track where customers go and what steps they take in making a purchasing decision. According to Aleksi, positioning cannot be about forcing customers down a predetermined path designed by the business. Instead, the focus must be on enabling customers to buy easily by aligning the process with their expectations and behaviors. The message here is clear: the process must reflect the customer's experience, not the company's agenda.

Positioning is also deeply connected to the ease of buying, and Aleksi points out that businesses often forget about the ease of selling. From a marketing and sales standpoint, it's crucial to ensure that sales teams have access to unified customer data. When the sales team is equipped with comprehensive information about the customer's journey, they can better serve the customer at the right time, optimizing the messaging and approach for maximum impact. Aleksi believes that when marketing, sales, and product teams are aligned around this unified view of the customer, it facilitates smoother sales enablement and more effective messaging.

Aleksi also touches on the importance of having authority over the go-to-market process, which allows product marketers to continuously advocate for the customer's needs. In his view, the ability to influence product decisions and adjust messaging based on real-time customer feedback is critical to the overall success of positioning. The challenge, he acknowledges, lies not in creating a better product but in fine-tuning all the minor aspects of the customer experience—from marketing and product design to sales and enablement—to ensure alignment around the customer's needs.

In sum, Aleksi reinforces that the key to successful positioning and messaging lies in maintaining a consistent focus on the customer throughout every decision. His approach is rooted in the belief that when companies design their processes with customer centricity at the core, they can more effectively communicate their value proposition and drive successful market outcomes.

David LaCombe (New York City, NY, USA)

Bio

David LaCombe is a seasoned Chief Marketing Officer based in New York, specializing in driving growth for B2B startups and scaleups. With a focus on healthcare and life sciences, David excels in bridging marketing, sales, and customer success to create scalable go-to-market strategies. He has a proven track record in brand management, strategic partnerships, and driving sales through customer-centric marketing initiatives. David is also a B-Corp evangelist and is authoring a guidebook on business acumen for marketers. His expertise spans across pricing strategy, demand capture, and community building, making him a valuable leader in delivering sustainable business growth.

Positioning & Messaging Insights from David LaCombe

In his interview with me, David LaCombe emphasizes that true innovation must always be paired with impact to succeed in the market. He stresses that for any innovation to gain traction, it must clearly demonstrate value and relevance to customers. His insights highlight the importance of effective positioning and messaging in communicating that value to potential users.

David outlines three common pitfalls that can hinder the success of innovations, which product marketers must address through clear messaging and strategic positioning. The first pitfall is the "nonstarter situation," where customers struggle to see how the innovation is superior to their current solutions. This occurs when the new product or feature doesn't resonate with the existing needs or preferences of the target audience. David uses the example of Google Glass, which failed to gain widespread adoption because it didn't clearly solve a significant problem for users. For product marketers, this underscores the importance of positioning innovations as solutions to real, tangible problems that customers face, ensuring the messaging makes it easy for potential customers to understand the benefits.

The second issue is insufficient implementation. David points out that innovations often fail when the process of adopting them is cumbersome or slow. He mentions the example of American Airlines, which faced delays in receiving its Boeing 787 aircraft, leading to frustration and inefficiencies. Similarly, in product marketing, if the messaging around an innovation fails to effectively address the implementation process—whether through complicated onboarding, unclear usage instructions, or lengthy adoption periods—the impact of the innovation is diminished. Marketers must communicate not only the product's benefits but also how easily customers can start using it and realize those benefits in a timely manner.

The third pitfall is when the cost of implementing the innovation outweighs the perceived value. David gives the example of smaller businesses investing in a CRM system that ultimately doesn't deliver the expected results. This highlights the critical role of positioning an organization's innovation as a cost-effective solution that delivers measurable value. Marketers need to ensure that their messaging makes it clear how the innovation provides a strong return on investment (ROI) and justifies the costs associated with its implementation.

In sum, David's message is clear: innovation can only thrive when it creates a significant impact. Effective product marketing and messaging must position the innovation as a clear improvement over existing solutions, ensure ease of adoption, and highlight the tangible value customers will receive. By addressing these factors, marketers can avoid the common pitfalls that lead to innovation failure and instead drive real, impactful success.

Dom Einhorn (Los Angeles, CA, USA)

Bio

Dom Einhorn is a multilingual serial entrepreneur and tech innovator based in Los Angeles. As the founder of Masters of Trivia and Born2Invest, he specializes in creating engaging digital platforms that combine education, entertainment, and business news. With over two decades of entrepreneurial experience, Dom has launched successful ventures including the Startup Supercup tech conference and UNIQORN, the world's largest rural incubator-accelerator. His latest venture, Intelligent Games LLC, aims to revolutionize knowledge-based gaming through innovative trivia and quiz experiences. A polyglot fluent in five languages, Dom brings a global perspective to his entrepreneurial endeavors.

Positioning & Messaging Insights from Dom Einhorn

In his interview with me, Dom Einhorn shares timeless wisdom on crafting effective positioning and messaging strategies. Drawing from over three decades of experience in the digital marketing space, Dom emphasizes the value of focusing on what remains constant rather than chasing fleeting trends. This approach offers a foundation for building enduring brands and businesses.

Dom challenges the tendency of marketers and entrepreneurs to follow trends or attempt to predict the future, noting that such efforts often lead to failure. Instead, he advocates for anchoring strategies in unchanging human needs and values. For example, the desire for love, connection, community, and belonging remains fundamental, regardless of technological or cultural shifts. By centering messaging on these universal truths, brands can create authentic and relatable narratives that stand the test of time.

He warns against the pitfall of creating solutions for nonexistent problems—an outcome he attributes to trend-driven approaches. Instead, Dom encourages addressing real, present challenges. This mindset not only grounds messaging in relevance but also resonates deeply with audiences seeking practical solutions to their pain points.

Dom's approach to positioning is rooted in stability and foresight. He likens chasing change to pursuing an ever-receding horizon, where businesses expend significant effort without achieving sustainable results. Effective positioning, he argues, involves identifying and leveraging constants in consumer behavior and societal needs. For example, the growing emphasis on community and connection, even in a world increasingly influenced by AI, provides a reliable cornerstone for messaging strategies.

From a messaging perspective, Dom highlights the importance of authenticity and clarity. By focusing on universal human desires, businesses can craft messages that evoke emotional connections and foster trust. For instance, emphasizing themes of belonging or mutual care allows brands to transcend superficial trends and establish a deeper rapport with their audience.

Dom also ties these insights to investment strategies, explaining that businesses rooted in unchanging principles are more likely to succeed. He encourages entrepreneurs to position their brands as solutions to enduring problems, ensuring long-term relevance and market viability.

In summary, Dom's insights provide a powerful framework for positioning and messaging. By focusing on timeless human needs and steering clear of trend-driven strategies, marketers can craft messages that are authentic, impactful, and sustainable. This approach not only builds stronger connections with audiences but also ensures brands remain relevant amidst rapid change. For entrepreneurs and marketers alike, Dom's advice serves as a guiding principle: success lies in solving genuine problems and communicating solutions in ways that resonate with universal truths.

Liudmila Kiseleva (Washington, DC, USA)

Bio

Liudmila Kiseleva is the CEO of Rampiq, a B2B marketing agency specializing in revenue growth for IT and SaaS companies through expert SEO, content marketing, and lead generation. With over 17 years in digital marketing, Liudmila is renowned for her robust frameworks and her hands-on approach to managing a team of 20+ global professionals. She also hosts the B2B Tech Founders Lounge podcast, sharing insights from the industry. A passionate AI enthusiast and serial entrepreneur, Liudmila brings proven processes, strategic oversight, and a dedication to empowering tech founders and marketing leaders to achieve scalable results.

Positioning & Messaging Insights from Liudmila Kiseleva

In her interview with me, Liudmila Kiseleva offers crucial advice on positioning and messaging, particularly from the perspective of SEO (Search Engine Optimization) and its rapidly evolving dynamics. While SEO has long been considered a stable and traditional field, Liudmila emphasizes the importance of staying agile, as the landscape has undergone significant changes, especially over the past year. This insight speaks directly to the need for businesses to adapt their positioning and messaging in response to changes in search algorithms and other trends.

Traditionally, SEO professionals, particularly those in B2B sectors, have relied on established practices and stable algorithms to guide their efforts. However, Liudmila points out that even in these stable fields, things can shift unexpectedly. She mentions how long-established algorithms, such as those used by Google, or emerging new functions in AI platforms like ChatGPT Search have undergone substantial updates that may have caught some professionals off guard. While this might seem like a challenge, Liudmila advises that it's crucial to view these changes not as disruptions but as opportunities to improve and refine positioning and messaging strategies. Businesses should be ready to pivot, evolve, and embrace these shifts to maintain their competitiveness in a fast-moving digital environment.

Liudmila's wisdom is particularly relevant to product marketers who are responsible for crafting and maintaining a brand's messaging. In an ever-changing SEO landscape, maintaining effective messaging requires a dynamic approach. Marketers can no longer rely on old methods but must constantly optimize their content to keep pace with changes in user behavior, search algorithms, and content trends. This includes ensuring that their messaging remains aligned with the right keywords, phrases, and user intent—ensuring the right content is being discovered by the target audience.

Her advice also touches on being proactive and looking for ways to turn change into an advantage. With the speed at which digital marketing is evolving, there is no room for complacency. Marketers must continuously refine their approach, ensuring that their messaging resonates with the evolving needs of their audience. By remaining vigilant and adaptable, businesses can stay ahead of competitors, maintain visibility in search rankings, and effectively communicate their value propositions.

Furthermore, Liudmila emphasizes the broader impact of staying alert and prepared. By monitoring changes in SEO trends and adjusting messaging accordingly, businesses not only position themselves more effectively but also create better experiences for their clients and partners. A brand's ability to adapt its messaging to fit the times can help it connect more deeply with its audience, driving engagement, loyalty, and ultimately, growth.

In sum, Liudmila Kiseleva's insights underline the critical need for product marketers to be adaptable, especially with positioning and messaging in the SEO realm. By staying proactive, monitoring shifts, and refining messaging strategies in real time, businesses can ensure they remain visible, relevant, and competitive in an increasingly dynamic digital environment.

Paul Terrasson Duvernon (France & Sweden)

Bio

Paul Terrasson Duvernon is a versatile Product Designer and entrepreneur with expertise in UX/UI and Product-Led Growth. Based in Sweden, he has collaborated with over 30 leading startups across France and internationally, leveraging his background in computer engineering from INSA Lyon and Chalmers University. His career spans impactful roles from Chief of Staff to Product Lead at EdTech firm Augment.org, where he revamped the user experience. Passionate about tech innovation, Paul also co-hosted a top French DeepTech podcast, engaging global tech leaders. Fluent in multiple languages, he brings a unique blend of technical, creative, and business acumen to his projects.

Paul Terrasson Duvernon on Positioning & Messaging

In his interview with me, Paul Terrasson Duvernon shares a powerful perspective on positioning & messaging that emphasizes the importance of ethical practices in product marketing and design. Drawing on his experiences as both a product professional and a user, Paul advocates for a user-centric approach that prioritizes transparency and integrity over manipulation.

Paul identifies a concerning trend in the proliferation of dark patterns—design tactics that manipulate user behavior for short-term gains. These patterns, he explains, are increasingly accepted and even praised as "smart" strategies within the product and marketing communities. However, Paul warns against normalizing such tactics, as they exploit psychological vulnerabilities and erode trust. For him, positioning and messaging should not rely on trickery but should instead focus on fostering genuine value and long-term relationships with users.

Paul's advice is the reminder that behind every screen, interface, and click is a human being. Ethical positioning and messaging require marketers to view users as partners rather than targets. This perspective challenges product marketers to craft narratives that empower users to make informed decisions rather than manipulate them into actions they may regret. Paul urges his peers to consider the long-term implications of their strategies, emphasizing that trust and respect are essential to sustainable success.

Paul also highlights the importance of vigilance and self-awareness in ethical positioning. As professionals, he notes, it is easy to be swayed by industry trends or pressured into adopting questionable practices. To counter this, Paul encourages product marketers and designers to actively identify and reject dark patterns in their work. He also points to the abundance of resources available for understanding and combating manipulative tactics, suggesting that ethical marketing and design are both achievable and well-supported by the broader community.

The heart of Paul's message is that positioning and messaging should reflect the values of honesty, respect, and empathy. Instead of focusing on short-term conversions through deceptive methods, marketers should aim to build lasting relationships by presenting their products authentically and helping users choose them for the right reasons.

In summary, Paul's insights remind us that ethical positioning and messaging are not just about avoiding harm, but about actively contributing to a better user experience. By treating users with respect and focusing on genuine value, product marketers can foster trust and loyalty while also achieving sustainable business success. His advice is a call to action for the industry to prioritize humanity and integrity in every aspect of its communication.

Rob Kaminski (Austin, TX, USA)

Bio

Rob Kaminski is a product marketing expert and co-founder of Fletch PMM, where he supports early-stage founders by refining their product positioning and developing impactful messaging. With experience consulting over 300 venture-backed startups, Rob has a proven track record in strategic positioning for B2B businesses. His career highlights include founding an incubator acquired by Vista Equity Group, launching multiple software products, and leading go-to-market strategies at Oracle. Rob holds a master's in technology commercialization from Case Western Reserve University.

Rob Kaminski on Positioning & Messaging: Clarity through Deliberate Targeting

In his interview with me, Rob Kaminski highlights a fundamental but often misunderstood truth about positioning: it is dynamic and must adapt depending on the audience. He underscores the critical role of deliberate decision-making in crafting clear, interesting messaging that resonates deeply with specific target segments.

Positioning is not static, Rob explains; it shifts depending on the specific roles and personas within your target audience. This nuance is frequently overlooked, particularly by startup teams attempting to create a one-size-fits-all message. He warns that trying to appeal to everyone—CEOs, operations directors, and finance leads simultaneously—leads to vague messaging that resonates with no one. Instead, effective positioning requires teams to focus sharply on specific audiences and tailor messaging to their unique needs and challenges.

For Rob, the homepage is not just a marketing asset; it is a direct reflection of an organization's positioning strategy. He identifies it as the first critical asset to address when shaping go-to-market programs, particularly for early-stage startups post-funding. Mistakes often arise when teams try to accommodate multiple markets, audiences, or products on this single page, resulting in a diluted and ineffective message.

The core of Rob's advice revolves around making deliberate choices about positioning. Teams must decide not only who their product is for but also who it is not for. This focus prevents the common pitfall of trying to cater to everyone, which inevitably weakens the impact of messaging. A clear, targeted homepage becomes a rallying point for marketing and sales teams, ensuring consistency and clarity across all customer touchpoints.

Rob advocates for a collaborative approach to refining positioning, recommending that teams rewrite the homepage together, including key stakeholders like founders. This exercise forces teams to clarify their priorities and articulate their differentiated value in simple, interesting terms. By prioritizing specificity, teams can avoid overspending on scattered go-to-market programs and instead build cohesive, impactful messaging.

Key Takeaways

- **Positioning is dynamic**: Tailor messaging to specific roles and contexts rather than broad groups.
- **The homepage reflects strategy**: Use it as a testing ground and cornerstone of clear, deliberate positioning.
- **Focus is critical**: Define not just your audience but also who you are not prioritizing to sharpen your messaging.
- **Collaborate early**: Involve cross-functional stakeholders to align positioning and messaging from the outset.

By embracing this focused, collaborative approach, teams can craft positioning and messaging strategies that drive meaningful engagement and fuel sustainable growth.

Rob Kaminski (Austin, TX, USA)

Roger Lanctot (Herndon, VA, USA)

Bio

Roger C. Lanctot is a pioneering expert in automotive and mobility connectivity, specializing in integrating satellite and cellular technology across transportation sectors to enhance safety, efficiency, and cost savings. As the Founder of StrategiaNow and President of the Mobile Satellite Users Association, Roger's strategic insights drive innovations in connected vehicles, from cars to planes and ships. His extensive experience includes leadership roles at TechInsights and Strategy Analytics, where he shaped connected mobility solutions. An award-winning analyst and industry advisor, Roger is committed to advancing the future of connected mobility through strategic consulting and industry-wide collaboration.

Roger Lanctot on Positioning & Messaging

Roger Lanctot's analysis in his article "Elon Musk: King of Connectivity" offers a masterclass in positioning and messaging. Musk's approach exemplifies how an ecosystem-driven strategy not only fortifies a brand but also amplifies its value proposition across multiple markets. From Lanctot's observations, product marketers can glean actionable insights about positioning, differentiation, and market alignment.

Strategic Positioning: Owning the Ecosystem - Lanctot underscores Musk's mastery in ecosystem-building, with Tesla seamlessly integrating electric vehicles, charging infrastructure, home energy solutions, artificial intelligence, and autonomous driving technology. This interconnectedness positions Tesla not just as a carmaker but as a comprehensive mobility and sustainability brand. The brilliance lies in vertically integrating these elements to reinforce the customer experience and differentiate Tesla. For product marketers, the takeaway is clear: developing interconnected solutions can elevate a brand's perceived value and lock in customer loyalty, making switching costs prohibitively high for competitors.

Messaging Alignment: Shaping Market Perception - Musk's ventures rely on messaging that aligns technical innovation with aspirational goals.

BY NITIN KARTIK

Lanctot highlights how SpaceX's Starlink aligns with public-sector initiatives like rural broadband expansion and green energy, portraying Musk as a problem-solver. This messaging transcends technology, embedding Starlink within narratives of accessibility, sustainability, and national interest. For marketers, this reinforces the importance of crafting messages that resonate not just with immediate benefits but also with broader cultural or social values.

Market Differentiation: Connecting the Unconnected - Lanctot's discussion on Starlink's pivot from direct-to-consumer satellite internet to a broader infrastructure and commercial connectivity play is especially instructive. Musk leveraged government contracts, defense collaborations, and aviation and maritime markets to scale Starlink. By aligning with emerging FCC standards for satellite-cellular connectivity and addressing 5G rural backhaul gaps, Starlink differentiates itself as a multifaceted solution. This demonstrates how targeting underserved or niche markets with scalable potential can provide a strategic edge, especially when combined with regulatory or infrastructural alignment.

Anticipating Future Opportunities: Standards-Based Connectivity - Lanctot forecasts standards-based satellite-to-car connectivity within two years, offering ubiquitous coverage for safety, navigation, and infotainment. Musk's readiness to adopt 3GPP standards ensures that Tesla remains at the forefront of the evolving connectivity ecosystem. For product marketers, this illustrates the importance of staying attuned to industry standards and technological advancements to capitalize on first-mover advantages.

Key Takeaway for Product Marketers - Lanctot's insights illuminate how Musk positions his ventures as indispensable components of larger ecosystems. By integrating products into broader societal and infrastructural narratives, he creates a gravitational pull that fosters trust, loyalty, and market dominance. For product marketing leaders, the lesson is to craft positioning strategies that extend beyond features, rooting products within transformative, purpose-driven narratives.

Roger Lanctot (Herndon, VA, USA)

Ryan Sorley (Wayland, MA, USA)

Bio

Ryan Sorley is a seasoned leader in competitive intelligence, currently serving as VP of Win-Loss and Cofounder at Klue. With over two decades of experience in research, Ryan founded DoubleCheck Research in 2014, a leading win-loss analysis firm which he bootstrapped to $10M in revenue through organic growth. Following DoubleCheck's acquisition by Klue in 2022, he now leads Klue's integrated win-loss and competitive enablement program, helping organizations drive smarter sales and marketing strategies. Ryan's background spans roles at industry giants like Gartner, AMR Research, and Forrester, where he honed his expertise in business strategy and leadership.

Ryan Sorley on Solving Problems Through Focused Value Delivery

In his interview with me, Ryan Sorley shares his journey from a sales leader at Gartner to building a successful bootstrapped business, emphasizing how clear positioning and value-driven messaging underpin sustainable growth. His story demonstrates how understanding a specific problem, articulating its solution, and delivering measurable client value can create a firm foundation for success in any business.

Ryan's story begins with a critical insight he gained at Gartner, where he observed confusion between two key client groups: buyers and sellers of technology. Recognizing this disconnect, he identified a unique opportunity to bridge the gap by providing actionable insights from buyers to sellers. This laser focus on solving a pressing problem set the stage for his business. His ability to position himself as the right person to tackle the challenge stemmed from his deep industry experience and a clear understanding of client pain points.

Ryan's success stems from his ability to carve out a niche and focus on delivering unmatched value. Rather than scaling rapidly or relying on aggressive sales tactics, he positioned his business as a partner uniquely dedicated to solving a specific problem. His messaging emphasized the transformative impact of the insights he provided. By prioritizing client outcomes, he differentiated his services from others in the crowded landscape.

At the heart of Ryan's approach is a commitment to client value. His messaging consistently highlights the benefits his services bring, such as clarity in buyer-seller relationships and actionable insights for technology sellers. By communicating the "why" behind his services and aligning his business offerings with client goals, he created an interesting narrative that resonated deeply with his audience. This client-first messaging strategy not only fostered trust but also fueled organic growth through word-of-mouth and client referrals.

Unlike many businesses that chase rapid growth through external funding or aggressive hiring, Ryan chose a deliberate, organic path. He expanded his team only as needed, ensuring every addition supported his mission of delivering exceptional value. This focused, authenticity-driven approach allowed his business to grow sustainably and maintain its core promise to clients.

Lessons for Positioning & Messaging

- **Solve a specific problem**: Positioning begins with identifying and addressing a clear market need.
- **Differentiate through value**: Highlight the unique benefits your offering provides to clients.
- **Be client-centric**: Align messaging with client goals and outcomes to build trust and drive loyalty.
- **Scale intentionally**: Stay focused on the mission, expanding only when necessary to sustain quality.

Ryan's journey showcases how effective positioning and messaging, rooted in solving real-world problems, can lead to sustainable growth and long-term success.

Shoshana Kordova (Israel)

Bio

Shoshana Kordova is a 3x founding product marketer and Product Marketing Alliance Ambassador with over 10 years of experience in journalism. Specializing in customer-centric messaging for B2B tech startups, Shoshana leverages deep customer insights to shape impactful case studies, website content, and sales enablement assets that speak directly to target audiences. Through her consultancy, Peel Product Marketing, she helps growth-stage companies define clear positioning, develop competitive intelligence, and refine their ideal customer profiles. Previously, Shoshana served in senior product marketing roles at Nayax, Optibus, Scopio Labs, and Datarails, combining her storytelling expertise with a strategic approach to product marketing.

Shoshana Kordova on Positioning & Messaging

In my interview with Shoshana Kordova, she shares valuable insights on how to extract genuine, impactful feedback from customer conversations. According to Shoshana, the key to uncovering "gold nuggets" of information lies in treating customer calls not as rigid interviews but as fluid, open conversations driven by follow-up questions.

Shoshana emphasizes that the initial responses customers give are often generic or superficial. When asking, for example, "How do you like using our product?" customers might reply with broad answers like "It's useful" or "It's great." While positive, these responses lack the depth needed to uncover true customer value. Shoshana advises product marketers to use this initial answer as merely a starting point, not an endpoint. She suggests asking targeted follow-up questions to dig deeper into the customer's experience.

Questions like "How did you reach that goal before using our product?" or "How long did that take before, and how long does it take now?" allow marketers to draw comparisons, revealing powerful insights about the product's ROI from the customer's perspective. Shoshana explains these moments are where the "gold ROI nuggets" emerge—those insights that reflect the true impact of the product and can be used to shape messaging and positioning that resonates with other potential customers.

One of the most effective techniques Shoshana recommends is encouraging customers to explain their experiences in simple terms, almost as if they were speaking to someone unfamiliar with the product. This helps customers articulate why a particular feature or benefit is meaningful, often leading to revelations about the product's unique value in their daily lives.

Shoshana's advice highlights the importance of listening carefully to what the customer is saying and engaging thoughtfully with their replies. Rather than moving on to the next question after a quick answer, she suggests following up and encouraging the customer to elaborate. By digging deeper and exploring various angles of their experiences, product marketers can uncover valuable feedback that might otherwise go unnoticed.

Her approach serves as a reminder that in product marketing, sometimes the most insightful answers come not from a checklist but from thoughtful, responsive engagement. By prioritizing open-ended questions and follow-ups, marketers can gain a richer understanding of customer needs and experiences, transforming basic conversations into a treasure trove of insights.

Sid Khaitan (Chicago, IL, USA)

Bio

Sid Khaitan is a Senior Product Marketing Manager at Beekeeper, specializing in go-to-market (GTM) strategy and competitive enablement with extensive experience in content strategy and B2B partnerships. He has successfully led initiatives that boosted ARR by 217% at Chili Piper, designed high-impact campaigns at MarketingOps.com, and managed content strategy at Intouch Group, driving engagement and retention. Sid also founded The Cabin, a creative agency supporting high-profile clients in the SaaS, culinary, and healthcare sectors. With certifications in Product Marketing and Product-Led Growth, Sid brings a well-rounded skill set and strategic insight to the field of product marketing.

Sid Khaitan on Positioning & Messaging: Focusing on Customer Problems

In his interview with me, Sid Khaitan shares valuable insights into how to approach product marketing through a positioning and messaging lens. He stresses the importance of going beyond product features and understanding the customer and market problems that the product aims to solve. Sid believes that effective product marketing stems from being attuned to the pain points and challenges faced by customers, which should directly inform messaging and product strategy.

Sid highlights a common misconception in product marketing: that the primary focus should be on aligning with the product manager and promoting new product features. While product features are important, Sid argues that product marketers should shift their focus to solving the actual problems customers face. By deeply understanding these challenges, product marketers can craft messaging that resonates with the target audience and addresses their needs. Sid emphasizes that this approach leads to stronger positioning in the market, as it shifts the narrative from product-centric to customer-centric, creating more meaningful and relevant communication.

Aligning Messaging with Customer Needs

A key point Sid makes is that successful messaging is rooted in understanding the customer's pain points. As product marketers progress in their careers, they should focus more on what customers are experiencing rather than just aligning with internal product development timelines. By engaging with customers, understanding their struggles, and identifying patterns, product marketers can shape messaging that communicates the product's true value. This deeper connection with the market not only improves messaging but also ensures that the product is positioned as the solution to real, pressing problems.

Using Market Insights to Drive Product Development and Influence

Sid notes that staying attuned to the market and customer feedback also influences product development. When product marketers understand the real-world problems that customers are facing, they can provide valuable insights to the product development team, shaping future features and updates. This collaboration helps ensure the product evolves in a way that continues to address market needs effectively. By focusing on solving problems rather than merely pushing new features, product marketers can help drive both customer satisfaction and product success.

In Sum

Sid Khaitan's perspective on positioning and messaging underscores the importance of viewing product marketing through the lens of problem-solving. By deeply understanding customer pain points, aligning messaging with those needs, and influencing product development based on market insights, product marketers can create stronger, more impactful positioning strategies that resonate with their audience.

Thiago Neres (Ontario, Canada)

Bio

Thiago Neres is a Senior Product Marketing Manager at RouteThis with over five years of experience in B2B marketing for SaaS companies. With a background in journalism, he brings a curious, data-driven, and empathetic approach to his work, empowering teams to create interesting narratives that resonate with customers. His expertise includes product positioning, go-to-market strategy, and competitive intelligence, having successfully launched multiple products and driven market expansion initiatives. Thiago also mentors aspiring Product Marketing Managers through ADP List, and enjoys traveling, hiking, drumming, coding, and cooking in his spare time.

Thiago Neres on Positioning & Messaging

In his interview with me, Thiago Neres emphasizes the crucial role of message testing in validating product positioning. He explains that testing your messaging is essential to not only validate your product's value themes but also to ensure that the proof points supporting your positioning are interesting and persuasive. Thiago advocates for using tools like Wynter to conduct message testing, which allows product marketers to refine their messaging based on real audience feedback.

Thiago shares an insightful experience where, after redefining his product's value propositions and broader value themes, he began testing his messaging. While the feedback from the audience confirmed that his value propositions resonated with them, he discovered a significant gap: the website did not provide enough proof points to reinforce the product's value. Despite the audience's alignment with the messaging, the lack of case studies, interactive demos, and sufficient product differentiators on the website made it harder for potential customers to fully understand and appreciate the product's unique benefits.

This experience highlights the importance of ensuring that the messaging not only speaks to the audience's needs but also provides enough supporting evidence to build trust and credibility. Thiago notes that even when your audience agrees with your value proposition, the absence of clear proof points, such as case studies or product demos, can undermine the impact of your messaging. This lesson reinforces that positioning is not just about the words you use, but also about how you substantiate your claims and differentiate your product.

Thiago's perspective suggests that message testing is an indispensable step in the product marketing process. It ensures that your messaging is not just relevant, but also persuasive, making sure that your audience has enough context and proof to understand why your product is the right choice. Through continuous testing and iteration, marketers can refine their messaging to align with audience expectations, ultimately driving better customer engagement and more effective positioning.

In sum, Thiago's advice underscores that product marketers must prioritize message testing as a key part of refining their positioning strategy. It's not enough for a value proposition to simply resonate—it must also be substantiated with clear, impactful proof points that help potential customers see the unique benefits and differentiators of the product. By doing so, marketers can ensure their messaging is both interesting and credible, laying a solid foundation for successful product positioning in the market.

Once we have our Positioning and Messaging in a good place, we are prepared to tackle the next essential Product Marketing Skill: Go-to-Market Strategy.

WISDOM ON GO-TO-MARKET STRATEGY

WISDOM ON GO-TO-MARKET STRATEGY

A successful Go-to-Market (GTM) strategy is the backbone of any product's launch, dictating how it reaches customers, gains traction, and achieves business objectives. While frameworks and templates provide structure, real-world insights from experienced professionals bring GTM strategies to life by revealing the challenges, nuances, and decisions behind impactful executions.

Professionals with hands-on GTM experience share practical stories that illuminate the complexities of aligning stakeholders, anticipating market reactions, and navigating unforeseen obstacles. For instance, a seasoned product marketer might explain how they adjusted their GTM strategy mid-launch in response to a competitor's surprise move or how they tailored distribution channels to meet the unique demands of a regional market.

These real-world insights often uncover the gaps between theory and practice, such as managing cross-functional alignment or balancing speed-to-market with product readiness. They also provide invaluable lessons on how to prioritize resources, refine value propositions, and measure success post-launch.

Engaging with industry veterans through case studies, mentorship, or webinars equips product marketers with actionable knowledge that's hard to gain elsewhere. By learning from their experiences, marketers can design GTM strategies that are not only comprehensive but also agile enough to adapt to the unpredictable nature of real-world markets.

In the following sections, we examine the insights of industry titans and rising stars to understand these skills better in practice.

Akshaya Chandramouli (India)

Bio

Akshaya Chandramouli is a dynamic B2B brand strategist and Head of Brand at Storylane, where she crafts memorable brand experiences with a creative edge. Known for founding The Newsletter Nerd Show, Akshaya previously managed and elevated brand presence at Paperflite, developing a distinctive tone, UX copy, and engaging social content. Her expertise spans creative writing, content marketing, and communications, with a hands-on approach to storytelling that resonates with audiences. Outside of work, Akshaya enjoys capturing inspiring content moments and spending time with her toddler. Akshaya is based in the United States and has deep roots in brand-driven storytelling.

Akshaya Chandramouli on Go-To-Market Strategy

In her interview with me, Akshaya Chandramouli, reflecting on a recent product launch at Storylane, provides valuable insights into executing a standout go-to-market (GTM) strategy. Her approach underscores the importance of cross-functional collaboration, community celebration, and multi-channel amplification to drive successful product launches and measurable ROI.

At Storylane, Akshaya and her team reimagined the traditional product launch playbook. Instead of limiting the planning and execution to the product marketing team, they engaged all marketing functions from the start. This unified effort enabled the team to present a cohesive front and leverage diverse skill sets, creating a holistic GTM strategy. By involving stakeholders early, the launch effort was collaborative and synergistic, ensuring consistency across all touchpoints.

A cornerstone of this GTM strategy was their commitment to celebrating not only the product but also their community of champions and advocates. This led to the creation and distribution of custom gift boxes to community members worldwide containing fun socks, a mystery note to keep an eye out for the launch, some stickers, and other goodies. These thoughtful packages, including items like branded socks, delighted recipients and sparked organic support for the launch. This approach demonstrates the value of fostering relationships and leveraging community goodwill to amplify a product launch.

The GTM strategy comprised three core components. First, the team built a unique brand experience through the gift boxes, generating excitement and goodwill among their community. Second, they collaborated with micro-influencers to help amplify their message to a broader audience. These partnerships extended the launch's reach while building credibility.

Finally, the live product launch served as the grand finale. During the event, Storylane's cofounder, Nalin, unveiled the product, generating enthusiasm and providing a clear vision of its value proposition. This live engagement not only reinforced the product's messaging but also created a memorable moment that resonated with the audience.

The results of this comprehensive GTM strategy were remarkable. Storylane's product waitlist was fully booked within weeks, a testament to the campaign's effectiveness. This success highlights the ROI of investing in creative, community-centered strategies that resonate with target audiences.

Akshaya's GTM approach showcases how integrating cross-functional collaboration, community appreciation, and strategic partnerships can elevate a product launch. Her experience serves as a guide for product marketers aiming to achieve impactful launches that balance creativity and ROI, leaving lasting impressions on customers and advocates alike.

Archita Fritz (Dusseldorf, Germany)

Bio

Archita Fritz is a strategic growth catalyst and fractional leader with over 20 years of experience driving business transformation across industries. She specializes in leadership energy, growth transformation, and team reconfiguration, helping organizations unlock sustainable growth. Archita has led 25+ product launches, generating $2.1B in revenue across 128 countries. As a board member, speaker, and advisor, she collaborates with private equity and venture-backed firms to maximize performance. Archita also serves as a workplace culture advisor, focusing on diversity, inclusion, and belonging. She is the host of the Embracing Only podcast and an advocate for transformative leadership.

Archita Fritz on Go-To-Market Strategy

In my interview with Archita Fritz, she emphasizes the transformative power of customer centricity in product development. Archita, who started her career in engineering before moving into quality systems and then marketing, reflects on how centering decisions around the customer's perspective has been a key lesson throughout her journey. She explains that early in her career, when she did not consider customer needs during the engineering process, issues would inevitably arise. Quality engineers often had to address complaints related to products that missed the mark, and sales teams needed her to join them in the field to resolve problems. This taught her firsthand how crucial it is to keep the customer's voice central to product design.

As she transitioned into marketing, Archita brought this mindset with her, advocating strongly for a customer-first approach in all her work. She describes a video she often shares with clients: a sales representative highlighting numerous features of a product by pulling out different drawers, each with a specific purpose, yet none addressing the customer's primary needs. This illustrates the disconnect that can occur when companies develop products in isolation, relying on assumptions about the market rather than direct customer feedback. Archita believes that regardless of budget or scale, if a product is developed without true customer insight, it will probably fall short.

Archita underscores her point with a powerful personal example. She recalls a project that required her team to seek insights from markets outside the United States, despite initially thinking that a US-focused approach was sufficient. Through a year-long process of gathering feedback, they discovered critical insights from international markets, which ultimately led to a product that saved lives—including, remarkably, her own father's life in Bangalore, India. This experience reinforced for her the importance of listening to customers across a range of geographies and demographics, not just the usual suspects. By broadening the scope of customer input, her team developed a product that was more aligned with diverse customer needs.

Archita's story serves as a powerful reminder that the best products are those created with a deep understanding of customer challenges, preferences, and contexts. She urges product marketers to avoid the trap of relying solely on intuition or industry experience, as these can lead to misalignment with actual customer needs. Instead, she encourages a proactive approach to engaging with customers at every stage of development to ensure that the end-product truly serves its intended purpose.

In summary, Archita's advice is clear: prioritize customer feedback, listen closely to their needs, and remain adaptable to insights that may challenge initial assumptions. Her journey underscores the immense value of customer-centricity in creating impactful, life-saving products.

Björn W. Schäfer (Zurich, Switzerland)

Bio

Björn W. Schäfer is a seasoned entrepreneur and advisor specializing in scaling B2B SaaS startups. With over a decade of experience, he has helped over 100 startups grow from pre-seed to Series B, focusing on optimizing go-to-market strategies and sales methodologies. As the founder of Rowing8 AG, Björn supports early-stage companies in achieving sustainable growth through his proven GTM acceleration framework. He is also an angel investor, author of Funky Flywheels, and host of The SaaS Symphony podcast. Fluent in German, English, French, and Italian, Björn brings global expertise to scaling businesses efficiently.

Björn W. Schäfer on Go-To-Market Strategy

In his interview with me, Björn W. Schäfer discusses a critical component of a successful Go-to-Market (GTM) strategy: the strategic role of product marketing. Björn describes product marketing as the essential link between product development and commercialization, emphasizing that it's central to effective GTM execution. According to him, organizations of all sizes—whether startups or established enterprises—benefit significantly from a product marketing function that integrates seamlessly across teams to foster cohesion and drive results.

Björn explains that product marketing should not be perceived as a linear function, but as an orchestrating role that adapts fluidly to the needs of product, sales, and customer success teams. This adaptability allows for a dynamic GTM approach, where product marketers can pivot or refine strategies based on real-time feedback, market shifts, or evolving customer needs. In Björn's view, the role of product marketing is highly strategic and operational, requiring it to be a key part of decision-making in every stage of the product life cycle. GTM success, he argues, hinges on having product marketing closely aligned with both high-level strategy and day-to-day operations.

A core part of Björn's GTM philosophy is that product marketing is indispensable because of its role in strategy and execution. Product marketing effectively fills the critical gap between building and selling the product by actively aligning with teams. Organizations with a product marketing role can leverage their expertise to continuously drive alignment and iterate on product messaging, positioning, and sales enablement.

Björn emphasizes the need for product marketers to be deeply involved in strategic decision-making, mainly for SaaS businesses, which face rapid changes in customer expectations and competitive landscapes. By aligning directly with strategic goals and remaining operationally agile, product marketing supports scalable GTM efforts, ensuring that product launches are well-informed by customer insights and competitive intelligence. This results in a cohesive GTM strategy in which each launch and initiative is tailored to resonate with target markets and meet revenue objectives.

Björn's insights underscore that product marketing is central to an adaptable, integrated GTM strategy. By bridging product development and commercialization, product marketing enables cross-functional alignment, ensuring that strategic initiatives are impactful and relevant. Organizations that recognize and invest in this role early are better positioned to scale effectively, meet customer needs, and achieve sustained success. For GTM success, it's crucial to recognize product marketing as an orchestrator of strategic vision and operational execution.

Jonathan Pipek (Illinois, USA)

Bio

Jonathan Pipek is the founder of Blue Manta Consulting, a Chicago-based firm specializing in GTM strategy for B2B SaaS startups. Leveraging over a decade of experience, Jonathan partners with clients to refine positioning, packaging, and pricing, as well as execute product launches and sales enablement. He serves as a GTM mentor at 1871.com's FinTech Innovation Lab and has a proven track record in product marketing leadership across various industries, including cybersecurity and talent acquisition. Jonathan holds an MBA from Northwestern University's Kellogg School of Management and regularly contributes to the Product Marketing Alliance.

GTM Strategy Insights from Jonathan Pipek

In his interview with me, Jonathan Pipek underscores the pivotal role of a robust go-to-market (GTM) strategy in determining the success of a startup. He asserts that a GTM strategy can either propel a business forward or lead it to stagnation. At its core, an effective GTM strategy rests on understanding foundational elements such as the Ideal Customer Profile (ICP), target personas, and the specific problems or "jobs to be done" the product or service addresses.

Jonathan stresses the importance of knowing exactly who you are targeting and why. Without clarity on these elements, efforts in positioning, messaging, pricing, or even broader marketing initiatives are futile. He likens an unclear strategy to "lighting money on fire," as spending on advertising or experimenting with channels without foundational knowledge leads to wasted resources and missed opportunities.

The first step, Jonathan explains, is identifying and articulating the value the product delivers to the intended audience. This involves crafting positioning and messaging that resonate deeply with the identified ICP and personas. Coupled with thoughtful packaging and pricing strategies, these elements form the bedrock of a startup's GTM approach. Only when this foundation is established does it make sense to layer on additional tactics such as channel experimentation or advertising campaigns.

Jonathan also highlights the need for alignment between the startup's product offering and its pricing model. He notes that improperly aligned pricing can undermine customer trust and hinder adoption. By focusing on getting this right, startups not only position themselves for financial success but also build credibility in their market.

Once the fundamentals are secure, startups can explore more dynamic aspects of a GTM strategy. Jonathan emphasizes experimenting with various marketing channels to determine which avenues drive the most meaningful engagement and results. He also advocates for cultivating strategic relationships that can expand distribution opportunities. Partnerships and community are critical elements of GTM strategy that can significantly enhance reach and adoption rates.

Finally, Jonathan points to adoption as a critical metric for GTM success. Ensuring that customers find value in the product and integrate it into their workflows validates the strategy and drives growth. By focusing on adoption, startups can turn early customers into advocates, creating organic momentum in the market.

In summary, Jonathan Pipek outlines a disciplined, step-by-step approach to GTM strategy, starting with solidifying foundational elements like ICP, positioning, and pricing. By prioritizing these aspects before exploring broader tactics, startups can maximize their chances of sustainable growth and long-term success.

Kirsten Jepson (Florida, USA)

Bio

Kirsten Jepson is a Top 10 Product Marketing Consultant and 3X Top Product Marketing Leader with over 20 years of B2B experience. As a Fractional Product Marketing Leader, she specializes in building, scaling, and revitalizing product marketing strategies, having led over 150 product launches and 10 major acquisitions. Kirsten excels in Digital Transformation, AI, and Robotic Process Automation, partnering with tech leaders like UiPath and Automation Anywhere. With expertise in cross-functional leadership and go-to-market strategies, she helps organizations achieve market relevance and growth. Kirsten holds an MBA from Regis University and a BSBA from Creighton University.

GTM Strategy Insights from Kirsten Jepson

In her interview with me, Kirsten Jepson highlights the pivotal role that product marketing plays in the go-to-market (GTM) strategy, emphasizing how it sits at the intersection of marketing, sales, and product. Product marketers are crucial for ensuring that all these departments collaborate effectively to drive success. According to Kirsten, the key to a successful GTM strategy is collaboration—product marketing professionals must guide and support each department with foundational work that aligns with the broader organizational goals.

One of the most important lessons Kirsten has learned is the significance of collaboration in driving a successful GTM strategy. Product marketers need to understand and interpret the needs of the various departments—marketing, sales, and product—and ensure that the overall strategy addresses those needs while aligning with the company's objectives. The process starts with a logical point of view, followed by ongoing negotiation and alignment with other leaders across the company. This is where product marketers are crucial: they identify common ground and help bridge the gaps between departments, ensuring that everyone is working toward the same goals.

BY NITIN KARTIK

Kirsten provides several examples of how this collaboration manifests in a GTM strategy. For instance, when launching a new product, product marketers may need to flex on what can be delivered as part of the launch, depending on the needs and feedback of sales, marketing, and product teams. This adaptability ensures that the launch is successful and that each department is equipped with the right resources. Incorporating feedback from sales into enablement materials and providing marketing with the necessary backdrop for brand development are other key aspects of this collaborative process. By maintaining open lines of communication and continuously adjusting strategies based on real-time feedback, product marketing ensures that all aspects of the GTM plan are aligned and moving in the right direction.

Kirsten also stresses that while AI can automate many processes, the human aspect of collaboration cannot be replaced by technology. Product marketing requires empathy, adaptability, and negotiation skills—qualities that enable product marketers to navigate complex organizational dynamics and ensure that everyone is aligned. This human element is essential for creating a cohesive and successful GTM strategy that meets the needs of all departments and drives business growth.

In summary, Kirsten Jepson underscores the importance of collaboration in GTM strategy. By serving as a bridge between marketing, sales, and product, product marketers guide these departments toward a common goal. This collaboration ensures that all teams are aligned and that the strategy is adaptable, ultimately leading to successful product launches and a more cohesive organization.

Lesia Polivod (Elk Grove Village, IL, USA)

Bio

Lesia Polivod is a seasoned Senior Product Marketing Manager at Expandi with over 7 years of experience driving product growth in B2B environments. A Harvard Business School alum and mentor at Projector Institute, she excels in customer onboarding, retention programs, and go-to-market strategies, contributing to a remarkable 2X growth at Expandi. Lesia holds multiple certifications in product marketing and data-driven management, showcasing her commitment to continuous learning. She has previously held key roles at Veon, PandaDoc, and SplitMetrics, where she implemented innovative marketing strategies and built high-performing teams to enhance customer value and drive revenue growth.

GTM Strategy Insights from Lesia Polivod

In her interview with me, Lesia Polivod shares valuable insights into go-to-market (GTM) strategy, particularly for product marketers navigating different stages of a company's growth. Drawing on her extensive experience in product marketing, she emphasizes that the role of a Product Marketing Manager (PMM) is not universal and must be adapted to the specific context of the business. Lesia outlines two essential questions every PMM should answer before embarking on any project or activity to ensure the success of their GTM strategy.

The first key lesson is understanding the product's stage in its lifecycle. Lesia stresses that whether a company is in its early startup phase, a growing company, or a mature organization, the scope of work for product marketing varies significantly. Each stage of product development and business growth requires a different approach. In the early stages, for example, a product marketer might focus on building awareness, creating early adoption, and defining the product's unique value proposition. In contrast, in a mature company, the focus may shift to scaling efforts, optimizing existing processes, and refining the messaging. Recognizing the product's stage and aligning the GTM strategy accordingly is crucial for ensuring that the product resonates with the target audience and meets its objectives at that specific point in time.

The second critical question Lesia highlights is understanding the company's growth model. Whether the company is product-led growth (PLG), sales-driven, hybrid, or community-led, the GTM approach needs to reflect the model in place. Different business models dictate the type of marketing and sales efforts needed. For example, a PLG model might focus more on self-service, user acquisition, and building organic growth, while a sales-driven model might prioritize direct sales efforts, lead generation, and relationship-building. Understanding this model not only shapes the PMM's day-to-day operations but also helps in setting appropriate goals and metrics.

Lesia advises PMMs to be proactive in researching and asking questions about the company's product stage and growth model. This understanding helps ensure that the PMM's efforts are aligned with the broader goals of the business, resulting in more effective GTM strategies. Additionally, she emphasizes the importance of curiosity and continuous learning, urging PMMs to explore these aspects thoroughly before diving into any new projects or initiatives.

In sum, Lesia Polivod's approach to GTM strategy highlights the importance of context and alignment. A PMM's success depends on their ability to understand both the stage of the product and the business model, ensuring that the strategies they employ are tailored to the company's unique needs at any given time. This foundational understanding sets the stage for creating impactful, targeted go-to-market strategies that drive business growth.

Mark Assini (Ontario, Canada)

Bio

Mark Assini is a Senior Product Marketing Manager at Plooto with over 9 years of experience in product marketing, sales, and marketing. He has led successful go-to-market strategies, developed buyer personas, and collaborated with cross-functional teams to drive product adoption and revenue growth. Mark has expertise in FinTech, marketplace platforms, and creative industries, bringing a unique perspective to balance technical analysis with creative execution. He is also a Product Marketing Alliance Ambassador and former host of the "Product Marketing Life" podcast. Mark holds an MBA from Ivey Business School and has been recognized as a Top 100 Product Marketing Influencer.

GTM Strategy Insights from Mark Assini

In his interview with me, Mark Assini shares valuable insights into go-to-market (GTM) prioritization, emphasizing the need to assess product launches not only from an internal perspective but through the lens of both customer and business value. This approach, he believes, is critical for making informed and strategic decisions in GTM planning, ultimately leading to more successful product launches.

Mark reflects on the tendency in many organizations for decisions about GTM priorities to be driven by internal stakeholders. The product team might push for a feature launch because they believe it's the next logical step, or key customers might request specific features or updates. While these internal voices are important, Mark stresses they should not be the sole determining factors when deciding the priority of a product launch. Instead, businesses must evaluate what will have the greatest overall impact, both for customers and for the broader business strategy.

To make better prioritization decisions, Mark recommends evaluating potential launches based on two core questions: "What's the value to the customer base more broadly?" and "What's the value to the Business?" The answer to these questions will depend on the type of customer and the business objectives. In businesses that focus on maximizing profit, the priority may naturally fall on features that will drive higher revenue or improve operational efficiency. However, for customers, the priorities could be quite different, ranging from saving time to increasing revenue or improving win rates. Mark emphasizes that understanding these distinctions is essential for setting clear priorities that serve both customer needs and business objectives.

The key to prioritization, according to Mark, is assessing how each potential product feature will affect these two areas: customer value and business value. If a feature is expected to have a significant impact in one or both categories, it should be considered a higher priority than other projects that may not have as substantial an effect. This method ensures that product teams focus on features that will create the most value, rather than getting sidetracked by less impactful initiatives.

Ultimately, Mark believes that the art of prioritizing within GTM strategies requires a clear understanding of customer needs and business goals, and then using that understanding to guide decision-making. The more closely a feature or initiative aligns with increasing business or customer value, the higher its priority should be. By applying this approach, businesses are better positioned to launch products that make the most meaningful impact, ensuring the success of the go-to-market strategy in both the short and long term.

In sum, Mark Assini's advice on GTM strategy underscores the importance of balancing internal priorities with a strategic view of customer and business needs. By focusing on value-driven decision-making, companies can ensure that their product launches are well-prioritized, customer-focused, and aligned with overarching business goals.

Meenal Relekar (San Francisco, CA, USA)

Bio

Meenal Relekar is a seasoned Product Marketing Leader, Advisor, and Career Coach based in San Francisco. With over 16 years of experience in B2B and B2C sectors, including roles at DoorDash, Dropbox, and Adobe, she specializes in transforming PMMs into strategic partners from ideation to launch. A Certified Product Marketing Manager (CPMM) and an award-winning professional, Meenal has successfully launched several products and features, notably DoorDash's first ad product, generating millions in revenue. She is also a sought-after instructor and mentor, helping aspiring marketers refine their skills and navigate successful career transitions. Additionally, Meenal also teaches Product Marketing courses and offers career coaching services. Connect with her on LinkedIn.

Meenal Relekar on Go-To-Market Strategy

In her interview with me, Meenal offers valuable insights into the often-overlooked role that product marketing managers (PMMs) can play in shaping a company's go-to-market (GTM) strategy, particularly when it comes to pricing. She stresses that while pricing is typically viewed as a one-off task or a responsibility left to the finance or product teams, it is a critical component of the marketing mix, often referred to as one of the "Ps" in marketing. Pricing has a direct influence on market positioning, customer perception, and ultimately, the success of the product. As such, it's an area that PMMs should be deeply involved in, if not leading.

In her experience, one of the biggest challenges is that PMMs often lack pricing expertise because they are either not involved in the process or are not encouraged to take ownership of it. This gap in knowledge, according to Meenal, stems from a broader misunderstanding of the PMM role and its potential to influence key business decisions. She advocates for PMMs to proactively seek out opportunities to contribute to pricing discussions and projects, as it's an essential skill that can have a major impact on the success of the GTM strategy.

BY NITIN KARTIK

From a GTM strategy angle, pricing plays an essential role in defining a product's value proposition and setting the tone for its market entry. It directly impacts customer acquisition, retention, and brand positioning. PMMs, with their deep understanding of customer behavior, needs, and motivations, are uniquely positioned to lead pricing efforts. They possess insights that can help align the product's price with what customers are willing to pay and what they perceive as valuable. Pricing isn't just about setting a number; it's about making sure that the price reflects the product's value and meets customer expectations, which is critical for driving adoption and ensuring long-term success.

Meenal encourages PMMs to view pricing as an opportunity to deepen their expertise and broaden their contributions within the organization. Besides being the voice of the customer, PMMs are in a unique position to collaborate across departments—such as sales, finance, and product development—to create a unified pricing strategy that benefits the business. She also highlights that a pricing strategy should not be static but continually refined based on market dynamics, customer feedback, and competitive insights.

Ultimately, Meenal stresses PMMs should take ownership of pricing strategy as a core competency that adds immense value to their overall skill set. By leading pricing efforts, PMMs can play a pivotal role in driving both short-term and long-term business growth. They can ensure that the product's pricing is aligned with the broader business strategy and customer needs, resulting in a stronger, more competitive product offering in the market.

Norman Rohr (Munich, Germany)

Bio

Norman Rohr is an accomplished marketing and revenue executive with over 20 years of experience in the tech and digital media industries. He holds an MBA from Melbourne Business School and an Executive Marketing Degree from Wharton. Norman has led successful go-to-market strategies and scaling efforts for global tech companies like Google, Uberall, and Xentral ERP Software. He is the founder of Kiyomizu Growth Advisory and a founding partner of B2B Practitioners, Germany's leading B2B tech marketing advisory. Norman has a proven track record in driving growth, team leadership, and executing impactful marketing strategies across multiple regions.

Norman Rohr on Go-To-Market Strategy

In his interview with me, Norman Rohr shares insights into his innovative product marketing strategy framework, which he has developed to address the recurring challenges faced by product marketers.

Identifying Key Challenges and the Need for a Unified Framework

In discussing his framework, Norman highlights three familiar challenges: late-stage involvement of product marketing in strategy, mismatches between sales and marketing in go-to-market initiatives, and a lack of unified alignment among leadership teams. These challenges inspired him to create a digestible framework that fosters alignment across departments and ensures product marketing plays a foundational role in corporate strategy.

Building a Foundation for Go-To-Market Success

Next, Norman outlines the key steps product marketers should take. First, focus on defining product marketing fundamentals, such as identifying the ideal customer profile (ICP), understanding the buyer's decision process, and mapping the buying center. These fundamentals, Norman argues, should inform the corporate strategy before decisions about go-to-market, product, or marketing strategies are made. This approach places product marketing at the forefront of strategic planning, ensuring a smooth execution of value propositions, operational marketing, and go-to-market plans.

Driving Momentum with the Framework

Norman emphasizes the transformative impact of his framework. It fosters alignment across the organization, accelerates execution, and reduces friction between teams. By involving product marketing at the early stages, companies achieve faster go-to-market motions, improved market traction, and smoother collaboration between product teams and economic buyers. Norman cites a success story where his framework enabled a client company to revise its positioning, packaging, and pricing within two months, demonstrating the momentum and clarity it provides.

Practical Insights and Further Resources

Norman encourages us all to adopt this structured approach, highlighting its ability to preempt common issues like premature ad launches and misaligned messaging. He also invites the audience to connect with him on LinkedIn and explore his article, which provides a more detailed breakdown of his framework.

In Sum

Norman's insights underscore the power of strategic alignment driven by product marketing and leaves us with actionable insights to apply to our own roles. Norman's pragmatic approach, rooted in real-world results, offers a roadmap for achieving significant organizational efficiency and go-to-market success.

Partho Ghosh (Vancouver, BC, Canada)

Bio

Partho Ghosh is a strategic Product Executive with 10+ years' experience in B2B SaaS, specializing in MarTech, Product-Led Growth (PLG), and AI. Currently, as VP of Product at Uberall, Partho leads a 25-member team to drive Uberall's Product Strategy and roadmap in Location Marketing. With a proven track record of boosting ARR and orchestrating successful exits at companies like Hootsuite, Bananatag, and Unbounce, he is a customer-obsessed innovator who builds scalable processes for sustained market fit. Partho is also a sought-after keynote speaker and a passionate scuba diver, hockey enthusiast, and punk rock fan.

Partho Ghosh on GTM Strategy

In his interview with me, Partho Ghosh emphasizes the critical importance of early collaboration between product management and product marketing for effective go-to-market (GTM) strategies. Drawing on his experience in product management and product design, Partho underscores how proactive involvement of product marketers during the ideation and discovery phases can significantly influence a product's success in the market.

Partho identifies a recurring challenge: product marketers are often brought into the process too late—typically when the product is nearing launch. By this stage, the opportunity to shape the product's positioning, pricing, packaging, and user experience is limited. This reactive approach undermines the strategic potential of product marketing, reducing their role to tactical execution rather than strategic partnership. Partho asserts that involving product marketing only at the final stages is "way too late in the game."

For a robust GTM strategy, Partho advises that collaboration between product marketing and product management should begin during the discovery phase. This includes participation in crafting Product Requirement Documents (PRDs) and canvases like one-pagers, where foundational decisions about product development are made. He stresses that these early conversations are crucial for shaping critical aspects like monetization, pricing, packaging, and customer adoption strategies. Early involvement enables product marketing to contribute insights that can drive impactful changes to the product's development and user experience, setting the stage for more seamless market adoption.

One of Partho's key insights is the value of embedding GTM considerations—such as monetization strategies and customer adoption pathways—directly into the product development process. For instance, by collaborating early, product marketers can influence how features are designed and prioritized to support upselling opportunities or improve user engagement. This proactive alignment ensures that the final product resonates more effectively with target audiences and meets business objectives.

Partho also touches on the organizational dynamics of product marketing, noting that reporting structures can vary—sometimes product marketing reports to marketing, and other times to product. Regardless of where product marketing sits within an organization, the collaboration between product managers and product marketers must be seamless and integrated. He highlights that this partnership is pivotal in driving alignment on strategy, ensuring that both groups work toward shared goals from the outset.

Partho's advice underscores the necessity of treating product marketing as a strategic partner from the start of the product development lifecycle. By fostering early collaboration with product management, organizations can craft more effective GTM strategies, optimize monetization, and enhance customer adoption. This proactive approach positions both the product and its marketing efforts for success in the marketplace.

Partho Ghosh (Vancouver, BC, Canada)

Stuti Dutt (Canada)

Bio

Stuti Dutt is a seasoned product marketing leader with over 8 years of expertise spanning Canada, the UK, and India. Currently at Vidyard, she has a proven track record in product strategy, customer segmentation, and go-to-market execution. Known for her operational insights and strategic impact, Stuti has launched customer-centric campaigns by integrating customer feedback, win/loss analysis, and sales insights. She has successfully driven cross-functional collaboration across marketing and sales teams, focusing on enhancing product adoption and customer engagement. Her extensive toolkit includes Highspot, Tableau, and Mixpanel, reflecting her commitment to data-driven and human-centered marketing.

Stuti Dutt on Go-To-Market Strategy

In her interview with me, Stuti Dutt emphasizes key insights about the role of product marketing in aligning with business objectives, demonstrating ROI, and driving cross-functional collaboration to ensure GTM success. Here are the key takeaways from her approach to GTM strategy.

Stuti stresses that while aligning product marketing efforts with business OKRs is essential, the real challenge is demonstrating impact. Product marketers must not only align their strategies with overarching company goals but also continuously show how their efforts contribute to revenue growth. This helps in building credibility with stakeholders and reinforces the value of product marketing within the organization. Stuti shares she has found quarterly business reviews (QBRs) to be an effective platform to showcase product marketing's role in driving results. These reviews offer product marketers an opportunity to present data-backed insights on how their strategies are positively impacting the business, helping stakeholders see the tangible value of product marketing.

Communication and proactive sharing of insights are essential for effective GTM strategy. Stuti highlights the importance of regularly sharing product marketing insights through QBRs and monthly readouts, which keep cross-functional teams aligned. These updates offer a comprehensive view of how the marketing initiatives tie into the company's broader performance. By proactively disseminating this information, product marketers can ensure that all teams—sales, customer success, and product—are aligned and informed. Stuti also suggests monthly check-ins with cross-functional leadership to maintain alignment and address any emerging issues or opportunities. This frequent communication ensures that product marketing remains aligned with business priorities while maintaining visibility on its impact.

Stuti advocates for product marketers to be their product's biggest champions. She practices this by using Vidyard's AI avatar technology in her message delivery, which exemplifies her belief in using innovative solutions to communicate the value of products. By embracing the tools and technologies that the product offers, product marketers can not only advocate more effectively but also demonstrate the potential of the product firsthand. This approach encourages product marketers to stay authentic and passionate about their offerings, which resonates strongly with internal teams and customers alike.

Stuti Dutt's approach to GTM strategy underscores the importance of demonstrating impact, ensuring continuous alignment across teams, and championing the product with innovative tools. By integrating these strategies into daily practices, product marketers can drive better results, enhance their influence within the organization, and accelerate the adoption of their products in the market.

Tzufit Herling (Lisbon, Portugal)

Bio

Tzufit Herling is a community consultant and content strategist with over 10 years of experience in building and managing thriving communities. As the founder of Connecteur, she helps companies drive organizational transformation, enhance community members' engagement, and foster innovation through community-building strategies. Tzufit also specializes in mentoring entrepreneurs and professionals, and designing impactful training programs that boost learning, entrepreneurship, leadership, and DEI. With a background in journalism, sociology, and business, she has contributed to various global initiatives and led successful projects across sectors, including technology, entrepreneurship, and social impact. Tzufit is passionate about creating meaningful connections that drive growth and transformation.

Tzufit Herling on Go-To-Market Strategy

In her interview with me, Tzufit Herling shares how community-based ambassador programs can transform a company's go-to-market (GTM) strategy. With her expertise in community strategy development, she outlines how leveraging top customers as brand champions not only boosts loyalty but also amplifies brand reach and drives measurable business outcomes.

Tzufit highlights the critical role of exclusive ambassador programs in enhancing GTM efforts. By identifying and engaging the most loyal and active customers, companies can create a network of brand advocates who drive long-term business success. These ambassadors form a direct link between the company and its target audience, fostering trust and credibility.

At the heart of Tzufit's approach is the power of deeper customer relationships. By investing in loyal customers, brands foster a shared sense of purpose and alignment with the company's mission. Ambassadors become emotionally connected to the brand, reinforcing their commitment to endorsing its products. This loyalty often translates into sustained advocacy, ensuring that the product remains visible in competitive markets.

Tzufit emphasizes ambassadors play a pivotal role in expanding brand visibility. When advocates share their positive experiences through social media, online forums, or word-of-mouth, they provide authentic social proof of the product's value. This endorsement enhances the company's credibility, organically increasing its reach with no significant advertising spending. These trusted voices resonate strongly with potential customers, accelerating the adoption curve.

Beyond creating a buzz, ambassador programs can have direct revenue implications. Tzufit explains how some brands empower ambassadors to offer personalized incentives to their own networks, creating a ripple effect that boosts sales. These programs are not just about visibility—they can also be engineered to contribute to measurable sales growth. The dual impact of positive recommendations and incentivized offers creates a sustainable revenue stream.

Ambassadors, as Tzufit notes, are more than advocates; they are invaluable sources of insight. Their feedback informs product development and marketing strategies, ensuring that the company aligns with customer needs and preferences. This feedback loop strengthens the overall GTM strategy, making it more customer-centric and adaptable.

Tzufit's insights underscore the importance of integrating community strategy into the GTM process. By nurturing brand champions, companies can enhance their launch efforts, maintain engagement post-launch, and evolve based on real-time feedback. In today's competitive landscape, these ambassador programs act as a multiplier for brand awareness, customer trust, and sustained business growth.

Tzufit Herling (Lisbon, Portugal)

Yuliya Andreyuk (Portugal)

Bio

Yuliya Andreyuk is an accomplished marketing leader with over 11 years of experience in product and growth marketing. Known for her strategic expertise, she has launched products for global brands like Meta, Gucci, and Ubisoft, excelling in go-to-market execution and team leadership. At Banuba, Yuliya drove €40M in pipeline revenue and led a high-performing team of eight. As a Reforge alumnus and advisor, she's skilled in data-driven marketing strategies and full-funnel campaigns. Passionate about storytelling and differentiation, Yuliya has worked across Europe and North America, building impactful brands and mentoring the next generation of marketers.

Yuliya Andreyuk on Go-To-Market Strategy

In her engaging discussion with me, Yuliya Andreyuk delves into the intricacies of developing a Go-To-Market (GTM) Strategy. Drawing on her extensive experience launching global products, Yuliya outlines critical lessons on balancing sales-led and product-led growth strategies to optimize business success.

Yuliya highlights a pivotal misconception in GTM strategies: many companies misuse free trials as a lead-generation tool, assuming it automatically integrates with a product-led growth (PLG) model. She stresses free trials are not intended to replace sales-led motions but to complement them. For a successful GTM approach, companies must simultaneously maintain their sales-led funnel while carefully nurturing a product-led funnel. This dual approach ensures a seamless transition and maximizes lead conversion potential.

A second common pitfall Yuliya identifies is the assumption that free trial sign-ups are inherently product-qualified leads (PQLs). She emphasizes that a sign-up is merely an entry point, not a qualifier. Businesses must invest in creating comprehensive customer journeys within their products, including onboarding, awareness-building, monetization strategies, and differentiated services. These elements collectively nurture trial users and gradually convert them into qualified leads or accounts.

Yuliya underscores the importance of cross-functional alignment in executing a product-led GTM strategy. She observes that the failure of such strategies often stems from misaligned visions across sales, marketing, product, and business intelligence teams. To succeed, organizations must establish a unified understanding of PLG, ensuring all stakeholders work toward shared objectives.

Yuliya's insights offer a pragmatic blueprint for startups and established companies alike. By avoiding the pitfalls of over-relying on free trials and ensuring cohesive collaboration across teams, businesses can leverage the strengths of both sales-led and product-led approaches. This hybrid model allows for a more resilient GTM strategy, where free trials serve as an accelerator rather than a replacement for traditional sales methods.

Ultimately, Yuliya advocates for a balanced and intentional approach to GTM strategies. Companies should focus on refining customer journeys, aligning cross-functional teams, and combining sales and product-led efforts to drive sustainable growth. Her expertise emphasizes that success lies not in choosing between sales-led or product-led models, but in integrating both to create a robust, adaptable strategy.

This conversation serves as a critical reminder: A successful GTM strategy is not about leaning on a single method, but about leveraging diverse tools and aligning teams to deliver value effectively. As Yuliya eloquently puts it, the synergy between sales-led and product-led motions can be the key to unlocking a company's full potential in the market.

If a good Go-To-Market Strategy gives us the skeleton of our marketing plan, it is our Storytelling and Content Strategy that adds meat to the bones.

WISDOM ON STORYTELLING AND CONTENT STRATEGY

WISDOM ON STORYTELLING AND CONTENT STRATEGY

Storytelling and content strategy are crucial for engaging audiences and building lasting brand connections. While theories offer a solid foundation, the insights of real-world professionals provide the nuanced understanding needed to create content that resonates in a crowded marketplace.

Experienced marketers share stories of how they've crafted narratives that go beyond selling products to building emotional connections. Their real-world examples illustrate how to identify a brand's unique story, align it with customer needs, and deliver it effectively across channels. For instance, a seasoned content strategist might explain how they transformed customer pain points into an interesting campaign narrative, driving both engagement and conversions.

Professionals also shed light on timing, platform choice, and content format. They reveal practical tips on adapting strategies for evolving trends, such as using short-form video to connect with younger audiences or leveraging thought leadership articles to build credibility in B2B markets.

By learning from these experiences through interviews, webinars, or case studies, product marketers gain actionable insights that extend beyond generic templates. Real-world wisdom equips us to develop content strategies and storytelling techniques that not only capture attention but also forge meaningful connections, fostering loyalty and long-term brand success.

In the following sections, we explore the perspectives of industry leaders and emerging talents to better understand these skills in the real world.

Andrew Wood (Montreal, Quebec, Canada)

Bio

Andrew Wood is the founder of Grammar Ghost, a company specializing in helping businesses create email funnels that convert clients seamlessly. With a background in software engineering and web design, Andrew has worked for notable companies such as SSENSE, Alpaca, and ExactBuyer, honing his skills in technical writing, software development, and content marketing. He is passionate about personal branding and ghostwriting, leveraging his technical expertise to help clients craft interesting email marketing strategies. Andrew holds a BASc in Computer Engineering from the University of Alberta and is based in Montreal, Quebec.

Storytelling & Content Strategy Insights from Andrew Wood

In his interview with me, Andrew Wood discusses an emerging content strategy that leverages personal storytelling to strengthen brand identity, particularly on professional platforms like LinkedIn. He highlights the shift from traditional company-driven content to content driven by personal brands, explaining how this trend creates a unique opportunity for individuals and businesses alike to engage audiences more authentically. According to Andrew, personal content—stories, experiences, and lessons learned—offers a powerful way to connect with an audience on a deeper, more personal level.

Andrew suggests that the easiest way to start creating personal content is to tap into one's own life experiences. He encourages individuals to select five meaningful photos from their collection, each tied to a personal story or lesson. By sharing the story behind each photo, along with the lessons learned and advice related to that experience, individuals can begin crafting LinkedIn posts that resonate with followers. This strategy not only enhances personal connection but also positions individuals as relatable and approachable figures within their professional network.

The key to success in this approach is consistency. Andrew explains that by continually posting personal content, individuals can create a steady stream of high-quality content that helps to transform their brand into a more authentic and engaging presence. This shift towards personal content helps bridge the gap left by the impersonal nature of business-centric platforms. In Andrew's view, the real value of this content is that it adds human elements to an otherwise professional space, fostering more genuine connections with an audience.

Additionally, Andrew emphasizes the power of storytelling in content strategy. By sharing personal experiences and insights, individuals can demonstrate vulnerability and authenticity, which are often more interesting than typical promotional content. The narrative element allows individuals to share not just what they do, but who they are—creating a more holistic and memorable brand image. For Andrew, storytelling is not just about conveying information; it's about connecting with others on an emotional level and providing value through lessons learned.

In summary, Andrew Wood advocates for integrating personal storytelling into content strategy to create a more relatable and human brand presence. His approach is simple but impactful: by sharing personal stories tied to meaningful moments, individuals can foster stronger connections with their audience, improve engagement, and build a brand that is both professional and personal. This shift towards authenticity is a powerful way to differentiate oneself in a crowded digital landscape, particularly on platforms like LinkedIn.

John Cook (Milton, WI, USA)

Bio

John Cook is a seasoned storyteller and technical writer with over two decades of experience specializing in healthcare and medical device industries. Known for his ability to translate complex technical details into engaging narratives, John brings expertise in user guides, system administration manuals, and regulatory-compliant documentation. He leads his own brand, JohnTheWordsmith LLC, where he helps clients craft impactful career stories. With certifications from IBM and hands-on experience in Agile, Jira, Confluence, and Adobe tools, John's unique blend of technical rigor and creative storytelling supports his work as a liaison between subject matter experts and end-users.

Storytelling & Content Strategy Insights from John Cook

In his interview with me, John Cook emphasizes the central role of storytelling in content strategy, focusing on its ability to create emotional connections with an audience. He explains that effective storytelling transcends the mere conveyance of information; it involves crafting narratives that resonate deeply with the audience by highlighting journeys, challenges, and transformations.

According to John, the key to impactful storytelling lies in making the audience see themselves in the narrative. This requires understanding their pain points, aspirations, and experiences and weaving these into the stories being told. By doing so, content becomes more relatable and engaging, fostering a sense of connection and trust between the storyteller and the audience.

John highlights that the structure of a good story includes three key elements: the journey, the challenges, and the transformation. The journey sets the stage, inviting the audience into a shared experience. The challenges provide tension and relatability, showcasing obstacles that align with the audience's own struggles. Finally, the transformation demonstrates growth, success, or resolution, offering inspiration and practical insights that the audience can apply to their own situations.

In the context of content strategy, John underscores the importance of aligning storytelling with brand values and audience needs. Stories should not only entertain but also reinforce the brand's mission and showcase how it can be a catalyst for the audience's own transformation. For example, case studies, customer testimonials, and behind-the-scenes narratives can all serve as effective storytelling formats, illustrating real-world applications of the brand's offerings.

John also advocates for adaptability in storytelling. He notes that different platforms and audiences may require tailored approaches to ensure the message is both impactful and contextually appropriate. Whether it's a long-form blog post, a short social media video, or a detailed whitepaper, the core narrative must remain consistent while being delivered in a way that resonates with the intended audience.

Finally, John touches on the emotional power of storytelling. By evoking emotions such as hope, determination, or empathy, stories become memorable and impactful. Emotional resonance not only strengthens audience engagement but also fosters loyalty, as people are more likely to connect with brands that understand and address their experiences on a human level.

In summary, John Cook illustrates how storytelling can elevate content strategy by creating emotional connections, highlighting relatable journeys, and inspiring transformation. By aligning narratives with audience needs and brand values, and adapting them to various platforms, storytellers can craft content that not only informs but also deeply engages and motivates their audience.

Jordan Rahtz (Denver Area, CO, USA)

Bio

Jordan Rahtz is a Senior Manager of Revenue Enablement at Procore Technologies and an Executive MBA graduate from Auburn University. Based in the Denver Metropolitan Area, she is a skilled leader with extensive experience in Sales Enablement, Risk Management, and Operations, having held key roles at RingCentral, Empower Retirement, and OppenheimerFunds. Passionate about coaching and team building, Jordan thrives on innovation, problem-solving, and enhancing the employee experience. She fosters an environment of growth, encouraging her teams to learn from challenges. Organized and strategic, Jordan champions integrity, continuous learning, and creating collaborative, empowered work cultures.

Storytelling & Content Strategy Insights from Jordan Rahtz

In her interview with me, Jordan Rahtz emphasizes the critical importance of alignment between product marketing and enablement teams, particularly when it comes to content creation and strategy. She believes that genuine success in these areas comes from a shared understanding of goals and a unified vision. The key, according to Jordan, is not just about producing content, but ensuring that everyone involved understands the why behind it and how it ties back to broader business objectives.

Jordan underscores that effective storytelling in product marketing and enablement goes beyond just pushing out content. It's about being deliberate in shaping content that aligns with specific goals—such as driving cross-sells, upsells, or other key business targets. Rather than simply creating content for the sake of content, Jordan stresses teams must connect the content they create to tangible outcomes. By focusing on these business objectives, teams can ensure that the content they produce is not only relevant but also strategically aligned to make a real impact on the business. This clarity allows teams to measure and track their progress toward these goals, which ultimately drives both accountability and success.

For Jordan, content creation becomes most effective when there is a strong sense of purpose behind it. She argues that when both product marketing and enablement are working toward the same objective—whether that's supporting sales teams or driving customer adoption—there's a greater chance of success. Instead of working in silos, the two functions should unite and leverage their collective strengths. When product marketing and enablement are aligned, they can produce content that not only supports internal teams but also delivers real value to the customer. By creating content that resonates with the customer's needs, teams can ensure that their messaging is relevant and impactful, ultimately driving business results.

A key part of Jordan's approach to storytelling within a content strategy is making sure the narrative is clear and purposeful. This clarity ensures that both internal teams and external customers understand the value and impact of the product. Whether it's a piece of content that helps the sales team close deals or a resource that enables customers to better use the product, Jordan's focus is on ensuring that all content efforts are driving toward the same end goal. This strategic focus allows teams to produce content that resonates more deeply with their audience, leading to better engagement and ultimately better results.

In summary, Jordan Rahtz highlights the importance of goal alignment in content strategy and storytelling. By ensuring that both product marketing and enablement teams work toward shared goals, they can create content that is purposeful, measurable, and impactful. When teams unite with a clear vision, the content they produce becomes a powerful tool for driving business success, fostering greater collaboration, and maximizing the value of their content across all channels.

Laura Hall (Germany)

Bio

Laura Hall is a seasoned content marketing leader with over 15 years of experience in B2B marketing and communications across Europe. Currently the Senior Content Marketing Manager at Uberall in Berlin, Laura excels at crafting interesting local marketing narratives and engaging social strategies. Her background includes Webgears GmbH, where she honed her expertise in storytelling and internal communications. With a CIM Professional Certificate in Marketing and a BA in Journalism and Media Studies from the University of Staffordshire, Laura brings a strong journalistic approach to marketing, consistently building brand stories that resonate and drive impact.

Laura Hall on Storytelling & Content Strategy

In her engaging interview with me, Laura Hall shares key insights on transforming SaaS product storytelling on LinkedIn. Laura's central message revolves around breaking free from traditional, feature-heavy posts and crafting narratives that captivate, inspire, and entertain audiences. She emphasizes LinkedIn has evolved from a purely business-focused platform into a dynamic space where both individuals and companies seek engaging, relatable content. For Laura, storytelling on LinkedIn must create a personal connection with the reader, combining educational value with a sense of enjoyment, or "infotainment."

Laura's storytelling strategy for SaaS products is built around conveying the grand vision of the product rather than focusing solely on features. She suggests that product marketers should aim to communicate how the product fits into the larger aspirations or day-to-day realities of the customer. Rather than presenting a laundry list of functionalities, Laura encourages highlighting how the product can help users achieve significant personal or professional goals, earn recognition, or solve meaningful challenges. The technical features can still be shared, but only after capturing attention and creating a sense of excitement about the product's potential.

Visual elements play a major role in Laura's approach. She recommends that images or videos accompanying LinkedIn posts should incorporate people, inviting viewers to see themselves in the journey and feel an emotional connection. Content should resonate with audiences by including relatable scenarios and aspirational outcomes, as these can help drive an emotional connection with the product. This is especially crucial given the sheer volume of content on LinkedIn—posts that lack a human touch or relatable context may struggle to stand out in the crowd.

Laura also addresses the value of balancing education and entertainment. As professionals are increasingly pressed for time, they seek content that informs but also leaves them feeling uplifted or inspired. To meet this demand, Laura advocates for creating posts that are both insightful and enjoyable to read, allowing audiences to learn without feeling bogged down by technical details. By adopting a more playful, visually engaging approach, SaaS companies can transform typically dry product updates into engaging stories that resonate on an emotional level.

In sum, Laura's advice represents a shift toward a storytelling strategy that is more human and emotionally engaging. By aligning product content with the audience's journey, aspirations, and values, companies can create LinkedIn posts that go beyond mere information-sharing to build genuine connections. Laura's approach encourages product marketers to view their products as part of a larger, more personal narrative that appeals to the desires and goals of their audience. Her insights provide a practical guide for content creators looking to adapt to LinkedIn's changing landscape and deliver memorable, effective stories that engage and inspire.

Lauren Parker (Oakland, CA, USA)

Bio

Lauren B. Parker is a seasoned Product Marketing Leader currently at TextNow, with past roles at Uber and Strava. Based in Oakland, CA, she brings over a decade of strategic marketing experience, spanning customer retention, product positioning, and cross-functional collaboration. Known for her purpose-driven, customer-first approach, Lauren is dedicated to creating products that resonate deeply with users. Her accolades include multiple AdWheel Awards and a 40 Under 40 recognition. A passionate public transit advocate and fitness enthusiast, Lauren also founded the Black Girl Magic podcast, highlighting empowerment and current events for women of color.

Storytelling & Content Strategy Insights from Lauren Parker

In her interview with me, Lauren Parker shares valuable insights into how storytelling and content strategy differ between B2B and B2C markets. With nearly 8 years of experience in consumer PMM, Lauren highlights the critical shift from focusing on features to connecting with emotions—a shift that plays a crucial role in developing interesting, human-centered marketing strategies.

According to Lauren, the key distinction between B2B and B2C product marketing lies in the decision-making process. In B2B, particularly when dealing with large organizations or government clients, decisions are often driven by logic and practicality—focused on features like cost savings, efficiency, and tangible outcomes. These clients are typically "headier" and more analytical, weighing factors like ROI and business impact. In contrast, consumer product marketing (B2C) operates at a deeper emotional level. Here, the decision-making process is often driven by feelings, personal values, and how the product aligns with an individual's life and identity.

BY NITIN KARTIK

A major lesson Lauren has learned over her career is the importance of shifting the focus from features to feelings when communicating value propositions. In the consumer space, it is not enough to simply talk about the practical benefits of a product, such as timesaving or cost reduction. Instead, it's crucial to understand the consumer's personal context and how the product fits into their life. The challenge is to distill the high-level features of a product and translate them into content that resonates with the consumer's deeper desires and aspirations. This transformation from features to feelings is at the heart of effective storytelling in consumer product marketing.

Lauren emphasizes that understanding the target audience is central to this process. Whether you're dealing with B2B clients or individual consumers, it's important to align the messaging with their values and needs. For consumers, this often means tapping into emotions, highlighting how the product improves their life, reflects their personal values, or helps them become the best version of themselves. In B2B contexts, the focus might be on efficiency, profitability, and practicality, but even here, understanding the human side of the decision-making process can lead to more interesting content that resonates with decision-makers on an emotional level.

In sum, Lauren Parker's approach to storytelling and content strategy emphasizes the importance of connecting with audiences on a deeper emotional level. Whether in B2B or B2C marketing, content must go beyond features to address the human side of decision-making, aligning with the audience's values, aspirations, and needs. This approach leads to more engaging, impactful storytelling that drives stronger connections with the target audience.

Madhav Bhandari (San Francisco, CA, USA)

Bio

Madhav Bhandari is an experienced B2B technology marketer with over 10 years of expertise in driving demand and growth for SaaS companies. Currently the Head of Marketing at Storylane, he specializes in SEO, content, and demand generation strategies. Madhav has successfully scaled multiple companies, including Hubstaff, where he grew revenue from $200K to $5M ARR, and Bonsai, where he tripled ARR in two years. With a background in both bootstrapped and VC-backed startups, he excels at converting strategic plans into action and has a proven track record of driving significant revenue growth across various marketing channels.

Madhav Bhandari on Storytelling & Content Strategy

In his interview with me, Madhav Bhandari shares valuable insights into content strategy, particularly emphasizing the growing importance of snack videos in today's content distribution landscape. His approach highlights the need for succinct and engaging content that caters to the ever-decreasing attention span of audiences, which is especially important today.

According to Madhav, the traditional model of long-form-content, such as one-hour podcast episodes, is becoming less effective in capturing the attention of audiences. Many listeners invest time into long podcasts, only to realize that they have gained little value, leading to a sense of wasted time. This growing apprehension around long-form content has led to a shift toward shorter, more digestible formats, such as snack videos, which fit well into the modern, fast-paced content consumption habits.

He notes that while there might be a handful of people willing to commit to a full hour of content, there are many more who are likely to engage with shorter episodes, such as 5-minute or even 1-minute videos. This shift is essential for maximizing content reach and distribution, as shorter videos can be consumed more easily, leading to a higher volume of views and impressions. By embracing snack-sized content, brands can more effectively engage with a broader audience, including those with limited time or attention.

Madhav took this insight and applied it to his own LinkedIn video series, GTM on the Go, where he interviews top go-to-market (GTM) operators and condenses their wisdom into 5-minute, 5-question episodes. This format allows him to capture the essential takeaways quickly and efficiently, offering value to viewers in a brief and engaging manner. By focusing on the 80/20 principle—providing the most critical insights in a short time—Madhav's content becomes more accessible and valuable to a wider audience.

He also points out the strategic advantages of platforms like LinkedIn, YouTube Shorts, and Instagram Reels, which are increasingly prioritizing video content. These platforms provide excellent opportunities for content creators to distribute short-form videos that can reach a vast audience with minimal effort. Madhav's success with GTM on the Go shows that when content is designed for quick consumption, it can significantly increase its distribution, leading to more impressions, viewers, and engagement.

In sum, Madhav Bhandari's approach to snack videos underscores the importance of brevity and relevance in today's content landscape. Short-form videos are not just a passing trend but a strategic tool for increasing content reach, engagement, and distribution. As the content consumption habits of audiences evolve, marketers and content creators must adapt by focusing on bite-sized, impactful content that delivers key insights in an easily digestible format.

Nora Stark (Israel)

Bio

Nora Stark is a Senior Product Marketing Manager at Walnut, where she specializes in crafting interesting narratives that drive adoption, strengthen market positioning, and generate new business for B2B SaaS brands. With a strong background in psychology and a unique skill set in go-to-market strategy, messaging, and competitive intelligence, she excels at turning complex product stories into engaging, accessible content. Nora's experience spans prominent roles in product marketing and content strategy at companies like Hibob and Cellebrite, where she leveraged her storytelling prowess to support sales teams and develop impactful campaigns for global audiences.

Nora Stark on Storytelling & Content Strategy

In her conversation with me, Nora Stark shares a key insight on how to approach storytelling in product marketing: keeping things simple by focusing on the customer's journey and needs. She emphasizes that while product marketing can sometimes seem complex, the core of effective communication lies in straightforward storytelling that aligns with customers' pain points.

Nora begins by drawing a powerful analogy between product marketing and storytelling in books and movies, noting that the most engaging stories follow a familiar structure. They start with a challenge—a central problem or goal—and continue through a series of obstacles before reaching a solution. Similarly, in product marketing, the goal is to convey the product's value by connecting deeply with the audience's struggles and demonstrating how the product effectively addresses those challenges.

To successfully connect with customers, Nora advises product marketers to truly understand their audience by "getting into their shoes." This involves diving into their needs, concerns, and the day-to-day difficulties they face. Instead of merely presenting features and benefits, a marketer's role is to empathize with the customer's perspective, making it easier to tell a relatable and relevant story. By focusing on what matters most to the audience, marketers can avoid unnecessary jargon and complexity, ensuring that their message resonates with clarity and authenticity.

Nora suggests that rather than complicating things with industry buzzwords or technical terms, product marketers should stay focused on the problem and solution. When the customer's pain points are clearly identified and addressed, the marketing message becomes far more interesting. This approach allows the story to feel natural and intuitive, drawing the audience in by addressing their real-life challenges.

She also highlights the flexibility in storytelling, encouraging marketers to break down their narrative into formats that suit their target audience's preferences. Whether it's a case study, blog post, or product demo, adapting the story to the audience's consumption habits can maximize engagement. For Nora, it's less about adhering to a strict format and more about conveying a clear, resonant message that remains consistent regardless of the medium.

In closing, Nora's message to product marketers is clear: avoid the temptation to overcomplicate things. By homing in on the customer's problem and showing how the product offers a solution, marketers can craft a story that not only captures attention but also builds trust and loyalty. Nora's emphasis on empathy, simplicity, and clarity reflects her belief that successful product marketing isn't just about promoting a product; it's about telling a story that the audience can connect with on a personal level.

Omprakash Karuppanan (Bengaluru, India)

Bio

Omprakash Karuppanan is a seasoned Account-Based Marketing (ABM) and demand generation leader with over a decade of experience working with Fortune 500 companies. As the founder of Fuego Systems, he helps B2B SaaS and IT firms to design personalized, omnichannel ABM strategies that drive measurable pipeline growth and improve conversion rates. Omprakash's approach has delivered remarkable results, such as a 300% engagement increase for Fortune 500 clients. He also hosts "The ABM Way" podcast, sharing transformative insights on modern ABM strategies. Based in Bengaluru, Omprakash speaks multiple languages, including English, Tamil, Hindi, and Spanish, and has been recognized as "Digital Marketing Person of the Year."

Omprakash on Rethinking Today's B2B Buyer Journey

In his interview with me, Omprakash challenges conventional marketing practices. He highlights a fundamental misstep in today's fast-paced, AI-driven business environment: many marketers rush to pitch their solutions without understanding the complexities of the modern B2B buyer journey. This impatience often leads to misaligned strategies, missed opportunities, and suboptimal results. Omprakash emphasizes that the B2B buyer journey, especially for enterprise companies, is not linear and cannot be compressed into a short sales cycle. He breaks it into three critical phases.

Low Buying Intent (4-6 months): At this stage, buyers are not actively seeking solutions. Marketers pushing for conversions here are often met with resistance. Instead, Omprakash advises focusing on building trust and familiarity. "When buying intent is low, the goal is not to sell but to make your brand follow-worthy," he explains. He recommends (a) encouraging prospects to follow your content; (b) nurturing interest using webinars and events; and (c) sparking engagement with high-value, educational content.

Medium Buying Intent (2-3 months): As buyers identify their challenges, they search for solutions. Omprakash explains, "This is when buyers think, 'Our ad spend rose 30%, but conversions haven't improved' or 'Our inbound leads are low quality.'" Marketers should use this phase to (a) share case studies and proof points; (b) align messaging with specific pain points; and (c) position their brand as a trusted problem-solver.

High Buying Intent (1-3 months): Finally, buyers are ready to make decisions. By this point, they've acknowledged their problems, evaluated options, and are actively seeking a partner or solution. Omprakash stresses that marketers who have built trust early on will be well-positioned to close deals. The focus here should be (a) delivering compelling proposals; (b) providing ROI projections; and (c) offering seamless sales experiences.

Omprakash observes, "With AI and automation tools, it's tempting to chase quick wins, but this approach often overlooks the trust and intent necessary for sustainable growth." For example, many teams push for product demos or aggressive outreach before a prospect is ready to engage. This both wastes resources but also damages long-term relationships.

Omprakash introduces the concept of **"strategic patience"** as a guiding principle for marketers navigating today's buyer landscape. Strategic patience doesn't mean passivity—it's about making intentional, well-timed moves that align with the buyer's readiness. "By practicing strategic patience," he explains, "marketers can focus on nurturing prospects, refining their narrative, and delivering value at each phase of the journey." He encourages marketing leaders to (a) use data to identify signals of intent; (b) invest in brand-building activities that create trust over time; and (c) resist the urge to push for immediate results without groundwork.

Omprakash's insights serve as a powerful reminder for marketers in an "instant results" culture. His approach combines the agility of modern tools with the discipline of thoughtful planning. By understanding the buyer's journey and exercising strategic patience, marketers can achieve not just conversions but lasting customer loyalty and scalable growth.

For Omprakash Karuppanan, success in marketing is not about rushing to the finish line—it's about pacing the race, building trust, and ensuring every step aligns with the buyer's journey. His philosophy continues to inspire marketing teams to rethink their storytelling and content strategies and embrace the long game in achieving impactful results.

Omprakash Karuppanan (Bengaluru, India)

Oren Blank (Israel)

Bio

Oren Blank is the VP of Product at Walnut, where he leads product strategy and development. With over ten years of experience, he has held key roles in companies like Grubhub, Monday.com, and ironSource, where he advanced product management and innovation. Oren co-founded and served as VP of Product & Business Development at Warranteer, a cloud-based eWarranty platform. He has a strong background in strategic planning and problem-solving, and holds an MBA in Technology, Innovation, and Entrepreneurship from Tel Aviv University. Oren is passionate about building products that meet user needs and drive business success.

Oren Blank on Storytelling & Content Strategy

In my interview with Oren Blank, he highlights the central role of storytelling in product marketing and product management. He explains that while a product may contain numerous complex details, the essence of successful marketing lies in crafting an interesting narrative that connects with the audience's pain points and resonates with their needs. According to Oren, storytelling is an art form that, when mastered, can elevate any product, enabling it to achieve a far greater impact than technical features alone might convey.

Oren begins by emphasizing the importance of keeping the audience's experience at the forefront. He believes that product marketers and product managers should collaborate closely to create cohesive stories around products. For Oren, storytelling isn't merely about listing a product's features but about shaping a narrative that speaks directly to what customers care about most—their challenges and the specific ways the product can address them. This approach not only attracts potential customers but also strengthens their understanding and connection with the product, which can enhance brand loyalty and drive adoption.

He points out that some great products fail to gain traction because they do not tell an interesting story, while other products with a strong narrative find greater success, even if they aren't as technically superior. In his experience, a well-told story can sometimes be more influential than the actual quality or capabilities of a product. The right story can punch above the product's technical weight, achieving what Oren describes as a "disproportionate impact" in the market.

In his role at Walnut, Oren focuses on ensuring that each product's story aligns with the core value proposition and effectively addresses the audience's needs. This alignment, he argues, is crucial for both product managers and marketers, as it provides a clear path for communicating the product's benefits, not just its features. Oren encourages product teams to avoid getting bogged down in technicalities and instead to focus on creating narratives that make an emotional connection and convey the product's unique value in a way that is both accessible and memorable.

Oren's insights underscore that, in today's market, a product's success is often determined less by its specifications and more by the way it is presented. This perspective aligns with my own experiences and reinforces the importance of storytelling in driving product marketing effectiveness. His advice is a reminder that, while the details matter, they should support the story, not distract from it.

Overall, Oren Blank's wisdom highlights storytelling as a critical skill for product marketers and product managers alike, one that can turn even an average product into a market leader when wielded effectively.

Puru Mehta (San Francisco Bay Area, CA, USA)

Bio

Puru Mehta is a skilled product strategist currently leading product initiatives at TikTok in the San Francisco Bay Area. With a background in product management and marketing, he has contributed to the development of various ad products and audience management tools. Previously, Puru held roles at LinkedIn, Uber, and Citrix, where he honed his expertise in growth marketing and analytics. He holds a master's in management information systems from the University of Arizona and has completed executive education in Strategy and Leadership at Harvard Business School. Fluent in Hindi, Gujarati, and English, Puru brings a diverse perspective to his work.

Puru Mehta on Storytelling & Content Strategy: Crafting for the Modern Audience

In his interview with me, Puru Mehta sheds light on the evolving nature of storytelling and content strategy, emphasizing the need for brevity, clarity, and adaptability in the age of information overload. Drawing from his experience in AdTech within big tech, Puru shares insights on how product marketers can better connect with audiences through interesting, digestible content.

Puru identifies a key question for marketers today: how to create content that is both easy to understand and widely appealing. The modern audience faces a deluge of information, with every brand vying for attention and creators producing entertaining material across platforms. This saturation, coupled with declining attention spans, demands a shift in content strategy. Traditional, lengthy content formats often fail to engage users who now prefer concise, actionable, and impactful messaging.

Puru observes a significant trend toward short-form content as the preferred medium for storytelling. Platforms designed for quick consumption—such as TikTok, Instagram Reels, and YouTube Shorts—highlight this shift. These formats cater to users' limited attention spans by delivering crisp, focused content that leaves them wanting more. Puru underscores the importance of crafting content that resonates immediately, capturing interest in moments rather than minutes.

He advises product marketers to prioritize accessibility in their messaging. Content should be simplified without losing depth, ensuring that users can seize its essence. The goal is to make complex ideas approachable while still retaining a clear call to action or takeaway.

At the heart of this strategy lies storytelling. Puru emphasizes that storytelling must evolve to fit these shorter formats, requiring creativity and precision. Marketers should focus on presenting key narratives upfront, sparking curiosity and offering value in a way that compels audiences to engage further. It's not about overwhelming with detail but delivering just enough to drive interest and interaction.

Key Takeaways for Marketers

- **Embrace Short-Form Content**: Focus on creating snackable, impactful content tailored for platforms where brevity is key.
- **Simplify Messaging**: Avoid jargon and complexity; instead, craft narratives that are universally understandable and relatable.
- **Prioritize Engagement**: Develop content strategies that align with audience habits, leveraging data to understand what works across different platforms and demographics.

Puru's advice serves as a vital reminder that storytelling and content strategy must evolve alongside audience preferences. By focusing on clarity, brevity, and emotional resonance, product marketers can cut through the noise, deliver value, and build meaningful connections in today's crowded digital landscape.

Ran Blayer (Tel Aviv-Yafo, Israel)

Bio

Ran Blayer is the Co-Founder and CEO of Percepto, a leading strategic reputation management and digital PR agency. With over 18 years of experience, Ran has advised top CEOs and business leaders on navigating corporate and reputational challenges, amplifying their key messages across diverse platforms. He holds an MA in Conflict Management and Resolution from Tel Aviv University and a BA in Communications and Political Science from the University of Haifa. Ran's passion for helping businesses build and maintain strong reputations drives his success at Percepto, where he leads a team of communications and digital experts.

Ran Blayer on Storytelling & Content Strategy

In my interview with Ran Blayer, he shares invaluable insights on the importance of proactively managing and owning your brand's narrative and online footprint. He emphasizes brands must be vigilant about their digital presence and take control over how they are perceived online, a practice that can enhance brand resilience and mitigate future risks.

Ran begins by suggesting a simple but powerful exercise: search for your brand name online to assess what others see when they look up your company. He encourages brands to look closely at the top search results, links, and information being presented. This approach offers a snapshot of how the brand story is unfolding online and helps identify gaps or inconsistencies in the narrative. Ran advises that brands consistently assess and update their key messages and online content to ensure they accurately reflect the brand's mission and values.

To further strengthen brand presence, Ran advocates for a multi-platform approach, utilizing various online channels to maintain a cohesive brand story. He highlights that a well-rounded digital strategy includes owned web assets, public relations, media coverage, business profiles, review sites, and social media. By diversifying the platforms on which a brand appears, companies can reach a wider audience and reinforce their narrative from multiple angles, amplifying their message and increasing brand recognition. This strategic approach, Ran points out, gives brands greater control over their digital footprint, ensuring that positive and consistent messaging dominates the online landscape.

Additionally, Ran underscores the importance of leveraging each marketing initiative to bolster the brand's online visibility. Brands must ensure that their online assets are not only created but also made highly accessible and prominent, maximizing each opportunity to shape the audience's perception. Ran believes that managing a brand's digital presence involves more than simply posting content—it requires a strategic alignment across channels to ensure a unified, interesting, and resilient brand image.

Ran also discusses the critical role a strong online presence plays in safeguarding a brand against potential negative publicity or crises. According to him, establishing a solid, positive online foundation helps brands to better weather crises, as their carefully crafted image can act as a buffer against negative events. This proactive approach can offer a brand a layer of protection, making it more resilient to challenges that may arise in the future.

Overall, Ran Blayer's advice underscores the importance of actively managing and owning a brand's narrative, staying visible and relevant across platforms, and strategically reinforcing a brand's story to build long-term resilience. His approach resonates deeply in the digital age, where a brand's online presence is often its most visible and influential asset.

PRODUCT MARKETING WISDOM

Tarun Kishnani (New York, NY, USA)

Bio

Tarun Kishnani is a dynamic strategist and expert negotiator reshaping financial services through innovation and transformative leadership. An alumnus of Harvard and Wharton, he excels in strategy and emerging technologies like AI, blockchain, and neuromarketing. As Chief Evangelist at LTIMindtree, Tarun collaborates with C-level leaders to revolutionize financial services at scale. Previously, at ICICI Securities, he led North America operations, achieving 6X revenue growth by blending innovation with relationship-driven sales. Passionate about financial markets and continuous learning, Tarun's success stems from his deep understanding of people, markets, and future technologies.

Neuromarketing—The Art and Science of Influence

In today's fast-evolving market, where consumer preferences shift rapidly, neuromarketing—the intersection of neuroscience, psychology, and marketing—has become a powerful tool. In a recent conversation with Tarun Kishnani, I explored how businesses can leverage neuromarketing strategies to enhance brand perception, improve customer experiences, and create impactful advertising campaigns. Here are three essential content strategies that can help product teams build lasting customer connections while driving engagement.

The Power of Color Psychology: Color plays a crucial role in shaping consumer behavior and perception. Red, for example, sparks urgency and excitement, which is why retailers like Target use it prominently. In contrast, blue promotes trust and calmness, making it ideal for financial brands like JP Morgan and Citi. A notable example of color psychology is Google's "50 Shades of Blue" experiment. By testing different shades of blue for their links, Google discovered subtle changes led to a $200 million revenue increase. So, color choices can directly influence behavior and impact your bottom line.

Less is More: Simplifying Choices - The paradox of choice reveals that too many options can overwhelm consumers, leading to "analysis paralysis." Neuroscience shows that when faced with excessive choices, customers may end up choosing nothing at all. A study found that adding an extra pricing option could reduce sales by 10%. Brands like Calendly and Google offer just three pricing options. They provide enough variety without overwhelming customers. By targeted selection, brands can streamline decisions and boost conversions.

Engage All the Senses: Engaging multiple senses enhances brand experiences and fosters emotional connections with customers. When Spotify launched in India, they worked with Neurons Inc. to identify the perfect tune for the Indian market, creating a unique sensory experience that resonated deeply with their audience. Other sensory elements, such as scent and texture, can also influence customer perceptions. Starbucks, for example, uses the smell of fresh coffee to create a welcoming atmosphere that enhances the overall customer experience.

The Ice Cream Truck Example: On a hot summer day in New York, a modest ice cream truck appeared, playing a nostalgic tune that drew kids and parents alike. Its menu offered just three flavors—vanilla, chocolate, and strawberry—making choices simple and quick. But the real magic was in the aroma: the truck diffused the smell of freshly baked waffle cones, triggering fond memories. Parents lingered, children smiled, and sales soared. This small truck showed how simplicity, sensory appeal, and emotional triggers can transform an ordinary moment into an unforgettable experience—neuromarketing in action.

Closing Thought: Neuromarketing is not just a theory—it's a practical and powerful tool. By leveraging emotional triggers, simplifying choices, and appealing to the senses, brands can create memorable experiences that drive results. Additionally, techniques like inducing Theta Waves, which enhance creativity, can help unlock fresh ideas and further improve content strategies.

Having worked on our Storytelling & Content Strategy, we are ready for Sales Enablement & Training to bring our hard work to life.

WISDOM ON SALES ENABLEMENT AND TRAINING

WISDOM ON SALES ENABLEMENT AND TRAINING

Sales enablement and training are pivotal for bridging the gap between product marketing and sales success. While theoretical approaches provide structure, real-world professionals offer actionable insights that stem from experience in driving sales team alignment, equipping them with the tools, content, and confidence to close deals effectively.

Experienced practitioners reveal the nuances of crafting sales enablement programs that resonate. For example, they might share how they tailored sales collateral to address specific customer objections or how they leveraged data-driven insights to refine training programs for underperforming teams. These stories bring clarity to what works—and what doesn't—when empowering sales teams in diverse industries.

Real-world insights often highlight the importance of collaboration. Professionals emphasize how close partnerships between product marketers and sales leaders ensure that training materials, messaging, and tools align with real-world customer needs and sales scenarios. Additionally, they offer tips on using feedback loops from the sales floor to iterate on enablement strategies.

Engaging with these experts through case studies, workshops, or mentorship helps marketers build robust sales enablement strategies that go beyond generic solutions. By applying their wisdom, marketers can better equip sales teams to deliver interesting product narratives, ultimately driving revenue and building stronger customer relationships.

In what follows, we examine the thoughts of established and up-and-coming industry figures to better understand these concepts.

Ashley Herbert Popa (Amsterdam, Netherlands)

Bio

Ashley Herbert Popa is a dynamic product marketing leader based in Amsterdam, currently serving as the Head of Product Marketing at Sendcloud. With a proven track record in scaling global SaaS companies, Ashley excels in storytelling, customer experience, and strategic planning. She is known for her role in building effective product marketing teams and fostering collaboration across departments. As a founding member of the Product Marketing Alliance, she is passionate about empowering product marketers worldwide. Ashley's accolades include the ISAM Rookie of the Year and the Sustainability Hackathon CEO Award, showcasing her commitment to innovation and excellence in the field.

Ashley Herbert Popa on Sales Enablement & Training

In my interview with Ashley Herbert Popa, she shares insightful advice on a core product marketing skill: prioritization. Ashley explains that prioritizing effectively is crucial for product marketers, especially if they aim to establish themselves as leaders within their organizations. She highlights that, regardless of whether someone is a solo product marketer or leading a team, the ability to manage a diverse workload through prioritization can define their success and professional growth. Product marketing, by nature, demands juggling multiple responsibilities, and Ashley emphasizes that mastering prioritization is essential to navigate these demands efficiently and strategically.

Ashley points out that product marketing roles often lack substantial staffing support, which intensifies the need to be strategic with time and resources. In her experience, many product marketers find themselves managing a "wide scope" with a lean team, often with new tasks adding to their workload without additional bandwidth. This environment requires an approach to prioritization that not only maintains productivity but also reinforces a product marketer's ability to operate at a high strategic level.

To achieve this, Ashley suggests utilizing tools like the "impact-effort matrix" or other priority matrices. By mapping out tasks based on their impact and effort, product marketers can make clearer, data-driven decisions about where to focus their time and resources. She explains that this method enables product marketers to make deliberate choices about what to pursue or delay and communicate these priorities transparently to colleagues and managers. For example, if a new initiative is suggested, the priority matrix can help illustrate the existing workload and spark conversations on what could be de-prioritized.

Ashley emphasizes that effective prioritization is not only about managing tasks, but also about building credibility as a strategic leader. A product marketer who can focus on the most impactful projects and make decisions based on company priorities stands out as a proactive and thoughtful contributor. This approach also allows product marketers to "manage up," fostering alignment with leadership while maintaining realistic workloads.

Concluding the discussion, Ashley's advice is especially valuable for product marketers in small organizations or for those working within small teams. For these individuals, prioritization is even more critical to success, as they may frequently find themselves as "teams of one." By consistently focusing on the most impactful tasks, product marketers can ensure they are contributing effectively to organizational goals while managing expectations across teams.

Ashley's emphasis on prioritization offers valuable lessons for sales enablement and training. Prioritizing high-impact initiatives ensures that sales enablement materials are timely, relevant, and aligned with current company strategies. Additionally, by applying prioritization to training, product marketers can tailor sessions to address the most pressing needs of the sales team, maximizing the value of each training effort and supporting the overall business objectives effectively.

Ashley Herbert Popa (Amsterdam, Netherlands)

Catie Ivey (Atlanta, GA, USA)

Bio

Catie Ivey is a tech-savvy revenue leader and diversity advocate dedicated to elevating B2B sales and empowering future leaders in the tech industry. Currently the Chief Revenue Officer at Walnut, Catie, has spent over a decade driving revenue growth and leading sales teams at companies like Pendo, Demandbase, and Marketo. Passionate about bridging the gender gap in sales leadership, she champions diversity and inclusion as essential components of successful teams. Catie is committed to empowering sales professionals to reach their potential and fostering cultures of engagement, resilience, and mutual success.

Sales Enablement & Training Insights from Catie Ivey

In her interview with me, Catie Ivey emphasizes the critical importance of making a product central to every stage of the customer journey, especially in sales enablement. She stresses that, particularly in SaaS companies, the product itself is one of the most valuable assets an organization has, yet many companies fail to effectively showcase their product to customers and prospects. Catie believes that an interactive product experience—such as demos or product tours—should be at the forefront of any customer interaction and should be integrated into every part of the sales and customer lifecycle.

Catie's main point is that product exposure should start early in the buyer's journey and continue throughout the entire customer experience. From the first touchpoint during demand generation to the ongoing efforts in customer success, the product should always be a part of the conversation. This includes incorporating interactive demos or product tours as key components of outbound sales efforts and ensuring they are easily accessible on websites. She highlights how many companies still neglect to place these interactive elements front and center, despite their proven effectiveness in driving engagement and conversions.

She also underscores the role of sales enablement in this process. Sales teams need to be equipped with the right tools and knowledge to engage prospects with the product as soon as possible. This requires integrating product demonstrations into sales cadences and making sure that sales reps have easy access to these tools to effectively move prospects through the funnel. By showing the product in action early on, companies can generate more interest, shorten sales cycles, and increase conversion rates.

Moreover, Catie stresses that product exposure should not stop after the sale. Post-purchase, the product must continue to play a role in educating customers about new features, ensuring they are successfully onboarded, and providing ongoing value. This reinforces customer satisfaction and helps drive long-term success, fostering a deeper connection with the product. Catie encourages organizations to think of product demonstrations not as a one-off but as a continuous part of the customer journey—integrating them into every stage of the sales and customer experience process.

In sum, Catie's advice revolves around making the product a central, accessible asset throughout the entire customer lifecycle. By integrating interactive product demos and tours at every stage—sales, onboarding, and beyond—companies can better engage their prospects, provide better training, and ensure customers are successful. She advocates for a more intentional and consistent approach to product exposure to maximize the product's value as both a sales and educational tool.

Deon Jamy Joseph (Milpitas, CA, USA)

Bio

Deon Jamy Joseph is a data-driven Product Marketing Manager based in Milpitas, California, specializing in B2B SaaS and AI. With an MBA and engineering background, he combines technical expertise with strong market insights to drive business growth. Deon currently leads product marketing efforts at Quantumverse AI and has a track record of enhancing user engagement through strategic initiatives. His experience spans various sectors, including Edtech and social networking, where he has successfully executed go-to-market strategies and optimized product positioning, achieving significant user growth and market competitiveness.

Sales Enablement & Training Insights from Deon Jamy Joseph

In his interview with me, Deon Jamy Joseph shares valuable lessons on pricing strategies from his internship experience at Illumio, a leader in cybersecurity. His insights emphasize the critical role of sales enablement and training in ensuring that pricing strategies are effectively communicated and executed.

Deon starts by highlighting the importance of aligning pricing with the value a product provides to customers. He stresses that pricing is not simply about covering costs but about reflecting the value of the product. At Illumio, he took part in a comprehensive market analysis to ensure that the product's pricing was competitive and matched the advanced cybersecurity protection it offered. This market-driven approach is essential for positioning products effectively in a competitive landscape, ensuring that sales teams can confidently communicate value to customers.

Transparency is another key takeaway from Deon's experience. He explains that creating a clear and detailed pricing and licensing guide was crucial for educating the sales team. With complex products like those in the cybersecurity space, simplifying and clarifying the pricing structure helped build trust with both customers and internal teams. This transparency not only facilitated a smoother sales process, but also helped eliminate confusion when interacting with potential customers, making it easier for the sales team to explain pricing with confidence.

Collaboration between product marketing and sales is another essential element Deon emphasizes. By involving the sales team early in the pricing process, the marketing team ensured they were aligned with the strategy and had the necessary knowledge to effectively communicate the pricing to customers. Regular training sessions were held to keep the sales team updated on any pricing changes, ensuring they had the most current information to facilitate customer discussions. This ongoing enablement ensured that the sales team remained well-equipped to sell the product in a competitive market.

Flexibility in pricing is also critical, especially in a rapidly changing industry like cybersecurity. Deon points out that the ability to adjust pricing based on market dynamics allows a company to remain competitive and responsive to customer needs. Flexibility ensures that the company's pricing remains aligned with evolving market conditions, giving sales teams the tools they need to stay relevant and maintain competitive advantage.

Last, Deon discusses the importance of continuous feedback loops. By collecting feedback from both customers and internal teams, Illumio was able to refine its pricing strategies over time. This data-driven approach enabled the company to make informed decisions that aligned with overall business goals, ensuring that their pricing strategy continuously supported growth and market competitiveness.

In summary, Deon's experience reinforces the idea that effective sales enablement and ongoing training are crucial for ensuring that sales teams are equipped to communicate and sell based on a customer-centric pricing strategy.

Dillon McDermott (Boston, MA, USA)

Bio

Dillon McDermott is a seasoned SaaS revenue and GTM leader with over 15 years of experience in B2B sales and management. Based in Boston, he has driven growth at both established public companies and early-stage startups by building and leading high-performance sales organizations. Dillon excels in GTM strategy, sales enablement, and pipeline generation, with a track record of doubling ARR, creating effective sales processes, and achieving significant revenue growth. Currently, he is the Director of Sales at Help Scout and is an Executive Member of Pavilion. His specialties include SaaS, generative AI, CX solutions, and professional development.

Sales Enablement & Training Insights from Dillon McDermott

In his interview with me, Dillon McDermott offers a valuable perspective on the importance of collaboration between sales and marketing, especially product marketing, in driving go-to-market success. While aligning these teams may seem fundamental, Dillon emphasizes that the most effective go-to-market teams foster tight integration and collaboration, which directly impacts revenue growth. This collaboration, he argues, is essential for product marketing to truly understand the challenges sales teams face and tailor their efforts to address these challenges.

Dillon draws a powerful analogy, stating that Sales is often referred to as the "tip of the spear" in the go-to-market strategy, while product marketing sharpens that spear. In this context, product marketing is responsible for equipping the sales team with the right content and tools to advance deals and close sales. However, for product marketing to do this effectively, it must go beyond the typical bi-weekly or monthly update meetings. Dillon's key recommendation is for product marketing to have a seat at the table during sales discussions—specifically during deal conversations, pipeline reviews, and forecast meetings.

By having a direct presence in these discussions, product marketers gain firsthand insight into the obstacles sales teams are encountering, such as losing momentum in deals or having difficulty engaging with key stakeholders. This level of involvement allows product marketing to create more targeted, actionable content that speaks to the real-time needs of the sales team. Rather than producing generic, persona-based materials, the content becomes highly relevant and tailored to help sales reps move deals forward.

The connection between sales and product marketing is crucial in creating content that not only resonates with the target audience but also addresses specific challenges that occur during the sales process. For example, by understanding why a deal is stalling or where Sales is encountering resistance, product marketing can develop resources that directly address those pain points. These resources can include case studies, objection-handling documents, or messaging guides that help sales teams navigate challenges more effectively.

Ultimately, Dillon highlights that the entire goal of the go-to-market team is to drive revenue. To achieve this, product marketing must be deeply integrated into the sales process, ensuring that the team is equipped with the tools and insights needed to close deals more effectively. This seamless collaboration between sales and product marketing leads to better sales enablement, improved deal progression, and, ultimately, more revenue. In summary, Dillon's nugget of wisdom encourages product marketers to move beyond traditional meeting cadences and work closely with sales to create real-time, actionable content that directly impacts the sales cycle.

Jaren Krchnavi (Munich, Germany)

Bio

Based in Munich, Jaren Krchnavi is a seasoned GTM and sales enablement expert having spent over 10 years driving global sales efficiency and revenue growth at Siemens. As Head of Sales Enablement for Siemens Smart Infrastructure, he has supported 10,000+ sales professionals in generating €10B+ in pipeline through programs, digital transformations, and innovative enablement strategies. Jaren is also a recognized thought leader, Sales Enablement Collective (SEC) Ambassador, and international speaker on sales enablement best practices. Fluent in English, German, and Spanish, he holds advanced degrees in business and international studies from Friedrich-Alexander-Universität and Sonoma State University.

Jaren Krchnavi on Maximizing Sales Enablement Impact

In today's challenging climate, Jaren Krchnavi explains sales enablers face the daunting task of driving revenue growth amidst tighter budgets, longer sales cycles, and increased customer hesitancy. As Jaren discussed at the Sales Enablement Summit, 2024 was a year of transformation for sales enablement—a call to reimagine strategies for thriving amidst scarcity.

Adapting Enablement for Lean Times

Economic constraints have forced enablement teams to deliver more value with fewer resources. While many organizations reduced budgets in prior years, those that strategically invest in enablement now have a unique opportunity to gain a competitive edge. Key strategies to overcome these challenges include:

- **Optimizing Existing Technology**: Fully leveraging AI capabilities within current tech stacks, rather than investing in new tools, is a cost-effective way to improve efficiency. Engage vendors to uncover untapped AI features.

- **Building Communities**: Establishing prospecting communities with dedicated activity days and recognition programs fosters collaboration, focus, and sustained motivation.
- **Knowledge Sharing**: Disseminating best practices from top-performing sellers can help uplift the entire team, as revealed by the Pavilion/Ebsta 2024 Sales Benchmark study.

Shifting to a Seller-Centric Mindset

To maximize impact, Jaren says enablers must shift to a seller-centric approach that prioritizes relevance, precision, and alignment with broader business goals. This requires a deep understanding of the Sales, Marketing and Product teams. Collaboratively refining Ideal Customer Profiles (ICPs) and identifying high-potential accounts ensures the ability to deliver measurable outcomes.

Empowering sellers is another critical priority according to Jaren. Training focused on confidently engaging C-suite executives and navigating complex conversations equips sellers with the tools to succeed. Comprehensive account planning and customer success strategies demonstrate value and build trust.

Avoiding Common Pitfalls

Jaren says Enablement efforts should not overwhelm sales teams or detract from core selling activities. By avoiding one-off initiatives and scrutinizing new programs, teams can maintain focus on initiatives that truly drive results.

Thriving Amidst Scarcity

In sum, Jaren's recommendation is that sales enablement must balance resource constraints with strategic execution. As Jaren emphasizes, success requires meticulous planning, cross-functional collaboration, and an unwavering focus on empowering sellers. By leveraging AI, fostering alignment, and adopting a seller-centric approach, enablement teams can transform challenges into opportunities, setting the stage for growth even in uncertain times.

Jaren Krchnavi (Munich, Germany)

Joe Parlett (Danville, CA, USA)

Bio

Joe Parlett is the CEO and Co-Founder of Amplify10, an AI-powered Sales Enablement company designed to elevate sales performance by changing the way we enable revenue teams, Amplify10 is moving enablement out of the classroom, and into the flow of each unique sales engagement. With over 20 years of experience in sales & leadership, he has held senior sales roles at companies like Veloce and Apttus. Joe specializes in cloud computing, Quote-to-Cash solutions, and applications that help with revenue team productivity. He is dedicated to improving sales execution and leveraging advanced technologies to drive growth and performance in organizations. His career also includes positions at Indymac Bank, Ownit Financial Solutions, and Oracle Corporation, where he honed his expertise in enterprise sales.

Sales Enablement & Training Insights from Joe Parlett

In his interview with me, Joe Parlett sheds light on the transformative role of AI in enhancing the effectiveness of B2B sales teams, drawing on his own experiences and lessons learned. He emphasizes B2B selling is inherently challenging, requiring deep product knowledge, an understanding of customer needs, and the ability to navigate complex buying processes. To address these demands, Joe advocates for integrating AI into sales enablement and training strategies.

Joe explains, AI can be a powerful tool for sales teams by streamlining research, preparation, and knowledge dissemination. In today's competitive environment, customers expect sales professionals to act as trusted advisors. To fulfill this role, sellers must not only master their own products but also deeply understand the customer's industry, pain points, and the broader competitive landscape. AI helps sales teams achieve this by providing timely insights, organizing complex data, and enabling better decision-making.

One key area where AI adds value is in research. By leveraging AI tools, sales teams can gather and analyze information about industry trends, customer challenges, and market dynamics more efficiently. This allows them to approach conversations with buyers armed with relevant, actionable insights. For example, AI can track industry-specific developments or identify patterns in customer behavior, helping salespeople anticipate needs and position solutions more effectively.

AI also aids in preparation, allowing sales professionals to customize their pitches and proposals. By analyzing data from past deals or customer interactions, AI can suggest tailored recommendations and talking points. This personalized approach not only builds trust but also increases the likelihood of successful outcomes by demonstrating a deep understanding of the buyer's unique situation.

In training, AI can support the continuous development of sales skills by identifying areas for improvement. Tools powered by AI can simulate real-world sales scenarios, offering real-time feedback on communication styles, objection handling, and persuasive techniques. Additionally, AI can track performance metrics across the team, highlighting trends and opportunities for targeted training initiatives.

Joe underscores that AI's goal is to enable sales teams to act as valuable resources for their customers, guiding the buyer through complex buying journeys with confidence and competence. By embracing AI, sales professionals can bridge gaps in knowledge and become the trusted advisors that are demanded by modern B2B buyers.

In summary, Joe Parlett highlights AI's potential to revolutionize sales enablement and training. By enhancing research, preparation, and skill development, AI empowers sales teams to meet the high expectations of B2B customers, improving both individual performance and overall team success.

Josh Britton (Harrogate, England, UK)

Bio

Josh Britton is a results-driven VP of Product Marketing based in Harrogate, England, focusing strongly on driving growth through strategic positioning and launch excellence. With extensive experience leading global teams, he excels in delivering impactful product launches and building market-leading brands. Currently at Cognism, he has successfully developed new messaging and positioning strategies that resulted in a significant increase in sign-ups. Josh's expertise includes P&L management, SaaS, and data analysis. He is passionate about creating interesting go-to-market strategies that align marketing and product teams to enhance customer satisfaction and product adoption.

Josh Britton on Sales Enablement & Training

In his interview with me, Josh Britton shares key insights on how product marketers can better enable and train sales teams by focusing on genuine customer insights. He emphasizes the importance of approaching customer research with as little bias as possible, as accurate, in-depth knowledge of the customer is foundational for effective sales enablement. Unlike traditional surveys, which can create confirmation bias and restrict responses, direct conversations with customers and prospects offer a richer understanding, allowing marketers to probe deeply and adapt their questions in real-time based on customer feedback. This approach, Britton argues, helps product marketers uncover real customer motivations that can significantly elevate sales enablement efforts.

A central piece of Britton's approach is the need to look beyond common pain points. According to him, focusing solely on pain points is a limited approach that often fails to capture the broader goals of the customer's role and organization. He highlights the classic example of Henry Ford, who famously said that if he'd asked customers what they wanted, they'd have requested faster horses instead of cars. Similarly, Britton believes product marketers should strive to understand how their products fit into the customer's broader objectives and aspirations, rather than relying on customers to define the role of the product. For sales enablement, this insight is invaluable, as it arms sales teams with a deeper understanding of how to position products within a larger vision rather than just addressing surface-level concerns.

Britton also stresses the importance of aligning sales enablement content and training with the customer's broader goals. By understanding a customer's end objectives—whether they're tied to the goals of a marketing director, a sales director, or the company itself—product marketers can craft messaging that resonates on a strategic level. This strategic alignment enables sales teams to present products as solutions that contribute directly to the customer's long-term vision, fostering a consultative selling approach. In training sessions, product marketers can emphasize how these insights should guide every sales conversation, helping the team to connect the product with the customer's overarching ambitions rather than just their immediate needs.

Josh Britton's method provides a blueprint for enhancing sales enablement through refined customer insight techniques. By encouraging sales teams to think beyond basic pain points and instead focus on the customer's broader objectives, product marketers can equip sales with nuanced knowledge that makes them more effective and credible advisors. Britton's emphasis on unbiased, dynamic customer conversations helps sales teams become more adaptive and aligned with customer needs. This approach not only sharpens messaging but also empowers sales teams to make authentic connections, positioning them as partners in the customer's success journey. Ultimately, Britton's insights underscore the power of thorough customer understanding as a cornerstone of effective sales enablement and training.

Nitya Kirat (Los Angeles, CA, USA)

Bio

Nitya Kirat is the Founder and President of YOSD Consulting, where he empowers sales teams to achieve remarkable growth using his proprietary Tiny Sales Habits Process™. With over 15 years of experience, Nitya has worked with industry giants like Google, BlackRock, and PIMCO, delivering custom sales training rooted in sales science and behavioral design. He has also served as a Mastery Faculty Partner at Google, guiding sales teams to unlock their potential. An MBA graduate from UCLA Anderson, Nitya combines strategic expertise with a deep commitment to performance improvement, helping clients win bigger, faster, and more consistently.

Nitya on Sales Enablement & Training

In his interview with me, Nitya Kirat explores the vital connection between marketing, product marketing, and sales, emphasizing the need for sales enablement to ensure successful sales conversations. While the trend of product-led growth (PLG) continues to shape the marketing landscape, Nitya stresses it doesn't eliminate the need for sales teams. In fact, there is still a crucial role for salespeople in engaging with prospects and clients, particularly when marketers equip them with the right tools, content, and training.

Nitya explains that, while PLG suggests products should sell themselves, many businesses still require salespeople to guide prospects through the decision-making process and close deals. However, he argues that marketing content must be built with the sales conversation in mind. By considering how a salesperson would use the content in a client-centric discussion, product marketers can craft materials that are not only informative but also tailored to facilitate smoother sales interactions. If content can help sales teams engage with prospects in a way that speaks directly to their needs and pain points, sales cycles will shorten, and the likelihood of successful conversions will increase.

BY NITIN KARTIK

A key challenge Nitya highlights is how sales teams often struggle to transform static content—like product decks or brochures—into an engaging, personalized conversation. Marketers might produce well-crafted content, but without guidance on how to use it effectively, salespeople may find it difficult to have dynamic and organic discussions with potential clients. This issue can be addressed by product marketers providing sales enablement tools and training to bridge this gap. For example, marketers can offer guidelines on how to integrate key messaging into sales conversations or provide example scripts that align with different customer personas. The goal is to ensure that the content isn't just informative, but also flexible and applicable to real-world client interactions.

Nitya also emphasizes the importance of understanding the unique challenges sales teams face. When marketers collaborate closely with sales teams and understand the context in which they operate, they can create more useful resources. Regular feedback from sales teams is crucial to refine content, making sure it is continually optimized to serve the needs of both the product and the customer. This feedback loop ensures that the content remains relevant, resonating with prospects at every stage of the sales funnel.

In sum, Nitya highlights that a successful sales enablement strategy requires strong collaboration between marketing and sales. Product marketers should create client-centric content that empowers sales teams to have meaningful conversations with prospects. By focusing on content that is adaptable, provides clear value, and is easy for sales teams to incorporate into their workflow, marketers can help salespeople close deals faster and more effectively. This strategic alignment between marketing and sales is essential to improving sales cycles, boosting conversions, and ultimately driving business growth.

Nitya Kirat (Los Angeles, CA, USA)

Russ Somers (Pflugerville, TX, USA)

Bio

Russ Somers is a seasoned marketing executive with extensive expertise in online marketing, e-commerce, and marketing strategy. As VP of Marketing at Quantified.ai, he leads growth through innovative solutions like the Sales Simulator, designed to expedite onboarding and certification. With a proven track record in driving demand generation, corporate strategy, and product marketing across various leadership roles, Russ also serves as a fractional CMO for early-stage companies, offering strategic guidance without the need for full-time hires. Based in Pflugerville, Texas, Russ advises startup leaders, mentors marketers, and continually aims to make a positive impact in his field.

Russ Somers on Shifting Focus from Quantity to Quality

In his interview with me, Russ Somers highlights the evolving role of AI in sales enablement, urging a departure from the traditional focus on quantity toward improving the quality of sales efforts. Drawing from years of experience training and enabling sales teams, he shares insights into how product marketers can empower sales teams to be more effective, not just busier.

Russ observes that many AI-powered sales enablement tools focus on scaling outreach—sending more emails, entering more data into CRMs, and automating workflows. However, this relentless push for volume leads to diminishing returns. Sales representatives bombard prospects with communication that often lacks personalization or persuasiveness, filling inboxes with noise rather than value. This approach does not address the real challenges sales teams face: effectively connecting with their audience and converting leads into customers.

Russ challenges product marketers to rethink how AI tools are leveraged in sales enablement. Instead of prioritizing tools that enable teams to do more, he advocates for solutions that help them perform better. AI can play a transformative role in areas such as pitch refinement, messaging accuracy, and understanding customer pain points. For instance, AI-driven tools could analyze recorded sales calls to identify strengths and weaknesses, enabling tailored feedback that elevates the team's skills. By focusing on quality, sales teams can deliver more interesting, personalized pitches that resonate with prospects.

A key aspect of Russ's vision is helping sales teams master the fundamentals of persuasion and product knowledge. This involves equipping them with sharper messaging and the ability to articulate value propositions effectively. AI can assist by providing insights into customer behavior, recommending optimized messaging based on prospect profiles, and highlighting the most relevant product features for each audience segment. These tools empower sales teams to engage more thoughtfully, fostering meaningful connections with customers.

Russ underscores that product marketers must be allies to sales teams, not just suppliers of tools. By prioritizing quality over quantity, marketers can help sales teams improve outcomes and customer satisfaction. This approach builds stronger alignment between marketing and sales, fostering a culture of collaboration where both teams succeed together.

Key Takeaways for Sales Enablement & Training

- **Move beyond quantity**: Shift focus from scaling outreach to enhancing the impact of interactions.
- **Leverage AI for quality**: Use AI to refine pitches, improve messaging, and deepen product knowledge.
- **Prioritize persuasion**: Equip sales teams with tools and training that amplify their ability to connect with prospects.
- **Collaborate for success**: Foster alignment between product marketing and sales for mutual growth.

Russ's insights challenge the industry to rethink sales enablement, focusing on delivering smarter, more effective tools and training that truly empower sales teams.

Yitzy Tannenbaum (Israel)

Bio

Yitzy Tannenbaum is a seasoned product marketing professional currently serving as a Senior Product Marketing Manager at Palo Alto Networks. With extensive experience across notable companies like Meta, IBM, and NICE Ltd, Yitzy specializes in business strategy, go-to-market planning, and product-market fit. He excels in leveraging both qualitative and quantitative research to inform strategic decisions and drive successful marketing campaigns. Yitzy holds an MBA in Marketing from Bar-Ilan University and has a proven track record of collaborating with cross-functional teams and managing relationships with key analysts to enhance product visibility and market positioning.

Insights from Yitzy Tannenbaum

In my interview with Yitzy Tannenbaum, he shares a key lesson that drives his approach to product marketing: always ask "why." Yitzy explains that in the fast-paced world of product marketing, teams often receive requests from various stakeholders, including executives, to execute tasks or campaigns. These requests can range from creating marketing collateral like eBooks and infographics to developing new features for products. However, Yitzy emphasizes that simply accepting these requests without questioning their purpose can lead to misguided efforts. Instead, he advocates for a more thoughtful approach by asking why the task is needed and what value it brings.

Yitzy highlights how understanding the "why" behind each initiative helps clarify its broader objectives. When a product manager is excited about a new roadmap feature involving machine learning or AI, it's important to recognize that while the technological potential may be thrilling, it does not always translate to customer value. Therefore, it's essential to ask why the feature is being developed and how it will benefit customers. Similarly, when someone requests marketing content, it's crucial to understand its role in the marketing funnel—whether it's intended to generate leads, build awareness, or support customer retention. By probing the "why," product marketers can better align their actions with the overall business strategy and ensure they are prioritizing efforts that have the greatest impact.

Yitzy's perspective is particularly valuable for organizations that face resource constraints, especially smaller companies where priorities can easily get muddled. In such environments, where there are countless tasks and initiatives competing for attention, asking "why" serves as a powerful tool to stay focused on what truly matters. It helps product marketers avoid getting caught up in non-essential tasks and instead concentrate on initiatives that will drive meaningful results.

Ultimately, Yitzy believes that asking "why" isn't just about questioning requests; it's about making more informed, strategic decisions. Whether road mapping product development, creating marketing campaigns, or building new features, a deep understanding of why a task is necessary leads to smarter, more effective execution. By embracing this mindset, product marketers can ensure they are working on the right things, driving business success, and delivering value to both customers and the organization.

In summary, Yitzy's advice underscores the importance of clarity, purpose, and focus for product marketing. Always asking "why" helps ensure that every action taken is purposeful and aligned with the company's larger goals.

While Sales Enablement & Training helps us arm our boots on the ground with the right assets to accomplish the mission, we must continuously partner vertically and horizontally across the organization to keep our engines humming smoothly. This brings us to the fine art of Cross Functional Collaboration.

WISDOM ON CROSS FUNCTIONAL COLLABORATION

WISDOM ON CROSS FUNCTIONAL COLLABORATION

Cross-functional collaboration is essential for successful product marketing, as it requires alignment across teams like sales, product, customer success, and engineering. While standard frameworks outline the importance of this collaboration, real-world insights from professionals highlight the challenges and best practices that make these partnerships truly effective.

Experienced professionals often share stories of how they've navigated the complexities of cross-functional work, offering strategies for breaking down silos and building trust among departments. For instance, a seasoned marketer might explain how they facilitated alignment between sales and product teams to ensure the right messaging was communicated during a product launch. These real-world examples reveal how communication, empathy, and shared goals are critical to overcoming the friction that can arise when different teams have varying priorities.

Professionals also discuss tools and techniques for fostering collaboration, such as using project management platforms to track progress, hosting regular cross-departmental meetings, and building logical processes for feedback loops.

Learning from these insights through interviews, workshops, or mentorship helps marketers understand the dynamics of collaboration and how to adapt strategies to fit their unique organizational cultures. By applying these real-world lessons, product marketers can drive greater alignment, improve outcomes, and ensure the success of their product initiatives.

In the following sections, we investigate the insights of established and rising industry figures to gain a better understanding of these concepts' practical implications.

Abby Rodrigues (Toronto, ON, Canada)

Bio

Abby Rodrigues is an experienced Product Marketing Manager with over six years of expertise in launching products, driving adoption, and building customer loyalty. Based in Toronto, she has worked across SaaS, eCommerce, and gaming, collaborating closely with Product teams to align on roadmaps and optimize messaging. Abby's multifaceted experience spans 0-1 product launches, customer enablement, GTM strategies, and lifecycle management, including successful partnerships with major brands like Apple Arcade and LEGO. She regularly leads customer-marketing workshops with the Product Marketing Alliance and writes about PMM trends, bringing creativity and strategic insight to every project she undertakes.

Abby Rodrigues on Cross Functional Collaboration

In my interview with her, Abby Rodrigues shares her perspective on the transformative role of cross-functional collaboration in product marketing during an insightful conversation. With her career focused on reporting to product teams, Abby emphasizes the unique strategic capabilities and value product marketers gain when working closely with technical and non-technical teams.

Abby explains that collaborating with product teams diversifies the scope of a marketer's responsibilities, balancing efforts between supporting current customers and driving new business. This often leans toward enhancing customer retention while still enabling sales motions. Her experience highlights the pivotal role of product marketers in inbound product marketing—shaping roadmaps, running product betas to validate messaging, and driving adoption rates. These activities, enabled by close collaboration with technical teams, contribute directly to improved revenue retention and healthier churn rates.

One key advantage of cross-functional collaboration is the ability to experiment. Marketers working on product teams have greater access to testing new features and introducing updates that cater to both existing and prospective customers. Abby observes that product marketers often work closely with growth product managers or assume this role informally. This involvement strengthens their strategic outlook and reinforces the critical bridge they form between technical teams, like engineering and design, and customer-facing teams, such as sales and support.

Abby underscores the importance of quickly mastering technical terminology to communicate effectively with development teams. This skill builds credibility and respect among technical stakeholders, facilitating smoother collaboration. At the same time, marketers must distill complex technical information into actionable insights for non-technical teams. This dual capability positions product marketers as translators and connectors, ensuring alignment across the organization.

On the much-discussed debate about whether product marketing should report to product or marketing, Abby offers a nuanced view: the answer depends on the specific needs of the business. Regardless of reporting structures, she advises product marketers to seize opportunities to work on product teams. Doing so enhances their technical fluency, strategic acumen, and ability to contribute to organizational growth.

Ultimately, Abby's insights demonstrate how cross-functional collaboration empowers product marketers to play a central role in driving success. By bridging the gap between technical expertise and customer-centricity, they not only elevate their careers but also create meaningful business impact. Abby's perspective serves as an interesting reminder that strong collaboration across diverse teams is key to thriving as a product marketer.

Alexandra "Sasha" Mitroshkina (Turkey)

Bio

Aleksandra "Sasha" Mitroshkina is a seasoned Product Marketing Leader based in Istanbul, Turkey, and a 2023 Tom Basil Award winner. With extensive expertise in SaaS and open-source software, she has successfully launched over a dozen go-to-market strategies, driving 200% annual contract value growth and 400% adoption growth. As a former Senior Product Marketing Manager at AlmaLinux, she built a vibrant community of 2,000 engaged IT professionals. Currently, she serves as Director of Product Marketing at Percona, where she oversees messaging and positioning for various database solutions, significantly enhancing team productivity and driving substantial revenue growth.

Sasha Mitroshkina on Cross Functional Collaboration

In her interview with me, Sasha Mitroshkina shares a valuable lesson learned over her seven years in product marketing. She emphasizes the importance of building powerful alliances when joining a new team, whether in a consulting or full-time role. According to Sasha, success in product marketing often starts with cultivating trust and collaboration across teams. Instead of immediately asking for help or making requests, she advises product marketers to begin by listening and providing valuable insights. By offering support and building rapport with colleagues, product marketers can create a foundation for future collaboration.

One of the key strategies Sasha uses to foster these alliances is conducting annual research on sales confidence. She utilizes a simple survey, easily accessible online, to assess how sales and customer success teams feel about the marketing efforts and where they think improvements can be made. While this is not traditionally seen as a product marketing responsibility, Sasha argues that taking the initiative to lead such a project can be incredibly impactful. By measuring sales confidence, product marketers gain direct insights into what front-facing teams believe is working and what isn't in terms of marketing support. This survey helps identify areas where alignment between sales, customer success, and marketing can be improved.

Sasha highlights that conducting a sales confidence survey provides a straightforward way to measure progress and gather valuable feedback without taking up too much time from the teams involved. The data collected can offer key insights into the effectiveness of marketing initiatives and reveal gaps in the support provided to sales teams. By focusing on these insights, product marketers can better understand how their marketing efforts are being perceived and where adjustments are needed to align more closely with sales goals.

Importantly, Sasha also sees the sales confidence survey to strengthen relationships with front-line teams. When product marketers actively seek input and offer solutions, they demonstrate their commitment to supporting the broader business. This collaboration can lead to product marketers being invited into customer-facing activities, such as customer interviews, or even becoming executive sponsors for key customers. By being directly involved in these interactions, product marketers can gain firsthand knowledge of customer pain points and better advocate for their needs.

Sasha's key takeaway is clear: building relationships and offering support before seeking help is crucial in product marketing. By using tools like the sales confidence survey, product marketers can gain valuable insights, foster stronger partnerships with sales and customer success teams, and position themselves as trusted allies within the organization.

Andrew Hatfield (Brisbane, Australia)

Bio

Andrew Hatfield is the Founder and CEO of Deepstar Strategic, with over 28 years of global IT experience in product marketing, technology, and communications. He specializes in GTM optimization for B2B SaaS, helping companies scale by identifying what's working, prioritizing what to do next, and aligning product, marketing, sales, and CS teams. With expertise in business strategy, product marketing, and solution architecture, Andrew has launched 15 products and generated $196M in sales and $1.34B in qualified pipelines. He has extensive experience in working with cross-functional teams, leading remote teams, and solving customer challenges in B2B enterprise markets. Andrew is also an expert mentor and Product Marketing Alliance ambassador. When he's not growing revenue, Andrew enjoys the subtle tones of Islay whisky, low 'n slow BBQ, and snowboarding.

Andrew Hatfield on Cross Functional Collaboration

In my interview with Andrew Hatfield, he shares an important lesson he has learned over the course of his career: the need to apply the same focus and skills internally that product marketers use to understand the market and customers externally. Andrew confesses it took him some time to realize this, as he had been fanatically focused on the buyer and the market, but he eventually discovered that successful product marketing isn't just about external engagement—it's equally about internal alignment and support.

Andrew explains that as product marketers, we often spend a great deal of time and energy understanding our customers' needs, motivations, and pain points, and shaping messaging, positioning, and go-to-market strategies accordingly. These efforts are typically outward facing, aimed at driving customer engagement and business growth. However, Andrew stresses that product marketing is not solely an external game. To truly succeed, product marketers must apply the same customer-centric skills internally to understand and support their peers across different departments—whether it be sales, product management, customer success, or other teams within the organization.

The key takeaway from Andrew's insight is that product marketers must extend the same attention to understanding the needs and challenges of internal stakeholders as they do when crafting strategies for external customers. Just as they would analyze and identify customer pain points to develop solutions that drive engagement, they should approach their colleagues with a similar mindset. By doing so, product marketers can foster collaboration, drive alignment, and support teams across the organization in a way that ultimately strengthens the overall product marketing efforts.

Andrew reflects on how, early in his career, he was so focused on customer and market research that he sometimes neglected the importance of internal communication and collaboration. As he gained more experience, he recognized that understanding what motivates and challenges his peers is just as essential to success. When product marketers are attuned to the internal dynamics of their teams, they are better positioned to create a unified strategy and to ensure that everyone is aligned toward achieving the same goals.

In essence, Andrew's lesson is that product marketing is both an internal and external game. Effective product marketers need to understand not only their customers' needs but also the needs of their internal teams, and address those with the same diligence and strategic thinking. By doing so, they can create a stronger, more cohesive product marketing strategy that drives success both inside the organization and out in the market. This approach ensures that product marketing isn't just about messaging to customers—it's about creating internal harmony and alignment that amplifies external success.

Elan Keshen (Toronto, ON, Canada)

Bio

Elan Keshen is an accomplished marketing leader with expertise in market analysis, go-to-market strategies, and cross-functional enablement. Currently the Head of Marketing at Distribute, he specializes in driving customer-centric insights to fuel awareness and adoption. With prior leadership roles at Magical, Shopify, and Ada, Elan has a proven record of product positioning, lifecycle marketing, and product education. He is passionate about blending technology with a positive impact, crafting clear narratives, and learning through experimentation. Elan holds an Honors Business Administration degree from Ivey Business School and has been recognized with multiple honors, including the Ivey Scholar and Dean's Honor List awards.

Cross-Functional Collaboration Insights from Elan Keshen

In his interview with me, Elan Keshen underscores the vital role of effective cross-functional collaboration in product marketing and highlights a key lesson: the art of saying no. This skill is not just about declining requests but doing so in a manner that fosters trust and enhances collaboration across teams.

Elan begins by addressing the broad and often misunderstood scope of product marketing. Product marketers are frequently expected to be all things to all people, leading to unclear boundaries and overextension. To navigate this, Elan emphasizes the importance of clearly defining the PMM role within the organization. By leveraging company data and strategic business metrics, product marketers can identify priorities and align their efforts with what truly matters to the business. This clarity ensures that cross-functional partners understand the PMM's focus and value, setting the stage for more effective collaboration.

A core aspect of this collaboration is the ability to say no strategically. Elan explains that product marketers often fall into the habit of saying yes too frequently, especially early in their careers or when trying to build goodwill with other teams. However, agreeing to tasks or projects that fall outside the scope of PMM can dilute focus and reduce the effectiveness of the team. Elan stresses that learning when, if, and how to say no is a defining trait of a great product marketer.

The "how" is especially critical in maintaining strong cross-functional relationships. Elan advises PMMs to decline requests with empathy and kindness, ensuring the rationale is clearly communicated. When saying no, it's essential to acknowledge the needs of the requesting team and explain how the decision aligns with broader company objectives or the PMM's strategic focus. This approach not only builds trust but also fosters a sense of mutual respect among teams, turning a potentially negative interaction into a constructive one.

Elan also highlights the importance of prioritization in cross-functional collaboration. By aligning priorities with organizational goals and data-driven insights, product marketers can focus their efforts on initiatives that deliver the most value. This prioritization enables them to work more effectively with other teams, ensuring that collaborative efforts are both impactful and aligned with shared objectives.

In summary, Elan Keshen's insights offer a blueprint for mastering cross-functional collaboration in product marketing. By defining the PMM role clearly, prioritizing strategically, and learning to say no with empathy, product marketers can build stronger relationships across teams while maintaining focus on their core responsibilities. This balance is key to driving business success and fostering a culture of trust and collaboration.

Hila Lauterbach (California, USA)

Bio

Hila Lauterbach is a Vice President of Product Marketing based in Silicon Valley, CA. with over 15 years of experience in leading high-performing go-to-market teams in global tech startups and enterprises. She specializes in positioning, pricing, sales enablement, win-loss, and product launch strategies, driving demand generation and customer acquisition. As a co-founder of multiple startups, Hila combines her entrepreneurial mindset with strong business acumen. An accomplished keynote speaker and recognized Top PMM Influencer, she excels in building win-win partnerships with industry giants like AWS, Salesforce, and Google. Hila holds an EMBA from Tel Aviv University.

Hila Lauterbach on Transforming Product Marketing into a Cross-Functional Powerhouse

In her interview with me, Hila Lauterbach shares interesting insights on elevating product marketing to a strategic, cross-functional driver of organizational growth. Her approach centers on aligning product marketing with company goals, fostering collaboration across departments, and focusing on high-impact initiatives that yield measurable results.

Hila underscores the importance of immersing product marketing leaders in organizational objectives. This entails understanding priorities across executive leadership, sales, customer success, and corporate marketing to ensure product marketing initiatives align with broader strategies. By embedding her team's work within the company's overarching goals, she ensures direct contributions to key bottom-line metrics.

A pivotal lesson Hila gained while expanding her team from 1 to 30 people was the value of establishing clear KPIs for every initiative and delineating ROI attribution. This involves identifying "orphaned projects"—complex initiatives like win-loss analyses, M&A integration playbooks, or retention plans—that lack ownership but hold strategic value. Successfully executing these projects allowed her team to demonstrate their impact and build a case for scaling efforts.

Cross-functional collaboration is at the heart of Hila's method. By uniting stakeholders across departments, her team surfaces gaps, aligns priorities, and drives cohesion. This collaborative framework positions product marketing as a vital connector, bridging silos to unify teams around shared goals.

Hila also emphasizes influencing executive-level strategy by showcasing product marketing's tangible impact on revenue growth, customer retention, and market share. Demonstrating measurable outcomes elevates the function's role as a strategic contributor.

Data and customer feedback play a crucial role in refining messaging, pricing, and offerings. Hila's data-driven approach empowers her team to address underperforming areas, identify changes, and capitalize on opportunities.

To manage competing priorities, Hila implements a tiered project management system. Tier-1 (MRR driving) initiatives receive top-tier focus, while lower-priority efforts are allocated fewer resources. This structure ensures her team remains focused on what matters most while addressing secondary needs.

Structured communication and a commitment to continuous improvement underpin her strategies. Quarterly business reviews enable her team to assess outcomes, share lessons learned, and refine approaches. Establishing clear OKRs and KPIs provides direction, while retaining flexibility ensures agility.

In summary, Hila Lauterbach's approach demonstrates the transformative potential of product marketing. By aligning efforts with organizational goals, fostering collaboration, and prioritizing impactful projects, product marketing transcends its traditional role to become a strategic growth driver. Her insights highlight the value of focus, integration, and continuous improvement in building a function that delivers sustained impact.

Leonard Burger (United Kingdom)

Bio

Leonard "Leo" Burger is a Senior Product Marketing Manager at Lenvi, leveraging over 12 years of international experience in product development, management, and marketing. With expertise in equity crowdfunding and angel syndicates, he has backed over 250 companies, including Chip, Monzo, and Nothing. A certified product marketer and Quantic Executive MBA graduate, Leonard is known for his T-shaped skills, creative problem-solving, and data-driven storytelling. He advises at Over Ventures and the FinTech Marketing Hub, with a focus on FinTech, sustainability, and innovation. Leonard also writes the "Product Burger" blog, sharing insights on product positioning and market communication.

Leo Burger on Cross Functional Collaboration

In his insightful interview with me, Leo Burger shares a strategic perspective on cross-functional collaboration and the essential interplay between brand, customer, and user experience. He envisions these three elements as interconnected components of a Venn diagram with Product at the core, forming the basis for a well-rounded and successful business. Leo underscores that, for any product to truly thrive, it must seamlessly align with these experiences to engage customers and mitigate churn. His approach highlights the need for close collaboration across brand, customer support, and product development teams to harmonize these essential dimensions.

Leo illustrates how brand experience extends beyond aesthetics or public perception; it's about creating a cohesive and recognizable image that customers feel connected to. He draws parallels between brands like Netflix and Amazon Prime, each with its unique appeal. For instance, Netflix might have a user-friendly interface, but Amazon's flexibility in customer support often sways customer loyalty. Leo stresses that brand teams need to work together with customer experience (CX) teams to identify brand elements that resonate with customers while also recognizing areas where competitors may excel in responsiveness or flexibility.

Leo continues by pointing out the necessity of linking customer and user experience (UX) to build a product that feels intuitive and supportive of users' needs. According to him, without collaboration between these teams, gaps are inevitable, which can create disjointed experiences. He sees this synergy as a means of providing continuity across the user's journey — from discovering the product and trying it out to long-term usage and potential advocacy. Leo's view aligns with the idea that customer service should not be a reactionary function but a proactive player, working alongside UX teams to preemptively address user needs through seamless design and responsive interfaces.

Central to Leo's approach is the role of product as the unifying force among these three dimensions. He believes that even the best-designed user or customer experiences can fall short if the product does not live up to expectations. A strong product at the center of this "holy grail," as Leo describes it, is one that not only fulfills its promises but also embodies the brand's values, meets customer expectations, and provides a satisfying user experience. Achieving this goal, however, requires active and ongoing collaboration between product managers, marketers, CX specialists, and UX designers.

Leo's holistic approach advocates for a cross-functional collaboration model where each team aligns its objectives with the others. By coordinating efforts and working as a cohesive unit, companies can deliver a well-rounded experience that truly captures customer loyalty and satisfaction. Leo's message is simple: aligning brand, customer, and user experience around a stellar product fosters a business ecosystem where customers feel understood, valued, and supported, driving growth and reducing churn.

Mary Lim (Austin, TX, USA)

Bio

Mary Lim is a dynamic Product Marketing Manager specializing in empowering customer success through innovative strategies. With over 7 years of experience in B2B SaaS, she excels in sales enablement, content creation, and program development. A passionate user advocate, Mary is dedicated to crafting optimized experiences for both internal and external stakeholders. She holds certifications in Product Marketing and KCS v6 Fundamentals, enhancing her ability to drive impactful initiatives. Outside of her professional pursuits, Mary enjoys exploring Austin's best bubble tea and coffee spots and spending time outdoors with her dog, Bernie.

Mary Lim on Cross Functional Collaboration

In her interview with me, Mary Lim delves into the vital role that cross-functional collaboration and internal communication play in the success of product marketing initiatives. She stresses that effective execution of tasks is just one part of the equation; equally important is the effort to showcase your work across departments. According to Mary, striking the right balance between executing and promoting work internally is key to making a meaningful impact. She believes that, in practice, about 60% of your time should be spent on execution, while the remaining 40% should be focused on communicating and showcasing your efforts to other teams.

Mary highlights that one of the key elements of successful cross-functional collaboration is ensuring that different leadership teams—whether from sales, product, or marketing—are kept informed and aligned. By doing so, you create a unified understanding of what is being worked on, which allows each team to see how their efforts fit into the broader picture. This alignment not only helps streamline execution but also ensures that everyone is moving toward the same goals. For instance, keeping leadership teams updated on the progress of campaigns and product initiatives helps them make informed decisions and allows them to integrate this work into the overall company strategy.

Mary's approach to showcasing work involves simple but effective methods, such as sending regular Slack updates to the sales team about new content, campaigns, and the results they are seeing. These updates are not just about informing the team but also about creating a feedback loop, where sales can learn about the outcomes of different initiatives and offer insights or ask for adjustments based on what they're hearing from customers. This transparency helps ensure that everyone—whether in product, sales, or marketing—is working with the same set of information, making it easier to collaborate effectively.

Through her experiences, Mary has learned that merely executing tasks is not enough to drive the recognition or support needed for success. She reflects on how she initially believed that great work would naturally speak for itself. However, she soon discovered that actively promoting and communicating her efforts within the organization was necessary to gain visibility and ensure her work had the desired impact. This insight is especially crucial in product marketing, where coordination across teams is essential for the success of launches, campaigns, and ongoing product initiatives.

In summary, Mary's perspective emphasizes that internal communication and visibility are as important as execution in driving successful cross-functional collaboration. By proactively showcasing work, product marketers not only ensure their efforts are recognized but also foster stronger alignment across teams. This helps create a more cohesive strategy, contributing to the overall success of the product marketing function.

Nicky Dibben (Cambridge, England, UK)

Bio

Nicky Dibben is a seasoned deep-tech marketing consultant, advisor, and mentor based in Cambridge, UK. With over 25 years of experience, she specializes in translating complex technology into interesting business narratives and scalable marketing frameworks to design and build businesses. Having worked with high-tech companies of all sizes, Nicky has also served as VP Marketing for a global telecom equipment company, where she helped double revenues in a year. Nicky's 360° Marketing framework helps startups get from lab to market in a structured fashion, covering areas from market analysis and business models through to positioning, messaging, and the development of comprehensive marketing plans. Her expertise spans both hardware and software sectors including clean tech, FinTech, Medtech and wireless, and she serves as a mentor with Deeptech Labs, the University of Cambridge, and NatWest Bank.

Nicky Dibben on Cross Functional Collaboration

In her insightful interview with me, Nicky Dibben emphasizes the critical importance of cross-functional collaboration, particularly in the context of product management and marketing within technology companies. Drawing from her extensive experience in deep tech, Nicky underscores how siloed thinking can undermine organizational success and shares strategies for fostering a more integrated approach.

Nicky begins by addressing the common perception of product management as a standalone "fiefdom" within many tech companies. While acknowledging the significance of product in driving innovation and growth, she points out that this dominance can sometimes result in neglecting other essential organizational functions. This imbalance creates blind spots, particularly in areas that are foundational to business success, such as business models, routes to market, positioning, messaging, competitive analysis, and customer journeys.

According to Nicky, effective product management and product marketing hinge on understanding their interfaces with other functions. She encourages professionals to adopt a more holistic approach by considering how product decisions impact—and are impacted by—other departments. For instance, product teams must align with sales strategies to ensure seamless go-to-market execution, while also integrating insights from competitive analysis and customer feedback. Ignoring these intersections risks an internal focus that can lead to misalignment with broader business objectives.

Nicky also highlights the danger of overlooking foundational business principles amidst a product-centric culture. While she has no issue with Product being viewed as "king," especially in tech-driven organizations, she cautions against letting the prominence of product overshadow the contributions of other marketing disciplines. A successful organization recognizes that product is part of a larger ecosystem, and all elements - marketing, sales, and customer experience - must work together to achieve sustainable growth.

Product teams should engage actively with other functions, ensuring their efforts are grounded in the organization's broader strategic objectives. Additionally, marketers and product managers alike must not lose sight of the fundamentals, such as clear objectives, well-researched customer journeys, and strong positioning. These foundational elements serve as guardrails, preventing costly missteps as teams push for innovation and growth.

Nicky's wisdom serves as a reminder that cross-functional collaboration is essential for creating a cohesive and effective organization. Product teams may play a central role, but their success depends on their ability to interface seamlessly with other departments. By embracing a holistic approach, teams can avoid pitfalls, leverage diverse insights, and achieve greater success in today's complex business landscape.

Rice Tong (London, United Kingdom)

Bio

Rice Tong is a Product Marketing Manager at Legatics, where she drives B2B SaaS growth through strategic, multi-channel campaigns. With an MSc in Strategic Marketing from Imperial College London, she brings a strong storytelling approach to building brand communities for tech startups. Her expertise spans product marketing, SEO, and social media, honed through roles at companies like Jupitrr and Oxygen. Fluent in Mandarin, Cantonese, and English, Rice has also managed global innovation campaigns, engaging communities for brands like Audi and Astellas Pharma. She's passionate about collaborative projects and enjoys connecting with mentors in her field.

Rice Tong on Cross Functional Collaboration

In her interview with me, Rice Tong shares valuable insights into the art of Cross-Functional Collaboration, particularly in the context of being the first product marketer in a company. Drawing from her personal experience, Rice highlights the importance of building relationships, defining priorities, and integrating efforts across teams to create impact from day one.

Rice begins by emphasizing the importance of defining the role of a product marketer clearly. As the first person in this role, she recognizes that it's essential to align her priorities with the company's challenges. By identifying gaps in processes and designing a targeted 30- or 90-day plan, she not only sets the foundation for her work but also ensures her efforts directly address the organization's pressing needs. This clarity helps position product marketing as a key strategic function.

A cornerstone of Rice's approach is speaking to as many people as possible within the organization. Through conversations across teams, she uncovers pain points, aligns expectations, and educates others about her role. These interactions serve as the basis for collaboration, helping others understand how product marketing can contribute to their goals. By fostering transparency and building trust early on, Rice ensures smoother collaboration, and a shared understanding of priorities.

Rice also stresses the importance of delivering visible, short-term outcomes. While foundational work like research and strategy development is crucial, quick wins help establish credibility and maintain momentum. For example, by contributing to ongoing projects from other teams and delivering results that are immediately appreciated, Rice builds goodwill and demonstrates the value of cross-functional collaboration. These efforts not only support the broader organization but also create opportunities to embed product marketing into ongoing workflows.

Besides aligning with existing team projects, Rice advocates for setting clear monthly outcomes. These short-term goals provide a measurable way to track progress and showcase contributions, keeping stakeholders engaged and supportive. This iterative approach balances the need for long-term strategy development with the company's demand for tangible results.

Ultimately, Rice's experience illustrates the vital role of cross-functional collaboration in establishing product marketing within an organization. By communicating openly, integrating with team efforts, and delivering value quickly, she not only defines her role but also helps her colleagues see product marketing as an indispensable function.

In summary, Rice's insights offer a roadmap for any product marketer stepping into a new organization, emphasizing that cross-functional collaboration isn't just a tool for success—it's the foundation of building trust, alignment, and shared achievement across teams.

Shobhit Bhutani (San Francisco Area, CA, USA)

Bio

Shobhit Bhutani is a seasoned product marketing and business development leader with over 20 years of experience and a record of award-winning performance in tech. Currently the Generative AI Product Marketing Lead at Broadcom for VMware's Private AI Foundation, Shobhit has driven transformative growth through strategic messaging, sales planning, and product positioning. Previously with VMware, Pure Storage, Rackspace, and Dell, he's crafted innovative market strategies, led multimillion-dollar campaigns, and spoken at industry events worldwide. Shobhit holds an MS in Industrial Engineering from Texas A&M and is certified in business and product marketing strategies, including Sirius Decisions and Pragmatic Marketing.

Shobhit Bhutani on Cross-Functional Collaboration

In his conversation with me, Shobhit Bhutani emphasizes the critical role of cross-functional collaboration in developing effective product messaging. He shares his insights on the importance of having a well-documented messaging document which is essential for aligning various go-to-market teams.

Shobhit begins by explaining that the messaging document serves as the foundation for all future product marketing efforts. The first step in developing the document is to understand the broader product category. This includes researching what analysts are saying about the category, providing credibility and context for the product. This background research is essential for positioning the product effectively.

Next, Shobhit highlights the importance of understanding the customer's challenges. It is crucial to have a deep knowledge of the pain points that customers face, as this directly informs how the product will be positioned as a solution. This customer-centric approach ensures that the messaging resonates.

The next step is to articulate how the product addresses customer issues and pain points, which is a product marketer's primary role.

For more complex products, such as software or hardware, Shobhit suggests diving into technical details and architectural elements. However, these details should not overshadow the core messaging of how the product benefits customers. The next step is to outline use cases—specific scenarios where the product provides tangible value to customers.

Shobhit stresses that the initial creation of the messaging document should be done in isolation, but it must not stay that way. Cross-functional collaboration is key to refining and validating the messaging. Product marketers should seek feedback from various stakeholders, including product management, engineering teams, IT directors, and other relevant departments. This collaborative input ensures that the messaging is aligned with business goals.

Shobhit also highlights the importance of securing executive leadership sign-off on the messaging document early in the process. This buy-in ensures that there is alignment at the highest levels of the organization, preventing issues down the line when the messaging is used in marketing collateral.

Lessons for Cross-Functional Collaboration

- **Develop a clear messaging document upfront**: This should be the starting point before creating any collateral.
- **Incorporate feedback from various stakeholders**: Collaboration with internal teams like product management, engineering, and IT is essential.
- **Secure executive-level buy-in early**: Ensure alignment with leadership to drive consistency across the organization.

By prioritizing early collaboration and a well-documented messaging strategy, Shobhit believes product marketers can set a firm foundation for success in their go-to-market efforts.

Stefan Gladbach (Seattle, WA, USA)

Bio

Stefan Gladbach is a Senior Product Marketing Manager and consultant based in Seattle, specializing in B2B technology and SaaS. Focusing strongly on storytelling, he transforms technical concepts into interesting narratives that resonate with target audiences, driving significant results—such as a 53% revenue increase in his last role. Stefan excels in creating engaging content that converts and developing effective sales enablement materials. As a passionate advocate for cross-functional alignment, he is dedicated to ensuring successful product launches. Additionally, he shares insights and best practices through his YouTube channel under his name, aiming to educate and inspire fellow marketers.

Stefan Gladbach on Cross-Functional Collaboration

In his interview with me, Stefan Gladbach shares valuable insights on the importance of cross-functional collaboration in product marketing. He emphasizes that building solid relationships across teams, especially with product management (PM), is crucial for success. His advice focuses on communication, ownership of messaging, and adaptability to ensure effective collaboration and alignment across different functions.

Stefan stresses that one of the most critical aspects of a product marketing manager's role is the ability to explain the "why" behind messaging and launch decisions. This requires building strong relationships across teams, particularly with product managers. While PM and product marketing managers (PMMs) have distinct roles, they must work closely to ensure alignment on the product roadmap and launch strategies. Stefan recommends frequent communication, ideally on a weekly or even daily basis, with the product team to stay in sync. He highlights the importance of understanding each other's perspectives and being able to delegate tasks effectively when roles overlap. By fostering these relationships and maintaining open communication, PMMs can ensure a smooth execution of product launches and positioning.

Another key point Stefan makes is the importance of taking full ownership of the messaging. After conducting the necessary research and crafting an interesting messaging statement, product marketers must be prepared to defend their decisions. Often, individuals higher in the organization may challenge aspects of the messaging or suggest changes. Stefan advises PMMs to stand firm in their convictions and use data to support their messaging decisions. He warns against a "messaging by committee" approach, where compromises dilute the effectiveness of the messaging, resulting in unclear or inconsistent communication. Product marketers should be able to explain every element of their messaging, backed by data, to ensure that the core message resonates clearly with the target audience.

However, Stefan also cautions against letting hubris impede improvement. He observes that some PMMs, after finalizing their messaging, may resist changes when new data or customer feedback emerges. Stefan encourages product marketers to remain adaptable and open to refining their messaging and positioning based on fresh insights. He stresses that product messaging and strategy are not static; they should evolve as new information becomes available. Embracing this adaptability ensures that the product marketing strategy stays relevant and responsive to the market's needs.

Stefan Gladbach's advice on cross-functional collaboration underscores the importance of communication, ownership, and adaptability. By fostering strong relationships with key teams, owning the messaging process, and staying open to change, product marketers can navigate internal dynamics and drive successful product launches.

Tanwistha Gope (Bangalore, India)

Bio

Tanwistha Gope is a seasoned Product Marketing Leader with 13+ years of expertise in B2B technology, specializing in Customer Data Platforms, AdTech, and MarTech. Known for developing targeted positioning and messaging, she has driven notable results, including a 20% increase in qualified leads and recognition in Forrester Landscapes. Her experience spans product launches, ABM campaigns, analyst relations, and sales enablement, with a focus on enhancing content marketing strategies. Currently leading Product Marketing and Growth at Zeotap, Tanwistha is also an active Ambassador for the Product Marketing Alliance and GTM Alliance, committed to driving market influence and customer engagement.

Tanwistha Gope on Cross Functional Collaboration

In my interview with Tanwistha Gope, she shares an interesting story about bridging the gap between product and go-to-market (GTM) strategies in her organization. Tanwistha explains how the absence of a dedicated product marketing role had created challenges at Zeotap, where strong features were developed, but their positioning both within the market and across internal teams remained unclear. Recognizing this gap, her organization introduced her solo PMM role, which she now leverages to align GTM efforts, enable sales and product teams, craft content, manage social media, partner collaborations, gather industry insights, and manage stakeholders.

Tanwistha recalls the early days in her role as overwhelming, as she faced a flood of requests from various departments, including sales, customer success, product management, and partnerships. Each team had its own needs and expectations, and the demand was intense, often leading her to work long hours with minimal direction. She quickly realized the necessity of bringing order to this complex role. By prioritizing her tasks and implementing Objectives and Key Results (OKRs), she began to gain control. Tanwistha emphasizes the importance of distinguishing each

OKR as either committed or aspirational, and of tying these OKRs to specific key performance indicators (KPIs). This approach has allowed her to balance workloads, focus on high-impact tasks, and gradually improve clarity in her role.

For solo PMMs, Tanwistha's advice is to take a step back and conduct an internal audit. By engaging with each department, PMMs can better understand immediate needs, identify gaps, and then prioritize their responsibilities according to OKRs. This prioritization not only helps manage workloads but also enhances the PMM's role as a valuable advocate for the product. As Tanwistha notes, setting clear priorities and aligning efforts with OKRs ultimately strengthens the product's positioning and maximizes the PMM's impact within the organization.

Through her insights, Tanwistha highlights how solo PMMs can navigate complex demands, become indispensable voices for their products, and make strategic decisions that align with organizational goals. Her story exemplifies the challenges of being a single PMM, yet demonstrates how proactive communication, prioritization, and clear metrics are keys to success. Tanwistha's journey serves as an inspiring reminder for PMMs to focus on building relationships with internal teams, conduct thorough audits, and remain committed to the goals that truly drive the product's value forward. This process, she believes, not only advances the product's market success, but also develops the PMM's own growth and effectiveness within the organization.

Vanisha Mittal (Boston, MA, USA)

Bio

Vanisha Mittal is a data-driven marketing strategist with a strong global perspective, holding both an MS in Marketing Analytics and an MBA in Marketing. Based in Boston, she has experience working across three continents, blending creativity with strategic insights to deliver impactful marketing campaigns. With expertise in data analysis tools like R, Python, and SQL, as well as platforms such as Google Analytics and Salesforce, Vanisha leverages her technical skills to drive growth and enhance customer engagement. She has worked in diverse industries, from enterprise marketing at Airtel to strategic consulting, and is passionate about using data to shape marketing strategies that resonate universally.

Vanisha Mittal on Cross Functional Collaboration

In her interview with me, Vanisha Mittal underscores the importance of cross-functional collaboration in the success of product marketing initiatives. She introduces the concept of "Collab-Achieve," emphasizing that collaboration is not just a trendy buzzword, but a foundational element behind every successful product launch and marketing campaign. Vanisha believes that collaboration in product marketing is essential for unlocking new opportunities, driving innovation, and ultimately ensuring the success of products in a competitive market.

Drawing from her experience, Vanisha illustrates how building strong, strategic partnerships across various teams, both internal and external, is crucial to achieving remarkable results. Throughout her career, she has seen the direct impact of effective collaboration in the success of GTM (Go-To-Market) strategies for diverse tech products. For instance, when leading GTM efforts, she successfully managed relationships with key stakeholders from product, sales, marketing, customer support, and analytics teams. By working together, they could synchronize efforts, define product features, craft interesting messaging, and create a unified customer experience.

One of the most critical aspects of cross-functional collaboration, as Vanisha explains, is leveraging the collective strengths of each team involved. Each department has its unique expertise, and by bringing them together, organizations can create a comprehensive strategy that drives product success. This approach ensures that every aspect of the product, from development to customer service, is aligned with the overarching business objectives. In her experience, collaboration goes beyond just working together—it's about making sure each team's contribution is integrated and maximized.

Vanisha highlights that this collaborative approach fosters a more agile and adaptive process, allowing product marketers to respond to market needs more effectively. Whether it is enhancing product features based on customer feedback, fine-tuning messaging for different target audiences, or ensuring excellent post-launch customer support, collaboration ensures all aspects of the product journey are seamless.

Moreover, Vanisha stresses that embracing collaboration allows teams to push boundaries and innovate more effectively. Innovation often arises from the intersection of different perspectives and areas of expertise. When cross-functional teams are encouraged to work together, they can think outside of the box and come up with creative solutions to complex challenges.

Vanisha's message is clear: by embracing and championing collaboration, product marketers can not only achieve short-term product success but also drive long-term growth and innovation. She believes that when teams work together, they unlock new growth opportunities, build better products, and deliver superior customer experiences. In her view, collaboration isn't just a key to success—it's the secret sauce behind truly transformative marketing strategies.

Yael Kahn (Germany)

Bio

Yael Kahn is an experienced business development leader specializing in AI and data solutions, currently working with AWS across EMEA. With a track record of launching and expanding partner networks in Germany, Austria, and Switzerland, she excels in new business development, relationship building, and strategic account management. Fluent in German, English, and Hebrew, Yael combines her multilingual skills and expertise to connect people, ideas, and technology. Passionate about coaching, mentoring, and fostering partnerships, she has successfully driven market strategies, created new pipelines, and enhanced brand presence across Europe. Yael holds an MBA in Business Innovation and Leadership from Business Trends Academy, Berlin.

Yael Kahn on Cross Functional Collaboration

In her interview with me, Yael Kahn highlights the critical role of emotional intelligence (EI) and emotional quotient (EQ) in fostering Cross-Functional Collaboration. Drawing from her experience, Yael explores how EQ strengthens connections, improves teamwork, and complements the rise of AI.

Yael begins by introducing Daniel Goleman's foundational work on emotional intelligence, emphasizing self-awareness, self-discipline, and empathy. EQ is a measure of emotional intelligence (EI), which refers to the ability to recognize, understand, manage, and influence emotions—both your own and those of others. EQ evaluates skills like empathy, self-awareness, emotional regulation, social communication, and conflict resolution. High EQ is associated with effective interpersonal relationships, resilience, and better decision-making, making it an important complement to cognitive intelligence (IQ) in personal and professional success. Yael explains these abilities are vital predictors of success and well-being. For Yael, EQ is not just a personal skill but a collective tool for navigating complex social dynamics and fostering collaboration.

BY NITIN KARTIK

As part of her work at AWS, Yael leads EQ and IQ sessions designed to enhance emotional awareness among partners, customers, and employees. She underscores that EQ is particularly important in a digital-first world, where virtual interactions often lack the depth and nuance of in-person communication. Emotional intelligence bridges this gap and fosters trust.

Yael also connects EQ to the ongoing evolution of AI, noting that while AI excels at optimizing efficiency and managing data-driven tasks, it cannot replicate the creativity and empathy inherent in human collaboration. As AI becomes more integrated into workplaces, the ability to build strong relationships and solve problems creatively will distinguish successful teams.

Moreover, Yael highlights the importance of embedding EQ into everyday work and interactions. By developing emotional intelligence, teams can better handle change, navigate challenges, and collaborate across functional boundaries. Creativity and problem-solving thrive when EQ is prioritized.

Yael's advice emphasizes a proactive approach: leaders and team members should actively develop their EQ by engaging with colleagues, partners, and customers empathetically. She recommends exploring resources on EQ to deepen understanding and applying these principles in both professional and personal contexts. Strong EQ drives success in any organization.

In summary, Yael's insights underscore the transformative power of emotional intelligence in fostering cross-functional collaboration. By prioritizing connection, empathy, and creativity, organizations can navigate the complexities of modern work environments even as AI reshapes the landscape.

Cross Functional Collaboration leverages our soft skills, which must be balanced by equally important hard skills—Key Performance Indicators (KPIs)—which we cover in the next chapter.

WISDOM ON KEY PERFORMANCE INDICATORS

WISDOM ON KEY PERFORMANCE INDICATORS

Key Performance Indicators (KPIs) are essential for measuring the effectiveness of product marketing strategies. While theoretical frameworks provide a starting point, real-world insights from professionals offer a deeper understanding of how to define, track, and optimize KPIs to drive business success.

Experienced professionals often share practical examples of how they selected and tailored KPIs based on specific business goals. For instance, a seasoned marketer might explain how they focused on customer acquisition costs and lifetime value to measure the ROI of a product launch. They may also share how they used product usage data and customer feedback to refine KPIs, ensuring they reflected changing market dynamics.

Real-world insights also highlight the importance of aligning KPIs with broader business objectives. Professionals emphasize how to work cross-functionally to ensure all teams are aligned with the same metrics, from sales and marketing to customer success. They also discuss how to create a balanced dashboard that tracks both leading and lagging indicators to provide a comprehensive view of performance.

Learning from these experts through case studies or mentorship allows product marketers to gain practical, actionable knowledge about setting and refining KPIs. Applying these insights helps marketers make data-driven decisions, optimize strategies, and achieve better business outcomes.

Subsequently, we examine the perspectives of industry giants and emerging talents to better understand these concepts in reality.

Aaftab Ahluwalia (Toronto, ON, Canada)

Bio

Aaftab Ahluwalia is a seasoned Product Manager and Marketer with over 10 years of experience in GTM strategy, product launch, and messaging for B2B and B2B2C SaaS solutions. Currently serving as a Senior Outbound Product Manager at Guidewire Software, Aaftab specializes in driving cross-functional collaboration, delivering impactful product launches, and managing multimillion-dollar marketing initiatives. His previous roles at FedEx, Gartner, and SHL have honed his expertise in growth strategy, sales enablement, and marketing analytics. With an MBA in International Business and a B. Tech in Computer Science, Aaftab is fluent in English, Hindi, and Punjabi, with elementary French proficiency.

Aaftab Ahluwalia on Key Performance Indicators

In his insightful interview with me, Aaftab Ahluwalia emphasizes the critical role of KPIs (Key Performance Indicators) in driving success in product marketing. With over a decade of experience spanning multiple geographies, Aaftab highlights the importance of adaptability and leveraging data-backed insights to optimize marketing strategies in dynamic market conditions.

Aaftab underscores that KPIs serve as the compass for evaluating the effectiveness of marketing campaigns and ensuring continuous improvement. He explains that product marketers must monitor KPIs like engagement rates, conversion rates, and the performance of different media channels and creative assets. Tracking these metrics enables teams to make informed decisions and pivot when necessary.

As an example, Aaftab describes a scenario where a marketing campaign is launched across three media channels using six creative sets. Initial KPIs such as click-through rates and conversions reveal that some channels and creatives underperform while others excel. A data-driven marketer doesn't stick rigidly to the original plan. Instead, they analyze the KPI trends, identify the outperforming channels and creatives, and reallocate resources accordingly. This strategic shift maximizes campaign impact, leading to improved engagement and higher conversion rates.

The conversation emphasizes actionable insights derived from KPIs. Aaftab explains that collecting data is only the starting point—its true value lies in its application to inform real-time decisions. Marketers who swiftly adjust their strategies based on KPI trends differentiate themselves by achieving greater campaign effectiveness and higher ROI.

Aaftab also highlights the iterative nature of effective product marketing. KPIs are not static; they evolve as campaigns progress and market conditions shift. Regular monitoring and a willingness to recalibrate strategies based on updated data are essential. This iterative process ensures that product marketing efforts remain aligned with consumer behavior and market demands.

Ultimately, Aaftab's lesson is clear: KPIs are not just metrics—they are tools for agility, adaptability, and impactful decision-making. His advice to aspiring product marketers is to immerse themselves in data analysis, continuously track KPIs, and embrace a culture of experimentation and responsiveness.

To me, the core takeaway here is that success in product marketing hinges on flexibility, strategic adaptation, and leveraging KPIs to drive impactful decisions. Aaftab's insights serve as a powerful reminder that data-driven strategies are fundamental to achieving measurable results and driving business growth in today's competitive landscape.

Aaftab Ahluwalia (Toronto, ON, Canada)

Aditi Salke (USA)

Bio

Aditi Salke is an accomplished Product Marketing Consultant based in the US, with a focus on transforming complex technical concepts into interesting customer narratives. She has collaborated with notable clients such as BeerBiceps Inc. and Zerion Inc., where she developed strategies that significantly boosted product demand and user engagement. Aditi is currently pursuing her Master's in Engineering Management at Duke University. With expertise in community management and a robust background in FinTech and SaaS, she excels in crafting audience-friendly content and implementing go-to-market strategies that drive growth and enhance brand visibility.

Aditi Salke on Key Performance Indicators

In her interview with me, Aditi Salke shares a key lesson about leveraging micro-moments to enhance marketing performance. Her insights highlight the importance of prioritizing quality over quantity in marketing strategies to achieve impactful results against key performance indicators (KPIs).

Aditi explains that in today's saturated digital landscape, where platforms like LinkedIn and Instagram overflow with content, marketers often struggle to capture audience attention. This creates a scenario akin to the small talk at networking events—plentiful but rarely memorable. To break through the noise, Aditi advocates for identifying micro-moments: specific, well-timed opportunities to deliver meaningful value to customers.

She emphasizes that the success of micro-moment marketing hinges on thorough data analysis and customer research. By understanding audience behavior, preferences, and pain points, marketers can pinpoint the right opportunities to engage. This targeted approach ensures that interactions resonate deeply with users, fostering brand loyalty and driving conversions.

From a KPI perspective, micro-moments help optimize engagement metrics by delivering content that aligns with customer needs at the right time. For instance, instead of bombarding users with generalized content, brands can focus on delivering high-impact messages during critical moments in the customer journey—such as when a user is exploring solutions or is ready to make a purchase decision. This tailored approach not only improves click-through rates and engagement, but also enhances broader KPIs like conversion rates, customer retention, and lifetime value.

Aditi underscores that achieving this level of precision requires a shift from volume-driven tactics to data-driven strategies. Marketers must invest in tools and techniques that allow them to uncover actionable insights from data, whether through audience segmentation, predictive analytics, or real-time performance tracking. This enables brands to allocate resources effectively and prioritize campaigns that align with measurable goals.

Moreover, Aditi's insights highlight the evolving role of product marketers in balancing creativity with analytics. While crafting interesting narratives remains essential, marketers must also be adept at interpreting data to inform their strategies. This dual focus ensures that marketing efforts not only resonate with audiences but also deliver quantifiable business outcomes.

Ultimately, Aditi's perspective offers a powerful reminder that success in product marketing is about more than creating content—it's about creating impact. By focusing on micro-moments, marketers can align their efforts with KPIs that matter, driving meaningful engagement and long-term brand growth.

Akshaya Ravi (USA)

Bio

Akshaya Ravi is a passionate GTM strategist and foundational SDR at Storylane, where she helps create interesting product stories through demos. Recognized as one of the "Top 100 Powerful Women in Sales 2024" globally, Akshaya brings a wealth of experience in outbound sales and customer communication. She has a background in building sales systems, generating revenue, and nurturing prospects at companies like Shifu Ventures and LeadSquared. A dynamic content creator on LinkedIn, Akshaya is actively engaged in communities supporting women in sales. She's also an avid reader and podcast listener, always open to conversations about GTM strategies.

KPI-Focused Insights from Akshaya Ravi: Backing Decisions with Data

In her interview with me, Akshaya Ravi emphasizes the importance of leveraging data, clear communication, and organized processes to drive key performance indicators (KPIs) in product marketing. Her advice focuses on building credibility, fostering collaboration, and maintaining a structured approach to achieving measurable outcomes.

Akshaya's first and foremost recommendation is to back all statements or suggestions with data. In a world where opinions are plentiful, data becomes the deciding factor that substantiates your viewpoint and earns buy-in from stakeholders. For product marketers tasked with meeting KPIs like conversion rates, adoption metrics, or customer retention, presenting data-driven insights is essential for making a persuasive case and aligning teams toward shared objectives.

Another critical aspect Akshaya highlights is the importance of preparation when seeking support from cross-functional teams. Instead of vague requests, she advises everyone to conduct preliminary research and document findings in detail. For example, if a marketer seeks input from a product team to enhance feature adoption KPIs, presenting insights into user behavior or feedback demonstrates initiative and provides clarity. This approach not only facilitates faster decision-making but also strengthens collaboration by showing respect for others' time.

Effective communication is another pillar of Akshaya's KPI-driven approach. She underscores the need to deliver concise, focused messages. When marketers articulate goals and strategies clearly, they minimize confusion and ensure alignment with stakeholders. This clarity is vital when tracking metrics like campaign performance or sales enablement outcomes, as it ensures all teams have a shared understanding of objectives and priorities.

Adding value to others also ties into achieving KPIs. Akshaya suggests being proactive in supporting colleagues by sharing relevant resources or insights. For instance, if a sales team struggles with closing deals, providing them with well-researched collateral or market data can improve win rates—an essential KPI for product marketers.

Akshaya also emphasizes documenting wins, losses, and lessons learned. This practice not only creates a repository of insights but also allows teams to iterate on strategies to optimize KPIs over time. By reflecting on past campaigns or product launches, teams can identify what worked, what didn't, and how to improve future outcomes.

Last, Akshaya advises everyone to set clear agendas when requesting meetings. This simple yet impactful practice ensures time is used efficiently and allows teams to focus on KPI-relevant discussions, such as campaign performance or product feedback analysis.

By aligning preparation, communication, and data-driven decision-making, Akshaya offers a roadmap for product marketers to achieve their KPIs while fostering collaboration and driving impactful results.

Alexandre Contador (The Randstad, Netherlands)

Bio

Alexandre "Alex" Contador is a seasoned CEO and co-founder of Videco.io, a SaaS platform transforming B2B sales with AI personalized video. Having spent over ten years across multiple continents, Alexandre specializes in digital growth, GTM strategies, and startup leadership. He has a proven track record of driving over $15 million in revenue and has held roles ranging from Head of Growth to GTM Advisor. Fluent in Portuguese and English, with a firm grasp of Spanish and French, Alex is recognized as one of Europe's most active marketeers on social media, and he actively mentors early-stage companies in achieving scalable growth.

Alex Contador on Key Performance Indicators

In my interview with Alex Contador, he shares key insights into how interactive and personalized video is transforming B2B commercial teams, drawing on his extensive experience with B2B tech companies. Having worked in the sector for over 10 years, Alex understands the common challenge of justifying the return on investment (ROI) for video content. Often, companies question the tangible benefits of video—particularly when it comes to lead generation and revenue impact. He explains that this skepticism stems from the high cost of producing corporate videos and the difficulty of proving their direct contribution to business outcomes.

Alex notes that the need for proof of ROI is especially important in B2B sales and marketing, where video production can require substantial investment. Even with interesting statistics showing how other companies have successfully used video for marketing or sales, it's still a challenge to quantify the exact impact on business growth. This is where Alex's team saw an opportunity to innovate. They began exploring AI personalized and interactive video solutions designed specifically for B2B companies, not just creating video content but also transforming it into an engaging, action-driven tool.

The core of their approach involves embedding interactive elements directly within the video, such as forms, surveys, clickable links, and even calendar integrations. For example, by embedding tools like HubSpot or Calendly within the video, viewers can immediately act—whether it's booking a meeting, filling out a form, or responding to a survey—without leaving the video. This interactive experience enhances user engagement and drives conversion.

The results have been impressive. Alex shares that businesses using these personalized and interactive video features have seen significant increases in conversion rates—up to 20 to 30 percent higher than traditional video content. Actions like downloading eBooks or scheduling meetings have seen substantial growth, and traffic to key landing pages has also increased. What makes interactive video so powerful, Alex emphasizes, is its ability to provide measurable results, something traditional corporate videos often lack. For example, a company may have spent $20,000 on a corporate video, but without interactive elements, it's difficult to track how well the video is performing or if it's leading to tangible business outcomes.

By contrast, personalized and interactive videos allow companies to track engagement more effectively and directly tie video content to revenue. The viewers who are most engaged are also more likely to take actions such as filling out forms or booking a meeting, making these videos far more impactful.

In summary, Alex's approach to personalized and interactive video is a game changer for B2B sales and marketing. By embedding actionable touch points in videos, businesses can turn passive content into a powerful lead-generation and conversion tool, yielding measurable results that justify the investment in video marketing. His experience underscores the importance of finding innovative ways to make video content more engaging, actionable, and ultimately more effective in driving business growth.

Ankita Chaturvedi (Gurugram, Haryana, India)

Bio

Ankita Chaturvedi is a seasoned GTM and product marketing expert with over seven years of experience across B2B SaaS, consumer internet, and media tech. With experience leading GTM strategy for SHOPLINE in EMEA, Ankita has a track record of crafting impactful messaging and executing campaigns that boost revenue and customer engagement. Previously, she has held pivotal roles at companies like Kuku FM and The Economic Times, where she achieved notable results in digital transformation and subscription growth. Ankita holds a BTech in Electrical Engineering and an MBA in Marketing and is certified in content marketing and inbound methodologies.

Ankita Chaturvedi on The Currency of Influence

In the world of product marketing, there are practitioners—and then there's Ankita Chaturvedi. With over seven years of experience spanning B2B SaaS, consumer internet, and media tech, Ankita has redefined what it means to be a product marketer.

From leading GTM strategies for SHOPLINE in EMEA to driving digital transformation and subscription growth at Kuku FM and The Economic Times, her career is a masterclass in creating impact.

Ankita's philosophy on product marketing is both refreshing and transformative. Over the years, Ankita has transformed the way organizations perceive product marketing, emphasizing the critical role of Key Performance Indicators (KPIs) in driving growth and shaping strategies.

"KPIs aren't just numbers on a dashboard," Ankita asserts. "They're proof of impact, a way to demonstrate how marketing drives not just awareness but real business outcomes." This perspective challenges the outdated notion of product marketing as a "launch-and-leave-it" team or a mere support system for sales. Instead, Ankita positions product marketers as strategic leaders—the "voice of the market"—bridging customer needs, competitive insights, and product evolution.

For Ankita, KPIs are the language of influence, and speaking that language clearly is non-negotiable. Among her go-to metrics is pipeline influence, which she calls the "north star" of product marketing. By linking marketing efforts directly to revenue, it highlights how strategies enable sales teams to win. She also champions metrics like customer adoption rates, campaign engagement, and even a product feedback loop that measures how effectively product marketing insights shape product development.

But Ankita's approach to KPIs goes beyond hitting targets; it's about educating stakeholders across functions—from leadership to product teams—on what these metrics mean and why they matter. "KPIs aren't just for us," she explains. "They're for everyone. They tell a story that aligns teams, drives strategy, and proves why product marketing is indispensable."

This storytelling is the cornerstone of Ankita's approach. She uses KPIs not just to measure success but to showcase how product marketing fuels everything from GTM engines to cross-functional collaboration. By doing so, she shifts the narrative: product marketers are not executors but architects of growth, shaping a company's trajectory with every decision.

The risks of neglecting this strategic foundation are clear to Ankita. Without metrics to guide and measure impact, product marketing can devolve into a tactical machine—churning out launches and slide decks without moving the needle. "The magic lies in using KPIs to show the depth and breadth of our impact," she says. "They're the currency of influence, unlocking the potential to take product marketing from misunderstood to mission critical."

Through her work, Ankita demonstrates KPIs are more than data—they're a tool for transformation, proving that when measured and communicated effectively, product marketing becomes the backbone of growth and innovation.

Deepika Tripathee (USA)

Bio

Deepika Tripathee is a Senior Product Manager at Walmart, where she leads E2E Order Fulfillment and Online Pickup and Delivery initiatives. With over 8 years of experience in product management, she combines technical expertise with a customer-first approach. A UC Riverside MBA graduate, Deepika previously held positions at Tieto and Infosys, where she focused on creating innovative, data-driven solutions. She specializes in agile project management, strategic vision, and cross-functional team leadership. Beyond her professional work, Deepika is passionate about community service, enjoys traveling, exploring different cultures, gardening, and spending time with her dog and family.

KPI Insights from Deepika Tripathee

In her interview with me, Deepika Tripathee provides essential guidance for product managers, particularly those in the early stages of their careers, about the importance of balancing user needs with business goals when designing Key Performance Indicators (KPIs). She highlights that while user empathy and meeting user requirements are vital, product managers must never lose sight of the larger business objectives, as these goals ultimately drive the company's growth and revenue.

According to Deepika, a common pitfall of budding product managers is an overemphasis on user-centric metrics. While understanding and addressing user needs is undoubtedly a foundation of successful product development, Deepika stresses that product managers must always consider how their efforts align with the company's strategic business goals. This balance is essential because, at the end of the day, business success drives revenue, which enables product managers to continue innovating and developing great products. The business goals provide the necessary context within which product managers should operate to ensure their work is directly contributing to the company's financial health and long-term success.

BY NITIN KARTIK

From a KPI perspective, Deepika's approach suggests that metrics should not just focus on user satisfaction and engagement, but also on their broader impact on business outcomes. KPIs must be carefully crafted to measure both the success of user-driven features (such as usage rates or customer satisfaction) and their contribution to business objectives like revenue generation, customer retention, and market growth. For example, when launching a new product feature, product managers should look beyond adoption rates and track how that feature affects customer lifetime value (CLV) or contributes to new customer acquisition. These business-oriented KPIs ensure that product development aligns with the company's overall strategy.

She also emphasizes the cyclical nature of product management: business success drives the resources and freedom for further innovation, which fuels product development that can further drive business success. This cycle requires careful monitoring through KPIs, ensuring product managers are not just tracking the performance of individual features, but also measuring the long-term impact of those features on business health. By setting KPIs that link user satisfaction with business outcomes, product managers can make informed decisions that keep their products aligned with both user needs and the company's financial objectives.

In sum, Deepika's message revolves around the idea that KPIs must capture the full scope of a product's impact, balancing user experience with the financial and strategic goals of the business. By setting KPIs that measure both the user experience and the business outcomes, product managers can ensure their work remains focused on both customer satisfaction and company growth, thereby fostering a sustainable and impactful product development process. This comprehensive approach to KPIs helps create a product strategy that supports continuous innovation and business success.

Div Manickam (California, USA)

Bio

Div Manickam is a renowned product marketing leader, mentor, and mindfulness advocate with over 13 years of experience in B2B SaaS across startups and Fortune 500 companies. As one of the Top 100 Product Marketing Influencers (2019-2023), she has led go-to-market strategies, product launches, and customer engagement initiatives. Div is also an expert in workplace well-being and authentic leadership, offering guidance through her mentor sessions. A prolific author, she has self-published six books on topics ranging from product marketing to mindfulness. Div is passionate about neurodiversity, mindfulness, and empowering individuals to embrace their authentic selves.

KPI-Driven Insights from Div Manickam

In her interview with me, Div Manickam emphasizes the critical role of key performance indicators (KPIs) and frameworks like Objectives and Key Results (OKRs) in driving focus, alignment, and accountability in product marketing. She explains how product marketers, adept at wearing multiple hats and managing shifting priorities, must also master the art of balance to ensure sustainable success. Her insights highlight the importance of clarity and structure in navigating the dynamic and often chaotic world of product marketing.

Div identifies one of the most essential skills in product marketing as the ability to effectively prioritize and manage expectations. This involves not only addressing immediate challenges but also maintaining transparency with stakeholders about current priorities and progress. To facilitate this, she advocates for the adoption of OKRs as a structured approach to goal setting and performance measurement. By establishing clear objectives and measurable outcomes, OKRs provide a roadmap that fosters transparency and credibility. Div underscores the importance of follow-through, as it builds trust and reinforces alignment across teams.

From a KPI perspective, Div explains that metrics should extend beyond mere outputs to reflect the true impact of product marketing initiatives.

Whether it's messaging and positioning, product launches, or sales enablement, each activity must be aligned with broader business objectives and measured for its effectiveness. Without this clarity, even the most well-intentioned efforts risk falling apart because of misalignment or lack of focus.

Div also highlights the universal applicability of her approach, noting that regardless of the company or industry, the principles of transparency, collaboration, and alignment remain vital. She stresses OKRs are not just a management tool, but a way to instill discipline and clarity into the product marketing function. By clearly defining what success looks like and tracking progress against these goals, product marketers can ensure they are delivering real value to the organization.

Moreover, KPIs and OKRs serve as a foundation for fostering collaboration across cross-functional teams. Div explains that product marketing often operates as a linchpin between teams such as sales, product, and customer success. Clear metrics and shared objectives help bridge gaps and create a unified vision. This alignment not only enhances team efficiency but also ensures that all efforts contribute to overarching business goals.

In summary, Div's insights underscore the importance of leveraging KPIs and OKRs to create clarity, foster alignment, and drive meaningful results. Her approach demonstrates how metrics can elevate product marketing from a reactive function to a proactive, strategic partner in achieving business success.

Gab Bujold (Quebec, Canada)

Bio

Gab Bujold is a seasoned product marketing expert specializing in message-market fit for sales-led B2B SaaS. As the founder of Press X to Market, he empowers startups by crafting effective messaging strategies that drive conversion and boost engagement. With experience across various tech sectors, Gab has held key roles at BizDev Labs, Sherweb, and V2 Cloud, leading initiatives in product positioning, market insights, and demand generation. As the co-host of We're Not Marketers, Gab also provides product marketers with practical guidance on securing executive buy-in, making complex marketing dynamics accessible to all. Fluent in English and French.

KPI Insights from Gab Bujold

In his interview with me, Gab Bujold highlights the critical role of data-driven decision-making in shaping go-to-market (GTM) strategies, particularly for product marketing managers (PMMs) in early-stage startups. His reflections focus on the importance of leveraging customer insights, aligning with sales teams, and refining messaging and positioning to drive measurable impact.

Gab emphasizes the power of trusting customer data to inform key aspects of the GTM motion. He notes that PMMs often face barriers in directly engaging with customers because of gatekeeping by sales teams. To overcome this, Gab introduces a strategic approach: integrating an additional step into the buyer journey, such as conducting customer interviews 30 days post-purchase. This tactic not only provides valuable insights into customer behavior, but also serves to gather actionable data that benefits both sales and marketing teams.

By analyzing these buyer journey interviews, Gab identifies trigger events that inform more relevant and timelier sales outreach. This alignment with sales ensures that lead engagement is both data-backed and effective, directly contributing to pipeline velocity and deal progression. He underscores that such collaboration between PMMs and sales can significantly enhance the precision of sales motions, leading to measurable KPIs like improved conversion rates and reduced sales cycle times.

The insights gathered from customer data extend beyond sales enablement, forming the bedrock of messaging and positioning strategies. Gab asserts that a robust GTM strategy is built on a clear understanding of customer pain points, motivations, and triggers. This data-driven foundation allows PMMs to craft messaging that resonates deeply with target audiences, creating a competitive edge in the market.

Gab's approach also highlights the iterative nature of refining positioning based on continuous data analysis. He stresses that customer feedback is not a one-time input, but an ongoing process that helps PMMs adapt to changing market dynamics. By regularly feeding customer insights into the messaging framework, PMMs can ensure alignment with evolving customer needs and expectations, which directly impacts KPIs such as customer satisfaction scores and net promoter scores (NPS).

In summary, Gab's lessons demonstrate how data can serve as a unifying thread across sales and marketing efforts, driving alignment and measurable outcomes. By prioritizing customer insights, fostering collaboration with sales, and anchoring messaging and positioning on solid data, PMMs can deliver significant results. These practices not only improve immediate GTM performance but also lay the groundwork for scalable strategies that yield sustained KPI growth over time.

Gab Bujold (Quebec, Canada)

Megan Pratt (Salt Lake City Area, UT, USA)

Bio

Megan Pratt is a seasoned product and content marketing leader specializing in customer-focused strategies. As the founder of Product Marketing House, she offers hands-on leadership in positioning, go-to-market execution, and customer intelligence, empowering businesses to refine messaging and drive product success. With extensive experience at companies like Alyce and Encamp, she has a track record of launching targeted campaigns and fostering alignment across teams to enhance brand visibility. An experienced coach and educator, Megan combines data-driven insights with storytelling, creating impactful sales enablement content. She is based in Salt Lake City and holds a BA in Mass Communications from the University of Utah.

Megan Pratt on Key Performance Indicators

In her interview with me, Megan Pratt dives into the ongoing debate within many organizations about whether to focus on competing with brand or product. This discussion often comes up when businesses are determining where to allocate their resources—should they invest in strengthening their brand identity or improving the product itself? Megan argues that product marketing is ideally positioned to resolve this debate because the right approach will vary depending on the organization's maturity, the stage of the product, and the competitive landscape.

At the heart of Megan's advice is the importance of Key Performance Indicators (KPIs) in answering the brand vs. product question. KPIs provide critical data points that reveal how well a product is performing and how it resonates with customers. A product marketer's deep understanding of these KPIs enables them to decode the signals that indicate where improvements are necessary. Megan uses two contrasting examples to illustrate how KPIs can point the way forward.

The first example revolves around a scenario where a business has a loyal customer base that loves the product but struggles with conversion rates. Here, the product may be great, but the challenge lies in attracting new customers. Megan suggests that the focus should shift toward strengthening the brand through better messaging, positioning, and targeted marketing campaigns. By refining the brand's appeal and emphasizing its value proposition, businesses can increase conversion rates and acquire customers.

In contrast, the second example involves a company with a strong conversion rate but high churn, meaning customers sign up for the product but leave shortly after. This is often a red flag that the product itself is failing to meet customer expectations or isn't solving their problems effectively. Megan recommends conducting win-loss analyses and churn studies to pinpoint the root causes of dissatisfaction. Based on these insights, product marketers can either refine the product offering or adjust marketing tactics to achieve product success.

Megan emphasizes that the role of product marketers is to use their expertise in both brand and product strategies to assess KPIs and guide decisions. Understanding what each metric tells you about the customer journey and product performance allows product marketers to make informed decisions on where to invest. By leveraging KPIs, product marketers can align the organization's go-to-market strategy, ensuring that efforts are directed in the areas that will create the most impact.

In sum, Megan advocates for a thoughtful, data-driven approach to marketing where product marketers use KPIs to inform strategic decisions. This approach not only helps resolve the brand vs. product debate but also supports a more cohesive and effective go-to-market strategy, ultimately contributing to the long-term success of the business.

Meeting and exceeding KPIs will help us in the present, but to keep us ready for the future, we need to also focus on Personal Development.

WISDOM ON PERSONAL DEVELOPMENT

WISDOM ON PERSONAL DEVELOPMENT

Personal development is a continuous journey that shapes not only your career but also your overall approach to challenges, leadership, and growth. Real-world insights from experienced professionals provide valuable lessons on how to cultivate key skills, develop a growth mindset, and navigate the complexities of professional life.

Veteran professionals often share their personal stories of overcoming obstacles, refining their leadership skills, and managing work-life balance. These real-world experiences can teach you how to adapt to shifting business environments, handle feedback effectively, and stay resilient in the face of setbacks. For instance, a senior marketer might discuss how they embraced continuous learning, such as taking courses or seeking mentorship, to stay ahead in a fast-changing industry.

Moreover, real-world professionals emphasize the importance of emotional intelligence, self-awareness, and time management in personal development. They offer strategies for setting clear goals, managing stress, and staying motivated.

Engaging with these insights through interviews, mentorship, or networking helps individuals better understand how to leverage their strengths and address areas for improvement. By applying these lessons, you can enhance your leadership qualities, build a stronger professional network, and navigate your career with greater confidence and purpose.

In the following sections, we examine the approaches of industry titans and rising stars to better understand these concepts in practice.

Anna Borbotko (Amsterdam, Netherlands)

Bio

Anna Borbotko is a seasoned Product Marketing professional with over nine years of experience driving B2B GTM strategies across organizations of all sizes. Currently, she is spearheading the creation of the Sales Enablement team at TomTom. Known as the "Jedi of Product Marketing," Anna is renowned for building high-performing teams and transforming sales experiences to enhance sales confidence, buyer engagement, and conversion rates. With extensive hands-on experience spanning Asia Pacific (APAC), North America (NAM), and Europe / Middle East / Africa (EMEA), Anna has successfully developed GTM strategies, launched proactive outreach initiatives, repositioned and introduced numerous products to market. Her expertise also includes a deep understanding of operational marketing. Connect with her on LinkedIn or explore her portfolio at annaborbotko.com.

Anna Borbotko on Personal Development

In my interview with Anna Borbotko, she shares an important lesson about the growth journey for product marketing leaders. Anna speaks from her experience, especially in aspiring to leadership roles in product marketing. She encourages those aiming for product marketing leadership positions, particularly millennials, to give themselves time to grow as managers and leaders. While the ambition to move up the career ladder quickly is understandable, Anna stresses the value of taking a slower, more deliberate approach.

Anna reflects on her own experience, noting that after two years as a team lead, she was eager to progress to the next role, such as Head of Product Marketing. However, looking back, she acknowledges that this desire for rapid advancement may have been premature. She explains that fast-tracking into higher leadership roles without the necessary time to learn can lead to mistakes, and the consequences of those mistakes can be significant. With 90% of product marketers not formally trained in product marketing, Anna points out that many leaders lack essential management skills or sufficient product marketing experience. This can create challenges when stepping into leadership roles too quickly.

She highlights that effective leadership requires learning how to manage up, how to motivate teams, how to structure teams for success, and how to collaborate effectively with others. Managing people, especially those with varying levels of education and experience, can be complex. Additionally, leaders need to be able to address a range of issues, from handling work performance to managing team members' personal challenges, such as balancing family life or navigating remote work dynamics. Anna emphasizes that these are skills that cannot be learned in just a couple of years. Leadership development takes time, and rushing into it without adequate experience can lead to struggles that are avoidable with patience and preparation.

Anna encourages product marketers to be honest with themselves about whether they are truly ready for the next leadership step. She believes it is perfectly fine to take the time to gain experience, improve in the current role, and confidently take the next step when the time is right. Her advice is a reminder that slow and steady growth can be more beneficial than trying to climb the career ladder too quickly.

In summary, Anna's lesson revolves around the importance of patience and self-awareness in the leadership journey. By taking the time to fully develop as a leader, product marketers can step into higher roles with the confidence and experience needed to succeed.

Bianca Stanescu (Bucharest, Romania)

Bio

Bianca Stanescu is Director of Product Marketing at SiriusXM's AdsWizz and Simplecast, based in Bucharest, Romania. With nearly a decade in product marketing, she expertly leads go-to-market strategies for digital audio and podcast advertising technology, combining strong cross-functional coordination with deep industry insights. Her career began in journalism, supported by a master's in media management, and evolved to include a certification in Innovation in Marketing. As a Product Marketing Alliance Ambassador, Bianca is passionate about mentoring others in the field. She is fluent in Romanian, English, and French, and enjoys outdoor sports and staying active in her community.

Bianca Stanescu on Personal Development

In my conversation with Bianca Stanescu, she shares profound insights on personal and professional growth in product marketing. From her experiences, Bianca emphasizes three core pillars for fostering personal development: leading with empathy, strategic alignment, and continuous growth opportunities. Together, these principles highlight how product marketers can grow into well-rounded, resilient, and strategic professionals while supporting the personal development of their team.

Bianca's first pillar is empathy, which she considers crucial for leaders in a high-demand field like product marketing. By creating a culture of empathy and trust, leaders encourage team members to perform at their best without feeling pressured to be perfect. Bianca advocates for supporting team members when they make minor mistakes, reminding leaders that an error, such as a typo on a landing page, is an opportunity to reinforce understanding and growth rather than perfection. This nurturing approach fosters a resilient mindset, enabling product marketers to focus on continuous improvement and emotional well-being. By valuing team members' efforts, leaders build a foundation of trust that ultimately enhances long-term performance.

The second pillar, Bianca highlights, is the importance of connecting all team members to the broader strategy of the company. Product marketers, she explains, need to understand that their roles go beyond managing operational details and creating presentations; they are strategic drivers within the organization. When team members understand the larger vision and goals, they can align their work with meaningful outcomes, giving them a sense of purpose and ownership. This alignment not only improves job satisfaction but also equips product marketers with the strategic insights necessary for advancing their careers. Bianca recommends leaders share relevant strategic updates with their teams, no matter their role, so everyone feels included and empowered to make a difference.

Bianca's third pillar is dedicated to continuous growth and learning. She advocates for supporting team members' career development through product marketing-specific training, budget allocations for industry events, and participation at conferences. Exposure to industry insights, she believes, is essential for building expertise, sparking new ideas, and staying current with trends. She further stresses the value of mentorship and coaching—both internally and through external networks like the Product Marketing Alliance. As a mentor herself, Bianca finds this role rewarding, benefiting not only her mentees but also her own growth through shared learning.

Bianca's approach to personal growth in product marketing is rooted in empathy, strategic alignment, and a commitment to lifelong learning. Product marketers who adopt these principles can build a resilient mindset, align their contributions with the company's broader goals, and embrace continuous learning opportunities. Leaders following these principles can cultivate high-performance, motivated teams that are well-equipped to navigate the dynamic landscape of product marketing.

Emily Pick (Bend, OR, USA)

Bio

Emily Pick is an accomplished product marketing leader with nine years in B2B SaaS, excelling in messaging, positioning, and revenue enablement. As Lead Product Marketing Manager at Clari, she's driven strategy for revenue operations and AI-driven sales engagement, surpassing revenue targets by over 100%. Emily's strategic expertise extends to Rattle, where she established a new category in Process Automation, and Clearbit, where she doubled user acquisition. Known for her results-oriented approach, she has also developed critical sales enablement tools and go-to-market processes that enhance engagement and fuel growth across SMBs to Fortune 500 clients.

Personal Development Insights from Emily Pick

In her interview with me, Emily Pick shares her journey of transitioning from a Series A startup to Clari, a more established organization, and reflects on the personal growth lessons learned during this shift. Her insights focus on adaptability, prioritization, and aligning with organizational goals as key elements of personal and professional development in product marketing.

Emily begins by highlighting the common perception of moving from a resource-strapped startup to a larger company: the expectation of abundant resources, time, and bandwidth to take a more nuanced approach to work. However, she quickly realizes that resource constraints are a universal challenge, regardless of company size. While larger organizations may offer more tools and support, the ability to effectively utilize available resources remains a critical skill. Emily's revelation underscores the importance of maintaining a "scrappy mindset"—a skill cultivated in the startup world that proves invaluable in navigating even enterprise environments.

This mindset involves leveraging limited resources creatively to deliver an outsized impact. Emily explains that the skill of resourcefulness learned in startups allows professionals to approach challenges with innovation and agility, skills that are transferable and beneficial in any organizational context. For Emily, this adaptability becomes a cornerstone of her success in her new role at Clari.

Another key lesson Emily emphasizes is the importance of prioritization. In both startups and established companies, the volume of tasks and initiatives can be overwhelming. Learning how to focus on what truly matters—the projects that align most closely with organizational objectives—is critical. Emily stresses that by demonstrating impact early on and ensuring that efforts contribute to broader company goals, professionals can build credibility and showcase their value within the organization.

Emily's reflections also highlight the broader theme of personal growth during career transitions. Moving to a larger organization involves navigating new challenges, understanding different team dynamics, and adapting to a more structured environment. For her, this transition reinforces the need to remain flexible, proactive, and aligned with the company's vision while continuing to apply the lessons learned in previous roles.

In summary, Emily's experience offers valuable personal development takeaways for product marketers and professionals alike. Her journey emphasizes the importance of adaptability, resourcefulness, and strategic prioritization in achieving success. By maintaining a scrappy mindset, focusing on impactful work, and aligning with organizational goals, individuals can thrive in new environments and continue to grow, regardless of the size or stage of the company.

PRODUCT MARKETING WISDOM

Eric Lindroos (Ocean Shores, WA, USA)

Bio

Eric Lindroos is a dynamic sales professional and enablement leader with over seven years of experience empowering individuals and businesses to achieve transformative success. Currently at Mobly, Eric excels at fostering meaningful relationships and delivering impactful sales strategies. As a Sales Instructor at Sales Impact Academy, he equips global B2B teams with essential go-to-market skills. A two-time Gong Employee of the Year and LinkedIn Sales Stars Top 100 honoree, Eric's expertise spans revenue enablement, strategic training, and cross-functional collaboration. Known for his creativity, commitment, and results-driven approach, Eric is a passionate advocate for growth, inclusion, and long-term success.

Eric Lindroos on Personal Development

In this insightful interview with me, Eric Lindroos covers a critical lesson in personal financial awareness. Drawing from his own journey, Eric emphasizes the importance of understanding the financial intricacies of equity compensation in early-stage startups, a lesson shaped by his own costly misstep.

Eric shares that during his tenure at Gong, he was offered equity—a common practice in startups to incentivize early employees. However, he lacked a clear understanding of the Alternative Minimum Tax (AMT), a complex tax rule that can impose significant financial burdens. When Eric chose to exercise his stock options at the vesting price while the company was still private, he unknowingly triggered an AMT event. This decision led to a staggering $152,000 tax bill, calculated as if he had realized income equal to the difference between his vesting price and the fair market value of the shares, despite no actual financial gain at that time.

As Eric reflects on his experience, he stresses the importance of proactive financial planning and the guidance of a qualified CPA or financial advisor when dealing with equity compensation. By consulting experts, employees can avoid triggering AMT thresholds, manage their equity strategically, and prevent devastating financial surprises. His advice extends beyond financial logistics; it underscores the value of seeking expertise, planning, and being informed in any critical decision-making process.

Eric's story offers more than a cautionary tale—it highlights the broader principle of self-education and the need to build a trusted network of advisors in both personal and professional spheres. Whether navigating the complexities of startup equity or making decisions that shape long-term success, his advice is clear: knowledge is power, and preparation is essential.

Eric's advice is a powerful reminder that personal development is not just about professional growth, but also about managing life's financial and emotional challenges effectively. His experience serves as a beacon for anyone working in startups or exploring equity options, urging them to take ownership of their financial education.

Eric welcomes professionals to connect with him for additional insights and strategies. Armed with his wisdom, they can make better-informed decisions, avoid unnecessary pitfalls, and focus on building a secure and successful future. Understanding and applying lessons like these are key to taking our personal development to the next level.

Eric Lindroos (Ocean Shores, WA, USA)

Esther Akinsola (Lagos, Nigeria)

Bio

Esther Akinsola is a travel marketing consultant and coach with expertise in building marketing systems that drive growth for travel and tourism businesses. As the founder of Zippa Marketing, a UK-based agency, she helps clients optimize ROI through simple, practical strategies. Esther has collaborated with global industry leaders, created content for top-ranking travel blogs, and led GuestChat's expansion into Africa. With a diploma in Journalism and ongoing studies in International Marketing, Esther shares her insights through her newsletter, Roam Revolution. Her skills in inbound marketing, SEO, and customer communication make her a sought-after expert in the travel industry.

Esther Akinsola on Personal Development

In her interview with me, Esther Akinsola shares a transformative perspective on personal and professional development. Speaking from her deep experience in the ever-changing marketing industry, Esther focuses on the importance of mindset in navigating trends and building lasting success. Her wisdom offers profound lessons that apply not only to marketers but to anyone aiming to thrive in a world of constant change.

Esther emphasizes that the marketing landscape is perpetually evolving, citing how once-dominant strategies like Yellow Pages advertising and mailed promotions are now obsolete. Similarly, today's booming content creation industry and startups' shifting budgets reflect the unpredictable nature of the future. Esther underscores that while trends come and go, the core principles and expertise that define a professional endure. This insight is a critical reminder for anyone working in fast-paced environments: adaptability is essential, but it must be grounded in foundational skills and knowledge.

Her advice to avoid jumping on every new trend resonates beyond marketing. Esther encourages individuals to focus on building systems and strategies that last, rather than chasing fleeting opportunities. This approach demands discipline and self-awareness, as it challenges the instinct to follow popular movements without critical evaluation. It also highlights the value of investing in one's expertise and confidence—qualities that empower leaders to chart their own course, even amid uncertainty.

Esther's perspective reflects a broader truth about personal growth: success requires balancing innovation with stability. Whether in marketing or life, short-term trends can be alluring, but true mastery lies in understanding when to adopt new tools and when to rely on proven methods. This mindset fosters resilience and positions individuals to lead rather than react to industry changes.

Esther's advice reminds us to "play the long game." By doing so, professionals can create meaningful impact and stand out as thought leaders in their fields. The conversation serves as an inspiring reminder to prioritize long-term vision over instant gratification, offering a roadmap for sustained growth and influence.

Esther's wisdom encourages listeners to view challenges as opportunities to reaffirm their core values and expertise. Her call to focus on enduring principles rather than fleeting trends is a powerful mantra for anyone seeking to navigate change with confidence and purpose. By taking Esther's advice to heart, we can help ourselves be motivated to embrace strategic thinking, cultivate a growth mindset, and ultimately, build something that truly lasts.

Julian Dawkins (United Kingdom)

Bio

Julian Dawkins is a seasoned Product Marketing leader, currently Senior Manager of Product Marketing at Infobip, with 10+ years in driving product strategy, GTM methodologies, and value proposition development across B2B and consumer sectors. His prior roles at Optimizely, Sodexo, and Sylvania Group honed his skills in product management, strategic marketing, and agile frameworks. Certified in PRINCE2® and Agile Project Management, Julian combines technical expertise with strong presentation and customer focus, delivering impactful growth. He holds a degree in English Language and Communication with Psychology from Kingston University and is a Product Marketing Alliance member.

Julian Dawkins on Personal Development

In this insightful interview with me, Julian Dawkins emphasizes the importance of intentional self-documentation as a vital personal development practice. He advises professionals, especially those transitioning into product marketing, to actively document their career journey, akin to maintaining a personal blog. According to Julian, mapping out one's professional experiences, lessons learned, and unique stories serves as an invaluable tool for identifying strengths, personal growth areas, and transferable skills. This process ultimately aids professionals in clarifying their direction and positioning themselves within their desired fields.

Julian views this practice as a means of self-discovery and self-confidence building. By systematically reviewing past roles and experiences, individuals can uncover connections between their existing skill sets and the demands of product marketing. This reflection highlights the relevance of past roles—even those outside of product marketing, such as customer success, engineering, or finance. He suggests these insights can reveal ways to leverage one's background and align it with product marketing, uncovering a unique value proposition in the field.

BY NITIN KARTIK

For those actively looking to transition into product marketing, Julian recommends completing this self-documentation alongside updating a LinkedIn profile and building a network within the industry. He suggests that understanding and articulating one's personal narrative before reaching out to others is crucial; it builds a foundation of self-assurance and enables professionals to communicate their skills effectively and authentically. He stresses that networking should be an extension of a confident self-presentation, rooted in clarity about one's strengths and aspirations. This self-awareness, according to Julian, not only strengthens one's personal brand but also supports lasting professional relationships, as connections will recognize the individual's clarity and genuine understanding of their own path.

Besides providing career clarity, Julian argues that a running professional document boosts self-esteem. This ongoing narrative helps individuals recognize their progress and areas of achievement, which fosters a mindset of growth and resilience. As they map out their journey, professionals gain insights into how they best contribute and where they can develop further. For product marketers especially, this self-awareness is critical in an industry that values adaptability, as it enables them to continuously refine their positioning and skill set.

Julian's advice encourages professionals to approach career growth as an ongoing journey rather than a destination. Through documenting experiences, professionals can find the intersections between their unique strengths and the opportunities within product marketing. This approach strengthens confidence and builds a roadmap for future development, making career shifts less daunting and more empowering. For those who apply his insights, Julian's strategy becomes a foundation for both personal and professional growth, transforming the process of self-reflection into an actionable plan for career advancement and sustained confidence.

Michal Lasman (Germany)

Bio

Michal Lasman is a dynamic marketing leader with over 10 years of experience in revenue-driven strategies across diverse industries. Currently a Coach-in-training and podcast host for CMO Convo, Michal is known for her strategic foresight, especially in B2BC, business-to-developer (B2D) and customer relationship management (CRM). She has a firm foundation in building and scaling marketing teams, managing end-to-end product positioning, sales enablement, and thought leadership. A certified product marketer and ambassador for the Product Marketing Alliance, Michal brings a people-centered approach to global marketing, emphasizing adaptability and proactive leadership in fast-changing environments.

Michal Lasman on Personal Development

In her insightful interview with me, Michal Lasman shares her personal development philosophy, emphasizing the power of a growth mindset. She believes that while technical skills like messaging or positioning are valuable in marketing, it's the cultivation of soft skills that truly drives success and fulfillment in one's career. For Michal, the journey of personal growth is deeply intertwined with self-reflection, an approach that she practices and encourages others to adopt.

Michal highlights journaling as a cornerstone of her personal development routine. By dedicating time each day to reflecting on experiences and asking intentional questions, she brings awareness to her progress and growth. She explains that her journey with journaling began with simple gratitude exercises, listing three things she is thankful for each day. This habit helped her recognize positive aspects of daily life and acknowledge small wins, even on challenging days. Over time, she expanded this practice, prompting herself to consider lessons learned and opportunities for improvement. According to Michal, this reflective process fosters a sense of accomplishment and encourages a growth mindset that is crucial for career advancement. This personal journey is what led Michal to become a certified coach. Michal strongly believes in human relationships and in the need to drive positive change.

Michal also emphasizes the concept of "design thinking" in both personal and professional contexts. She describes design thinking as a framework for approaching life with curiosity, empathy and problem-solving, which can be as impactful in one's personal development as it is in product marketing. She suggests that product marketers could benefit from integrating design thinking into their lives, using it as a tool to adapt and grow continually. This approach is rooted in understanding oneself and others, adapting to new challenges, and viewing obstacles as opportunities for growth.

A favorite resource Michal mentions is 'The Life Designer', a journal that combines motivational quotes with space for introspection. One quote from the journal that resonates deeply with her is, "The privilege of a lifetime is to become who you truly are." She believes this wisdom serves as a powerful reminder to pursue authenticity and continuous self-discovery. For Michal, the journey to becoming one's true self is not only a privilege but also a responsibility, especially for leaders who aim to inspire their teams. She encourages leaders to model this mindset, promoting a culture of learning and development within their organizations.

Through these personal development strategies, Michal demonstrates that building a successful career goes beyond mastering hard skills; it's about nurturing a mindset open to growth, reflection, and authenticity. Her insights offer a roadmap for professionals striving to improve themselves and inspire others, proving that adopting a growth mindset can be transformative both personally and professionally.

Natália Tóth (Budapest, Hungary)

Bio

Natália Tóth is a multilingual Product Marketing Manager based in Budapest, with three years of experience in the B2B SaaS industry. Currently at Ranking Raccoon, she has launched over 10 new features, managed paid campaigns across three platforms, pioneered the company's blog, and introduced product analytics to identify bottlenecks in the user journey. Natália's skill set includes competitive intelligence, segmentation, and channel marketing, complemented by proficiency in such tools as Mixpanel, Salesforce, HubSpot, and Figma. An alumna of the Product Marketing Alliance Scholar program, Natalia has also consulted for tech startups on go-to-market strategies, making her a versatile asset in global product marketing.

Natália Tóth on Personal Development

In her inspiring interview with me, Natália Tóth reflects on her recent career pivot into product marketing and shares her insights on building a successful personal development plan. For Natália, transitioning into product marketing was a journey driven by a deep desire for growth and an openness to hands-on learning. She emphasizes that acquiring practical product marketing experience is crucial for anyone looking to transition into this field, offering advice that highlights the importance of strategic self-development and proactive learning.

Natália's key lesson is simple yet powerful: gaining experience through real-world projects and tasks is invaluable. She encourages anyone pursuing a similar career change to start by connecting with a mentor who can provide guidance on the essential skills for success in product marketing. These mentors can help identify skill gaps and suggest a coherent plan for closing them, enabling the mentee to focus their efforts on areas that will make the biggest impact. For Natália, mentorship provides not only a roadmap for skill acquisition but also valuable support and encouragement during what can be a challenging transition.

Besides mentorship, Natália suggests gaining experience through practical projects, either within one's current role or through side projects. She advises aspiring product marketers to seek opportunities to volunteer for product marketing tasks such as market research, user analysis, competitive research, persona development, and even prototyping. For those unable to find such opportunities within their current company, she recommends reaching out to early-stage entrepreneurs or joining online groups where people are eager for marketing insights but may not yet have a dedicated product marketing team. By offering support for these "pet projects," individuals can acquire hands-on experience that is both relevant and impactful.

Natália stresses the importance of documenting this work in a portfolio or CV. This step allows prospective employers to see concrete examples of skills in action, which are often more persuasive than formal education or theoretical knowledge alone. For her, a well-assembled portfolio showcases not only her technical skills but also her commitment to her professional growth, making her a strong candidate for future roles.

Through her journey, Natália illustrates career transitions don't happen overnight; they require persistence, a willingness to learn, and an openness to untraditional paths. Her advice on volunteering for side projects reflects a proactive mindset that can empower anyone to gain practical skills, regardless of their current job. Natália's experience is a testament to the value of taking ownership of one's career, seeking learning opportunities, and embracing mentorship and collaboration as pillars of personal growth. Her story offers a practical roadmap for those aiming to make similar transitions, proving that a strategic approach to personal development can make career pivots not only possible but highly rewarding.

Nevine Ismael (Toulouse, France)

Bio

Nevine Ismael is a dedicated Product Marketing Manager at Scaleway, based in Toulouse, France, with a passion for helping fast-growing B2B SaaS companies identify and meet market needs. With extensive experience in positioning, messaging, and go-to-market strategies, she has previously held roles at Pigment, Sigfox, and Anaplan, where she led impactful product launches and developed competitive intelligence strategies. As a co-founder of the PMM Toulouse Hub and a Product Marketing Alliance ambassador, Nevine is committed to building a powerful community of product marketers. She is fluent in French and English, with a working knowledge of Spanish.

Nevine Ismael on Personal Development

In her engaging interview with me, Nevine Ismael shares her reflections on personal development through the power of connection. Based in Toulouse, France, Nevine's experience underlines the value of networking both within and outside of one's organization, which she believes is essential for growth in the often-misunderstood field of product marketing. By actively seeking these connections, she's found greater clarity and direction, a deeper understanding of her role, and new ways to bring value to her organization.

Nevine begins by explaining that product marketing is frequently seen as a "black box" profession. Because most people don't specifically study product marketing in school, many discover it only once they're in the field, learning and adapting along the way. This, according to Nevine, makes it especially important for product marketers to engage with peers across the industry. By doing so, PMMs gain diverse perspectives on what the role should entail and what unique contributions they can bring to their companies. Nevine emphasizes that this outside input allows her to refine her personal approach, as product marketing has varied interpretations—some see it as a purely marketing function, while others see it as product-focused.

Reflecting on her role in Europe, Nevine notes a general lack of understanding about product marketing, making her job both challenging and full of opportunities. Early in her career, she struggled to identify the full potential of the role and the contributions she could make. However, conversations with other product marketers helped her realize many professionals face similar struggles, especially with tasks like managing last-minute launches. By exchanging ideas and experiences with fellow PMMs, Nevine successfully navigated her role more confidently, often discovering solutions to common challenges in these discussions.

Nevine's involvement with the Product Marketing Alliance has been central to her growth. Through PMA, she connected with peers across Europe and even helped initiate a community gathering for product marketers. For Nevine, creating this space for dialogue has been empowering, providing a consistent avenue to share knowledge, offer support, and learn collectively. The insights she's gained from these interactions have helped her bring new, impactful ideas to Scaleway, enhancing her contributions to the company in ways she might not have otherwise achieved.

In summary, Nevine's story highlights that in a role as multifaceted as product marketing, personal development thrives through proactive connection. Building relationships with other PMMs has been transformational for her, fostering not only her own growth but also her ability to innovate within her company. Her advice is a reminder of the importance of building a network, as it can open doors to knowledge, community, and self-discovery in an ever-evolving field.

Prashanth Shankara (Ann Arbor, MI, USA)

Bio

Prashanth Shankara is a Senior Marketing Manager and a former aerospace engineer with over 13 years of expertise in B2B Product, Content, and Customer marketing. Known for transforming engineering software growth, Prashanth led product marketing efforts that drove revenue from $75M to $320M and supported a $1B acquisition. His innovative strategies have expanded market share, launched viral campaigns, and helped grow developer communities. With a unique blend of engineering insight and creative storytelling, Prashanth champions data-driven marketing while emphasizing storytelling's power to connect and engage. Currently with Salad, he drives GTM strategies, messaging, and campaign execution across sectors.

Prashanth Shankara on Breaking Out of Ruts for Creative Excellence

In his interview with me, Prashanth Shankara reflects on the personal development lessons that have shaped his approach to product marketing. Drawing on diverse experiences across teams and products, he emphasizes the importance of breaking free from repetitive patterns to unlock creativity and develop standout messaging.

Prashanth highlights a common pitfall in product marketing: the tendency to iterate endlessly on existing messaging without introducing significant differentiation. He describes how this habit can lead to a "sea of sameness," where products and campaigns lose their distinctiveness. For marketers, this stagnation can hinder innovation and prevent their messaging from resonating in competitive markets.

To combat this, Prashanth suggests an unconventional but powerful thought exercise: begin by imagining the opposite of your current messaging. By exploring ideas that initially seem extreme or even unacceptable, marketers can push the boundaries of their thinking and uncover fresh perspectives. This practice fosters originality and reinvigorates positioning strategies, making them more impactful.

Prashanth acknowledges that breaking out of ingrained thought patterns is easier said than done. Achieving this shift requires conscious effort and a willingness to embrace change. For him, physical and environmental changes play a crucial role in fostering creativity. Whether working remotely, traveling, or simply moving to a coffee shop, altering one's surroundings can spark new ideas and perspectives.

He draws inspiration from his travels, observing marketing in its most elemental forms—whether it's a small shop advertising sugarcane juice or a roadside vendor with a creative sales pitch. These experiences remind him that marketing exists everywhere, and that inspiration often lies in the simplest and most unexpected places.

Prashanth advocates for product marketers to step out of their comfort zones regularly. He advises everyone to engage with other marketers to exchange ideas, seek new environments, or travel to gain diverse perspectives. Even minor changes, such as shifting work locations or immersing oneself in different cultural contexts, can help break the cycle of repetitive thinking.

By challenging themselves to think differently and drawing from varied experiences, marketers can craft messaging that not only stands out but also connects meaningfully with audiences.

For Prashanth, personal development in product marketing hinges on continuous learning and embracing change. By disrupting familiar routines and actively seeking inspiration, marketers can escape creative ruts, develop fresh ideas, and elevate their craft. This approach transforms messaging from formulaic to interesting, helping products shine in crowded markets.

Shirin Shahin (Massachusetts, USA)

Bio

Shirin Shahin is a Boston-based product marketing consultant and leader with over 12 years of experience, including roles at Constant Contact and Brightcove. Known for her creative and customer-centered approach, she specializes in positioning and messaging, sales enablement, and product launch frameworks. Shirin has supported companies at various growth stages—from startups to established enterprises like Grammarly and Bitly—and has made significant contributions to their go-to-market strategies. A mentor with Techstars and an ambassador for the Product Marketing Alliance, Shirin is recognized for her integrity, strong communication skills, and immediate impact on product marketing teams.

Shirin Shahin on Trusting Your Intuition in Business

In her interview with me, Shirin Shahin, an experienced consultant and business owner, shares valuable lessons about personal development through her journey of building her consulting business over the past four and a half years. One of her key insights is on the importance of tuning into what feels right for you as a business owner, particularly when faced with overwhelming external advice and pressures.

When starting a business, there is no shortage of advice. Entrepreneurs are often bombarded with suggestions on everything from content strategies (such as how often to post on LinkedIn or write blogs) to operational decisions like whether to hire a team. Shirin reflects on how this flood of external opinions can lead to confusion, making it difficult to make rational decisions. The challenge lies not only in the quantity of advice but also in how to assess which pieces of advice are aligned with your vision and values.

Shirin's key lesson is to trust your own instincts and feelings when deciding about your business. She emphasizes that, while advice from others can be helpful, it's crucial to determine what feels right for you personally. Whether it's the pace at which you create content, the structure of your team, or the way you build your client pipeline, Shirin believes that aligning business choices with your personal comfort and conviction is essential.

If you're not fully bought into the decisions you're making, Shirin argues, the outcomes will probably be misaligned with your goals. It's about maintaining authenticity and staying true to what feels aligned with your values, rather than simply following trends or external pressures. This deeper sense of personal alignment ensures that the decisions you make will lead to growth and fulfillment in both your personal and professional lives.

By focusing on what feels right for her, Shirin has built a business that supports her values and long-term goals. Her approach is grounded in self-awareness and trusting her own process, which has allowed her to build sustainable success. Shirin notes that true personal development in business comes from understanding yourself and using that self-knowledge to guide decisions, even if those choices deviate from the traditional or popular paths others take.

Lessons for Personal Development

- **Filter external advice**: Recognize when external advice is overwhelming and focus on what truly resonates with you.
- **Trust your instincts**: Make business decisions that align with your values and comfort level.
- **Commit to your choices**: If you're not fully invested in your decisions, their outcomes may not align with your true goals.
- **Stay authentic**: Personal development in business comes from making choices that are authentically yours, not dictated by others.

Shirin's experience highlights how personal growth and business success are intertwined, encouraging entrepreneurs to prioritize their own insights over external noise.

Shruti Verma (Greater Toronto, ON, Canada)

Bio

Shruti Verma is a skilled B2B SaaS Product Marketing Manager with over 5 years of experience across AI, retail, finance, banking, and HR tech industries. Known as a 2x Top Product Marketing Voice, she has led go-to-market strategies, product positioning, and sales enablement initiatives for companies like Vue.ai and iDreamCareer, driving product adoption and user engagement across North America, APAC, and EMEA. Shruti excels in market research, customer insights, and digital marketing, with a track record of launching impactful campaigns that increase revenue, reduce bounce rates, and enhance brand perception in fast-paced, mission-driven environments.

Shruti Verma on Personal Development: The Power of Building a Personal Brand

In her interview with me, Shruti Verma shares a key lesson she's learned throughout her career—building a personal brand is essential for both personal and professional growth. With five years of experience in product marketing and having pivoted from a writing background, Shruti explains how cultivating a strong personal brand has played a crucial role in boosting her confidence, opening new opportunities, and helping her navigate career transitions.

Overcoming Self-Doubt and Embracing Your Value

One of the first hurdles Shruti addresses is the feeling of inadequacy that many professionals face, particularly when switching careers or fields. She encourages others to let go of the belief that they are "not enough" and emphasizes the importance of showcasing one's skills and strengths. Shruti's own journey from being a writer to transitioning into product marketing illustrates this process of self-discovery and confidence-building. By consistently demonstrating what she's good at, she has not only gained self-assurance but has also earned the respect of recruiters, colleagues, and potential employers. Shruti stresses that building a personal brand is not just about immediate job opportunities but is an investment that pays off in the long term.

The Long-Term Benefits of Personal Branding

While building a personal brand might not provide immediate career benefits, Shruti highlights it is a crucial part of personal development that creates new opportunities. She explains that even if you're not currently looking for a job, cultivating a personal brand opens doors for networking, visibility, and future career growth. For Shruti, focusing on her personal brand has been instrumental in building her confidence, especially after transitioning into a new field. She advises that product marketers and professionals in any industry should work on establishing their personal brand, as it acts as a superpower that helps gain recognition and trust within their industry.

The Confidence Boost of Personal Branding

Shruti credits her personal brand with helping her regain confidence, particularly after moving from a career in writing into the fast-paced world of product marketing. By developing a clear sense of her unique strengths and value proposition, she has gained credibility and recognition within her field. For Shruti, this newfound confidence has not only helped her in her current role but has also positioned her for future career opportunities.

In Sum

Shruti Verma's insight into personal development reinforces the idea that building a personal brand is crucial at every stage of your career. By embracing your strengths, overcoming self-doubt, and consistently showcasing your skills, you create opportunities that not only help you grow professionally but also boost your confidence and open doors to fresh paths. Personal branding, as Shruti puts it, is a superpower that all professionals—especially product marketers—should harness for long-term success.

PRODUCT MARKETING WISDOM

Shuja Hasan (Delhi, India)

Bio

Shuja Hasan is the Founder of Mahsheen, a creative agency based in Bengaluru, India, that crafts unique ads to bring a moment of joy and relief. He is also the founder of Brand Raps, where he creates marketing raps for brands. With a background in advertising, Shuja has an unconventional approach to creativity, blending humor with impactful messaging. An author of four books on Amazon, his works include The Subtle Art of Closing Sales and Understanding Sales Like Your Spouse. Shuja's interests extend to guitar teaching and talking to aliens, showcasing his eclectic passions.

Shuja Hasan on Personal Development

In my interview with Shuja Hasan, he shares valuable insights into the patience, perseverance, and self-belief needed to succeed in creative fields, especially as an entrepreneur. Brand Raps is Shuja's unique venture that uses rap to make corporate messaging "cool," and he emphasizes that achieving any meaningful result requires playing the long game.

Shuja begins by highlighting the importance of self-belief, especially before one can gain external validation. He explains that being his "own biggest supporter" was essential before gaining fans or followers. As an introvert, Shuja finds performing in front of people challenging, especially since he never initially envisioned a career in rap. Writing was his first passion, and he imagined himself working in fields like advertising or even becoming an author. However, he stresses the importance of embracing unexpected opportunities, even those outside one's comfort zone. When the chance to perform and engage with audiences through rap came along, he took it and, to his surprise, fell in love with it. This openness to unexpected paths led him to a career he could not have anticipated.

Shuja's journey highlights how progress in creative fields often unfolds in incremental steps rather than in grand leaps. He likens this process to moving from "1 to 1.1 and then 1.12," underscoring that growth doesn't always feel like a linear climb. Instead, progress can be slow and nuanced, requiring patience and commitment. He encourages individuals to focus on the day-to-day process rather than expecting instant success, suggesting that each slight improvement can lead to something significant over time.

Shuja's advice also touches on the resilience needed to push through challenging phases. He encourages others to focus on continually improving and nurturing a love for their craft, regardless of external recognition. He believes that if someone is genuinely passionate and committed to improving, the rewards will eventually follow. This long-term focus and passion-driven approach, he believes, "pays dividends" over time.

I found Shuja's advice profoundly relatable. His journey serves as a reminder of the "air hostess rule"—prioritizing self-belief before seeking external validation. This is particularly valuable for anyone looking to innovate or build something unique in their field. As Shuja says, no matter how many people support you, if you maintain a genuine love for what you do and remain focused on incremental progress, it can lead to long-lasting success.

Shuja's insights serve as a reminder that passion, resilience, and incremental growth form the foundation of meaningful, impactful work. His story is a testament to embracing unexpected paths, trusting the process, and believing in oneself through the ups and downs.

Stephanie Schwab (Barcelona, Spain)

Bio

Stephanie Schwab is a seasoned digital marketing expert, founder, and CEO of Crackerjack Marketing. With 20+ years in corporate and personal branding, she specializes in building powerful LinkedIn presences for B2B executives. She's worked with clients like HP, Medtronic, and Citizen Watch, aligning executive personal brands with corporate marketing strategies. As Co-Director and Faculty of Harbour.Space's Digital Marketing Programme in Barcelona, she mentors and teaches students in digital marketing, social media, and content strategy. Based in Spain, Stephanie is also the Editor-in-Chief of The Networkist, a weekly newsletter offering insights on LinkedIn strategy for personal branding.

Stephanie Schwab on Personal Development

In her interview with me, Stephanie Schwab emphasizes the profound importance of LinkedIn for personal and professional growth, sharing her wisdom rooted in years of social media marketing experience. She urges individuals, particularly product marketers, to harness the platform's potential to build a strong personal brand, expand their network, and secure future opportunities.

Stephanie highlights LinkedIn is more than a digital resume; it's a tool for long-term career development. She advises everyone to start with a firm foundation: an up-to-date profile featuring a professional photo, an interesting headline, and detailed information about skills and experiences. This polished presence forms the basis of credibility and visibility on the platform.

Beyond having a robust profile, Stephanie stresses the importance of active participation on LinkedIn. She suggests posting content regularly—whether weekly or biweekly—to remain visible within the platform's algorithm. Sharing insights, experiences, or even personal reflections can demonstrate expertise and authenticity, helping professionals connect with their audience on a deeper level. Additionally, she underscores the value of engaging with others' posts by leaving thoughtful comments, which fosters relationships and broadens one's reach.

Stephanie connects LinkedIn's growing importance to recent shifts in the professional landscape. The pandemic has increased reliance on digital networking, while the decline of platforms like Twitter has driven more professionals to LinkedIn. As a result, the platform has become a central hub for business connections, making consistent engagement crucial for staying relevant and top of mind within one's industry.

She also highlights LinkedIn's versatility, noting that its benefits extend far beyond job searching. Whether you're nurturing sales leads, seeking advice, collaborating on projects, or exploring alternative career paths, an active LinkedIn presence ensures that your network is ready when you need it most. Stephanie's advice resonates particularly in today's uncertain economic climate, where layoffs and shifting roles emphasize the need for a strong professional network.

By committing to even small, consistent actions—updating profiles, sharing insights, and engaging with others—professionals can cultivate a powerful LinkedIn presence. This proactive approach not only builds credibility but also positions individuals to seize opportunities when they arise.

Stephanie's guidance serves as a reminder that investing time and effort into LinkedIn is an investment in one's future. Whether for immediate gains or long-term benefits, staying active on the platform empowers professionals to take control of their personal development, expand their horizons, and thrive in an increasingly digital and interconnected world.

Zach Hoskins (Springfield, MO, USA)

Bio

Zach Hoskins is a strategic growth leader with over a decade of experience guiding businesses and individuals to clarity, impact, and growth. As CEO of The Efficiency Conductor, he specializes in streamlining operations to help leaders expand revenue and profit without sacrificing personal life. A USAF veteran with an Air Force Achievement Medal, Zach has co-founded communities like Harmony Growth Lab and LeadUp Growth Community, fostering personal and professional growth. Known for his role as a fractional Chief Strategy Officer, Zach has led strategic planning sessions globally, helping companies create $2M+ in annual recurring revenue and build resilient, impact-driven teams.

Zach Hoskins on Personal Development

In his interview with me, Zach Hoskins offers valuable personal development advice centered on the idea of a "north star"—a guiding principle that helps individuals navigate life's challenges and opportunities with clarity and purpose. Zach believes that by answering two crucial questions, individuals can establish this north star and unlock profound clarity in their lives.

The first question Zach encourages people to ask themselves is, "Why do I exist?" This question focuses on discovering one's purpose. By understanding why you wake up each morning and what motivates you to act, you gain insight into your true calling. Zach suggests that answering this question provides the foundation for a meaningful and focused life. With a clear purpose in mind, you can make decisions that align with your deeper aspirations, ensuring that your actions are intentional and contribute toward something greater than yourself. The clarity gained from this question allows individuals to filter out distractions and focus on what truly matters in the long run.

The second key question is, "What do I stand for?" This question is about defining your core values and principles—the things that shape how you interact with the world and the impact you want to have on others. By identifying what you stand for, you solidify your personal code of ethics, your beliefs, and your desired legacy. This clarity helps you approach challenges with integrity and aligns your actions with your moral compass. When faced with difficult decisions or opportunities, knowing what you stand for helps you evaluate whether they are in harmony with your values, ensuring that you remain true to yourself in all situations.

Together, these two questions create a north star that serves as a reference point for making decisions in every area of life. Zach explains that, with a clear sense of purpose and values, it becomes easier to evaluate new opportunities, relationships, and challenges. When something aligns with your north star, it's a sign that it's worth pursuing; if it doesn't align, you have the confidence to let it go without second-guessing yourself. This helps prevent distractions and keeps individuals focused on what truly contributes to their growth and well-being.

Zach also acknowledges that life is rarely a straight path. There will always be obstacles and changes in direction, but by staying connected to your north star, you can navigate through those trials with confidence. Whether faced with setbacks or new opportunities, keeping the answers to these questions at the forefront ensures that you're always headed in the right direction. In this way, the north star doesn't just guide your daily choices—it serves as a constant reminder of who you are and what you stand for, no matter where life takes you.

Besides developing ourselves personally, we also need to bolster our professional knowledge in our tradecraft by being always on top of the latest developments in AI & Technology.

WISDOM ON AI AND TECHNOLOGY

WISDOM ON AI AND TECHNOLOGY

AI and technology are rapidly transforming industries, and product marketers must understand how to leverage these innovations to stay competitive. While academic theories provide foundational knowledge, real-world insights from professionals reveal the practical applications, challenges, and strategies that make AI and technology truly impactful.

Experienced professionals share their journeys of integrating AI into their workflows, providing real-world examples of how these technologies improve efficiency and drive innovation. For instance, a product marketer might explain how they used AI-driven analytics to refine customer segmentation or enhance personalization strategies. These insights help clarify how to select the right tools, adapt to new technology, and measure its effectiveness.

Professionals also discuss how technology is reshaping product marketing practices. They might share how automation has streamlined repetitive tasks, freeing up time for strategic initiatives, or how data visualization tools have made complex metrics easier to interpret and act upon.

By learning from these experts, through case studies or mentorship, marketers gain a deeper understanding of how to embrace AI and technology as part of their toolkit. Real-world insights allow professionals to avoid common pitfalls, adapt quickly, and implement technology solutions that drive growth and efficiency in their product marketing strategies.

In the ensuing sections, we explore the perspectives of emerging talents and industry leaders to better grasp these concepts from a practical standpoint.

Akshita Kanumury (Dubai, UAE)

Bio

Akshita Kanumury is a global Top 100 Product Marketing Influencer and is part of Business World India's Marketing 30u30. She has 8+ years of marketing experience spanning across industries and is currently leading marketing initiatives for education and culture at Expo City, Dubai, UAE. She has led several impactful product marketing initiatives, including product and feature messaging and positioning, customer and market intelligence, customer and sales enablement campaigns, and global product launches. Known for her strategic marketing acumen, Akshita has delivered several talks and led workshops and panels on marketing across forums like GrowthSchool, Dubai Tech Talks, and more. An MBA graduate from Xavier Institute of Management and a Six Sigma certified professional, Akshita demonstrates expertise in full-stack marketing across domains like marketing strategy, product marketing, analytics, and brand management. She strongly believes in paying it forward for the next generation of marketers and entrepreneurs and actively mentors on platforms like ADPList, Abu Dhabi SME Hub, and Interview Club to name a few.

Akshita Kanumury on Product Marketing in SaaS

In her interview with me, Akshita shares a crucial lesson that many product marketers overlook: the power of in-product communication. Akshita explains that while marketers often focus on external channels such as social media, email campaigns, webinars and internal tools like Slack for awareness and communication, one of the most valuable yet underutilized channels is the in-product channel.

She points out that customers log in to the product frequently, making it an ideal space for delivering important updates, new features, or product announcements. According to Akshita, this is not just effective but also very cost efficient as it would just require minimal developmental effort or can also be self-served with the help of in-product tools.

Akshita emphasizes that in-product communication can be particularly impactful in a product-led growth (PLG) environment, where the product itself plays a central role in user acquisition, retention, and expansion. By utilizing in-product channels, marketers can inform users about new features or upcoming launches, creating buzz and excitement in real-time. This direct engagement at the point of use can foster deeper connections with customers, enhance their product experience, and drive adoption and engagement without relying on external communication that might get lost in users' inboxes or on social media feeds.

Akshita suggests several practical ways to leverage the in-product channel. These include using pop-ups, banners, and tooltips, which can appear at key moments during product usage. Additionally, incorporating how-to videos, product walkthroughs, and tutorials can further enhance the in-product communication strategy, helping users easily understand and engage with new features. These methods not only inform users about updates but also guide them through the experience, enhancing overall satisfaction.

By making better use of in-product communication, marketers can achieve several goals: improving user engagement, driving feature adoption, and ultimately reducing churn. Akshita further quips that the in-product channel offers a unique opportunity to engage users without interrupting their workflow and avoiding external distractions. This level of seamless communication can be particularly valuable for SaaS companies and product-led growth businesses, where creating continuous value and keeping users informed is key to long-term success.

Akshita's key takeaway is clear: product marketers must think beyond traditional channels and harness the potential of in-product communication. By tapping into this underutilized channel, marketers can better connect with users, create stronger brand loyalty, and ultimately drive product success.

PRODUCT MARKETING WISDOM

Chandrakumar "CK" Pillai (Brussels, Belgium)

Bio

Chandrakumar "CK" Pillai is a distinguished AI and blockchain expert with over 20 years of experience in IT strategy, enterprise architecture, and consulting. As a former Global Top 10 Coder, CK combines deep technical knowledge with strategic vision, advising organizations on digital transformation and innovation. With a master's degree in computer science, an MBA from IE Business School, and certifications in TOGAF and Java, he has led impactful IT projects at the European Commission and global firms like IBM and Tata Consultancy. CK is also an influential writer and speaker, inspiring professionals through insights on AI, blockchain, and leadership. He also contributes as a board member and advisor to numerous technology-driven startups, driving innovation and growth.

CK Pillai on AI & Technology

In my interview with him, CK Pillai delves into the transformative role AI is playing in product marketing. CK emphasizes that while AI technologies have existed for some time, they were previously accessible only to tech giants like Meta, Google, and Netflix. However, the recent arrival of tools like ChatGPT has democratized AI, bringing sophisticated, accessible tools into the hands of product marketers everywhere. This accessibility now enables product marketers at all levels to leverage AI's advanced capabilities, reshaping the landscape of how products are positioned, targeted, and optimized.

CK outlines three main areas where AI can significantly enhance product marketing. The first area is personalization. Through AI, product marketers can analyze detailed data about user preferences, behaviors, and engagement patterns, allowing them to deliver highly personalized and relevant content. This technology enables the creation of customer experiences that respond to individual needs and preferences, thereby improving engagement and driving loyalty. By interpreting data on what users like and dislike, AI empowers product marketers to develop and evolve products based on real-time feedback, making customer alignment an achievable goal.

The second core function CK highlights is customer insights gathering. With AI, product marketers can pull vast amounts of information from various platforms, such as social media and review sites like Google and Trustpilot. AI tools can parse user-generated data across multiple languages, distilling customer opinions into actionable insights regardless of the source or language. This functionality makes it easier to spot trends, understand user sentiment, and gauge overall brand perception, which helps marketers to fine-tune messaging, enhance product appeal, and align with customer expectations. By using these insights effectively, product marketers can adapt their strategies to resonate with a broader, global audience.

Finally, CK introduces the role of predictive analytics in product marketing. With access to data from past and current customer behavior, product marketers can now use AI to predict future trends, identifying patterns that signal where demand may be heading. Predictive analytics enables marketers to anticipate market shifts, position their products strategically, and identify emerging opportunities before competitors. By building forecasts based on data-driven insights, product marketers can make informed decisions on product launches, market entries, and customer engagement tactics, adding precision to their GTM strategy.

CK's insights demonstrate AI is no longer just an innovation for tech giants; it is now an essential tool for every product marketer. By enabling deep personalization, real-time customer insight collection, and predictive analytics, AI supports more precise, agile, and customer-centered product marketing. Through the democratization of AI, marketers are equipped to create tailored, data-informed experiences that evolve with customer expectations, positioning AI as a game-changer for driving product-market fit and competitive advantage in today's fast-paced market landscape.

Dalit Heldenberg (Israel)

Bio

Dalit Heldenberg is a visionary AI product executive and entrepreneur with over eight years of experience building AI-based solutions. As the Founder of Elevate AI and a co-founder of LeadWith, she leverages her expertise to drive innovation in AI strategy and workforce productivity, while promoting gender diversity in tech. Previously, Dalit held key roles at leading tech companies, where she focused on high-impact AI and data-driven product strategies. A frequent speaker and mentor, she is committed to fostering the next generation of tech leaders, especially women, by providing practical skills and mentorship in Israel's tech landscape.

Dalit Heldenberg on AI & Technology

In her interview with me, Dalit Heldenberg shares her insights on how organizations can effectively adopt generative AI. Dalit outlines six critical steps that help businesses not only integrate AI but also create a culture where AI can thrive and deliver meaningful results.

First, Dalit emphasizes the importance of building a unified understanding of AI within the organization. She advises leaders not to assume that all employees are naturally familiar with AI or how it can be applied in their daily tasks. Instead, organizations should focus on creating a baseline level of AI knowledge for everyone, establishing clear standards that define how AI should be understood and implemented across teams. This foundational understanding ensures that employees are well-prepared to work with AI tools confidently and effectively.

Second, Dalit suggests appointing an AI ambassador. This role could be filled by someone within the organization or an external expert who advocates for AI adoption and seeks opportunities for the business to leverage AI capabilities. The AI ambassador champions AI initiatives, identifying areas where AI could add value, and ensuring these efforts align with the company's goals.

Third, Dalit underscores the need to invest in employee training. Developing generative AI skills among employees is essential, she explains, as it empowers them to work with AI tools and applications effectively. Dalit notes that without intentional training, employees may lack the expertise or confidence to use AI in a way that benefits the organization. Training should focus not only on the technical aspects of AI but also on fostering a culture of curiosity and comfort with these emerging tools.

Fourth, Dalit advocates for a culture of innovation. She encourages organizations to create spaces for experimentation, such as hackathons, where employees can explore new AI tools and ideas. This type of environment enables teams to actively learn, experiment, and discover creative ways to use AI, which can lead to new business opportunities and innovations.

Fifth, Dalit highlights the need for robust data infrastructure to support generative AI applications. She explains organizations must prioritize data quality and security, as strong infrastructure is fundamental for AI success. Without reliable data, AI tools are less effective, potentially leading to inaccurate insights and poor outcomes.

Finally, Dalit stresses the importance of establishing a clear AI strategy. Organizations should define their specific goals for AI and ensure they have a structured approach to AI integration. This strategy helps guide AI investments and keeps the focus on sustainable, long-term impact rather than viewing AI as a short-lived trend.

Through these six steps, Dalit illustrates how organizations can maximize the potential of generative AI, creating a thoughtful and strategic approach that leads to real, lasting benefits.

Emmanuel Umoh (Oshawa, ON, Canada)

Bio

Emmanuel Umoh empowers small businesses to scale with actionable strategies. A certified Financial Modeling & Valuation Analyst (FMVA) and LinkedIn Marketing Insider, Emmanuel leverages over five years of experience in project coordination, customer service, and business development. Currently serving as Business Development Manager at SMASH ICT, he drives SEO optimization and content strategies to enhance engagement and lead generation. As Co-Founder of Chimney Global, he fosters entrepreneurial success, and as a Northeastern University Global Ambassador, he promotes inclusive campus recreation. Emmanuel holds a B.Sc. in Economics and an MS in Project Management.

Emmanuel Umoh on AI & Technology

In his interview with me, Emmanuel Umoh shares profound insights on leveraging AI for innovation and product development in his interview with me. Emmanuel emphasizes a crucial perspective: while AI advances rapidly, the fundamental pain points of customers remain constant and continually evolve with changing contexts.

Emmanuel highlights that one of AI's greatest strengths lies in its ability to simplify and enhance the collection and analysis of data. Unlike a decade ago, when businesses relied heavily on surveys and manual methods, modern technology enables companies to gather and interpret vast amounts of data efficiently. AI tools can now refine customer preferences, identify unmet needs, and process daily feedback streams to inform product strategies. Emmanuel underscores that this data-driven approach not only accelerates product development but also ensures solutions align closely with customer expectations.

A key takeaway from Emmanuel's insight is the importance of observing competitors. He cites an example wherein understanding how others market to shared audiences can uncover actionable strategies. AI, in this context, acts as a catalyst for innovation, enabling companies to analyze competitor data, mine trends, and identify gaps in the market. For

Emmanuel, the message is coherent: AI isn't the enemy—it's a powerful ally when used effectively.

Emmanuel also shares a practical mindset for businesses grappling with AI integration. By focusing on core customer pain points and allowing AI to help solve these issues, companies can drive meaningful outcomes. Technology, he argues, is only as valuable as the problems it addresses. This pragmatic approach demystifies AI for product owners and innovators, urging them to see it as a tool to complement their efforts rather than a disruptive force to fear.

Emmanuel's advice resonates with a broader truth: while technological tools evolve, customer-centricity remains the cornerstone of successful product development. By staying attuned to customer pain points and harnessing AI's capabilities to address them, businesses can create products that not only meet but exceed customer expectations.

Emmanuel's advice serves as a powerful reminder: AI and other emerging technologies should serve as enablers, helping businesses solve age-old challenges in innovative ways. As Emmanuel demonstrates, understanding and applying AI thoughtfully can transform obstacles into opportunities, making it an invaluable resource for modern product marketing.

Luka Kankaras (Vienna, Austria)

Bio

Luka Kankaras is a Product Growth Lead at Storylane, with expertise in driving product-led growth (PLG) strategies. With experience spanning multiple countries, he has successfully helped companies scale by focusing on user activation, retention, and engagement. Luka has led significant growth at Storylane, expanding its customer base fivefold and tripling revenue. He has also worked as a Senior Product Growth Specialist at Usersnap, assisting SaaS companies with customer validation and product decisions. Passionate about fitness, Luka believes in a balanced approach to work and life, advocating for equal opportunities and celebrating diversity.

Luka Kankaras on AI & Technology

In his interview with me, Luka Kankaras shares his insights on leveraging AI and technology in marketing to drive user engagement through interactive demos. Luka highlights how these demos, structured as demo chapters, effectively educate users about new features while optimizing conversions. This chapter-based approach provides marketers with a scalable tool to bridge product awareness and action. Luka emphasizes that with the right technological setup, interactive demos can serve as a powerful, AI-supported touchpoint, helping companies drive meaningful interactions that naturally lead users toward conversion.

Luka begins by discussing a recent successful campaign where, just days after announcing a new feature, Storylane's interactive demo garnered over 500 views, with a notable 20% conversion rate that translated to dozens of sign-ups and 40 calls booked. This impressive response, according to Luka, is largely because of Storylane's strategic use of tech-driven, segmented demo chapters that allow each user to explore content at their own pace and according to their specific needs. AI plays an integral role in this process. For example, AI is used to add voiceovers and generate engaging content, making the demos more dynamic and personalized, and enhancing the overall flow and accessibility. This approach personalizes the experience, holding user attention longer and providing digestible information about individual features, which strengthens user interest and engagement.

Luka also stresses the importance of keeping the demo ungated—allowing unrestricted access without sign-ups or other barriers. This strategy, often risky in terms of competitor access, reflects a tech-forward, customer-centered philosophy, where delivering value trumps gatekeeping. By removing this friction, Luka ensures potential users can experience the core of the product's value instantly. Engagement patterns and feature popularity are monitored through built-in analytics. These insights are then leveraged by Luka's team to refine future demo experiences and target specific user needs even more effectively.

Another key piece of advice Luka offers is adding a call-to-action (CTA) button that is consistently visible throughout the demo experience. Using real-time tracking and data on user behavior, Storylane monitors the placement, engagement, and effectiveness of these CTAs. This allows the team to adjust CTA visibility for maximum conversion. Luka reveals that over 90% of clicks came from users interacting with the CTA within the demo, underscoring the importance of well-positioned, tech-driven prompts for user action.

Luka's approach demonstrates how AI and digital technology can transform the traditional product demo into a more engaging, effective tool. By structuring demos as chapters and integrating AI to enhance specific aspects like voiceovers, videos, and content generation, Luka empowers marketers to create experiences that are intuitive and impactful. These interactive demos not only introduce new features but also guide users seamlessly toward the next step, laying the groundwork for successful product launches and continuous user engagement.

Spyros Tsoukalas (Athens, Greece)

Bio

Spyros Tsoukalas is a No Code expert and founder with a passion for building MVPs and products quickly. He has a background in computer engineering and has transformed from a tech founder to a passionate No Coder. Spyros is currently a PhD student at Ionian University, researching the impact of low code/no code in early-stage product development. He also leads Technology without Borders, a social enterprise focusing on startups and no-code solutions. Spyros has extensive experience in business strategy, product management, and social entrepreneurship, having co-founded several ventures and led award-winning teams in AI and tech innovations.

Spyros Tsoukalas on AI & Technology

In my interview with him, Spyros Tsoukalas emphasizes the transformative potential of no-code and low-code technologies in today's fast-paced business environment. Speaking from his experience, Spyros sheds light on how these tools, combined with the advancements in AI, are reshaping software development, accelerating time-to-market, and driving innovation.

Spyros highlights that no-code and low-code platforms democratize software creation, making it accessible to individuals and businesses without deep technical expertise. Unlike traditional development processes that require extensive resources and time, these solutions enable the rapid creation of software—ranging from startup applications to internal corporate tools—in just days or weeks. This agility allows businesses to save money, test ideas quickly, and iterate based on user feedback, fostering a culture of experimentation and continuous improvement.

A key advantage Spyros discusses is the ability of no-code and low-code platforms to address resource constraints. Startups and organizations with limited budgets can now develop robust solutions without the heavy investment traditionally associated with software development. This accessibility empowers entrepreneurs and teams to focus on innovation and market differentiation, rather than getting bogged down by technical hurdles.

Spyros also touches on the role of AI in amplifying the capabilities of no-code and low-code tools. AI enhances automation, streamlines workflows, and offers predictive insights, making these platforms even more powerful. The fusion of no-code, low-code, and AI ensures businesses can stay competitive in an ever-evolving technological landscape.

Moreover, Spyros underscores the need for professionals to explore and understand the potential of these technologies. Despite their growing popularity, many businesses and individuals remain unaware of the efficiencies and opportunities they offer. By embracing no-code and low-code platforms, professionals can bridge skill gaps, accelerate digital transformation, and unlock new avenues for growth and scalability.

In summary, Spyros's insights illuminate a paradigm shift in how software is developed and deployed. No-code and low-code solutions, complemented by AI advancements, empower businesses to innovate faster, operate more efficiently, and respond to market demands with unprecedented agility. His message is clear: the future of software development lies in leveraging these tools to reduce complexity, maximize resources, and create smarter, more adaptive solutions.

Spyros's advice serves as a rallying cry for businesses and professionals to embrace the possibilities of no-code, low-code, and AI—ushering in a new era of innovation that redefines what's possible in the world of technology.

Now that we have covered the many essential skills critical to Product Marketing, it is important to take a step back and look up at the horizon and consider the future of Product Marketing.

THE FUTURE OF PRODUCT MARKETING

THE FUTURE OF PRODUCT MARKETING

As we look into our crystal ball, below are some themes that lie ahead for the ever-evolving field of Product Marketing. From AI and automation to customer-centric marketing to cross functional collaboration to data-driven decision making to sustainability and fractional marketing - the best is yet to come.

AI and Automation in Product Marketing

Artificial Intelligence (AI) and automation are transforming product marketing, enabling marketers to work more efficiently, make smarter decisions, and deliver highly personalized experiences at scale. These technologies are reshaping how product marketers strategize, execute, and measure campaigns, offering new opportunities for targeted, data-driven approaches.

Personalization at Scale

AI enables marketers to create personalized experiences by analyzing vast amounts of customer data, such as behavior, preferences, and purchase history. Machine learning algorithms can segment audiences, allowing marketers to craft tailored messaging and product recommendations.

Automation amplifies this by ensuring that personalized content is delivered to the right customer, at the right time, across the right channel, without manual intervention. This streamlined approach enhances customer engagement and satisfaction while driving higher conversion rates.

Predictive Analytics for Smarter Decisions

AI's power in predictive analytics allows product marketers to forecast customer behavior and market trends. By analyzing historical data, AI algorithms help identify potential customer churn, optimal pricing strategies, and ideal product launch timing. Marketers can use these insights to adjust campaigns, prioritize customer retention efforts, and make smarter decisions about market expansion.

For example, AI can pinpoint early signs of churn, allowing marketers to intervene with targeted retention efforts, or it can predict which customer segments are likely to respond best to a new product.

Automating Routine Tasks

Automation reduces the burden of repetitive tasks like scheduling social media posts, generating reports, and crafting basic content such as email copy. AI tools can even assist with natural language generation (NLG) to create blog posts or articles.

Additionally, chatbots powered by AI can handle customer inquiries and gather real-time feedback, enhancing the customer experience. By automating these routine tasks, marketers are free to focus on higher-level strategic and creative initiatives, driving more value for the business.

Continuous Optimization

AI-driven tools enable continuous campaign optimization. Marketers can monitor real-time performance and adjust on the fly, improving targeting, messaging, and ad spend. AI can also analyze A/B tests and key metrics to provide insights into what works best.

In Sum

As AI and automation continue to evolve, product marketing will increasingly become a strategic, data-driven discipline. These technologies will allow marketers to engage customers more effectively, optimize campaigns continuously, and make smarter decisions, all while reducing manual workload. Product marketers who embrace AI and automation will be better equipped to thrive in a rapidly changing landscape.

BY NITIN KARTIK

The Shift to Customer-Centric Marketing

The shift to customer-centric marketing marks a fundamental change in how brands approach their audience. Unlike traditional marketing, which often centers on the product, customer-centric marketing prioritizes the customer's needs, desires, and experiences. This approach focuses on building lasting relationships by creating personalized, relevant, and engaging experiences at every stage of the customer journey.

Understanding the Customer Journey

A customer-centric strategy requires a deep understanding of the entire customer journey. Unlike the linear paths of the past, today's customers interact with brands across various touchpoints and channels, both online and offline. Product marketers must adapt by creating seamless, integrated experiences that span these touchpoints. This involves understanding the specific needs and behaviors of customers at each stage, from awareness to post-purchase loyalty, and delivering tailored messaging and engagement at every step.

Hyper-Personalization and Data-Driven Insights

Central to customer-centric marketing is hyper-personalization. With vast amounts of customer data available, marketers can now tailor messaging, content, and offers based on individual preferences and behaviors. By leveraging AI and machine learning, marketers can analyze this data to predict customer needs and deliver highly personalized experiences.

For instance, personalized product recommendations on e-commerce sites are powered by AI algorithms that predict what customers are likely to purchase based on past behavior. Similarly, email marketing campaigns are no longer one-size-fits-all but are dynamically generated to suit each customer's interactions with the brand, increasing engagement and conversion rates.

Building Trust and Loyalty

Customer-centric marketing also emphasizes building trust. Customers expect brands to be transparent, authentic, and reliable in their communications. To foster trust and loyalty, marketers must listen to their customers and respond to feedback in real-time. Engaging with customers through surveys, social media, and personalized outreach helps create a sense of connection and loyalty. Customers who feel understood and valued are more likely to remain loyal and advocate for the brand, leading to increased retention and lifetime value.

The Role of Customer Feedback

Customer feedback is crucial in refining customer-centric strategies. Product marketers must actively gather and use feedback to improve products, adjust marketing tactics, and enhance the overall experience. Tools like surveys, social listening, and customer satisfaction metrics provide valuable insights that guide decision-making and ensure continuous optimization of marketing efforts.

In Sum

The shift to customer-centric marketing is essential for brands aiming to thrive in today's competitive landscape. By focusing on the customer's needs and creating personalized experiences, product marketers can build stronger, more loyal relationships, ensuring long-term success.

BY NITIN KARTIK

Cross-Functional Collaboration in a Hybrid Workforce

Hybrid work environments, where teams operate both remotely and in-office, have become a standard in modern workplaces. For product marketing teams, which rely heavily on cross-functional collaboration with departments like product management, sales, engineering, and customer success, this shift presents unique challenges and opportunities. Adapting to this new normal requires a strategic approach to communication, alignment, and teamwork to ensure productivity and cohesion across locations.

The Role of Cross-Functional Collaboration

In product marketing, cross-functional collaboration is essential for aligning teams around shared goals, crafting comprehensive strategies, and executing successful product launches. Hybrid work introduces complexities, such as time-zone differences and reduced face-to-face interaction, that can hinder collaboration if not addressed proactively. However, with intentional planning and clear communication, teams can maintain alignment and ensure seamless execution.

Leveraging Technology for Collaboration

Technology is the backbone of effective collaboration in a hybrid environment. Communication tools like Slack, Microsoft Teams, and Zoom facilitate real-time conversations, while document-sharing platforms like Google Drive and Confluence centralize resources for easy access. Project management tools such as Asana, Monday.com, or Trello enhance transparency by tracking progress, deadlines, and responsibilities, ensuring everyone remains aligned with key objectives.

These tools bridge physical and digital divides, fostering real-time coordination and accountability across dispersed teams. To maximize their impact, organizations should establish consistent usage guidelines and ensure all team members are proficient in their operation.

Cultivating a Collaborative Culture

Tools alone aren't enough; fostering a culture of collaboration is critical in hybrid work. Regular check-ins, virtual meetings, and collaborative workshops help strengthen relationships and maintain open communication, ensuring remote workers feel as integrated as their in-office counterparts.

Clear roles and responsibilities are crucial to prevent confusion. Setting expectations upfront and ensuring mutual understanding of each team's contributions fosters trust and avoids miscommunication. Encouraging a feedback-friendly environment further supports collaboration by keeping lines of communication open and improving processes over time.

Overcoming Challenges

Hybrid work can create feelings of isolation for remote workers. Leaders must actively promote inclusivity through regular virtual face-to-face interactions, team-building activities, and transparent decision-making processes. Recognizing and addressing these challenges helps maintain engagement and morale across the team.

In Sum

Cross-functional collaboration in a hybrid workforce depends on a mix of technology, culture, and clear communication. By embracing these elements, product marketing teams can overcome challenges, maintain alignment, and drive impactful results. Organizations that gain expertise in hybrid collaboration will build more agile and cohesive teams, ensuring long-term success.

BY NITIN KARTIK

The Future of Data-Driven Decision Making

Data-driven decision-making and market intelligence are at the forefront of the future of product marketing, revolutionizing how teams develop strategies, create campaigns, and measure success. As technology advances, product marketers have access to an ever-growing volume of data and sophisticated tools to extract actionable insights. Leveraging this information will enable more informed, agile, and impactful marketing strategies.

Real-Time Data and Predictive Analytics

The future of data-driven decision-making lies in real-time analytics and predictive modeling. Marketers are no longer confined to historical data; instead, they can harness live metrics to make agile decisions. Tools powered by Artificial Intelligence (AI) and machine learning analyze customer behavior, market trends, and competitor actions as they unfold, enabling marketers to respond quickly to opportunities or threats.

Predictive analytics will become even more critical, helping marketers forecast customer needs, market demands, and revenue outcomes. For instance, AI algorithms can predict customer churn, enabling targeted retention strategies, or anticipate the success of a new product in specific market segments.

Hyper-Localized Market Intelligence

Market intelligence is evolving to become hyper-localized, enabling product marketers to adapt strategies based on regional and demographic nuances. Tools that integrate location-specific data, social sentiment analysis, and competitive benchmarks will empower marketers to tailor their campaigns with precision. This level of granularity helps brands resonate deeply with target audiences and gain competitive advantage in diverse markets.

For example, a global product launch might include region-specific messaging informed by localized market intelligence, increasing relevance and impact.

Democratization of Insights

Advancements in data visualization and accessibility will democratize insights across organizations. Self-service analytics tools, such as Tableau or Looker, allow cross-functional teams to interact with data without requiring technical expertise. This democratization ensures that insights are not siloed within specialized departments, but are available to everyone involved in product strategy, fostering greater alignment and collaboration.

Balancing Automation with Human Expertise

While automated tools are becoming indispensable, the future of market intelligence will depend on the balance between machine-driven insights and human intuition. Machines excel at processing vast amounts of data, but human marketers bring contextual understanding, creativity, and strategic foresight. This synergy will be critical in translating raw data into meaningful, actionable strategies.

In Sum

The future of product marketing lies in leveraging advanced data-driven decision-making and market intelligence. With real-time analytics, predictive modeling, and hyper-local insights, marketers can craft strategies that are precise, agile, and impactful. By combining automation with human expertise, organizations will unlock the full potential of data, driving innovation and maintaining a competitive edge in an increasingly dynamic market.

BY NITIN KARTIK

The Future of Sustainability and Ethical Marketing

Sustainability and ethical marketing are becoming essential pillars in the future of product marketing, driven by consumer demand, regulatory pressures, and corporate responsibility. Today's customers increasingly expect brands to address environmental and social challenges while maintaining transparency and integrity. As a result, product marketers must adapt their strategies to prioritize sustainable practices and ethical messaging, ensuring alignment with these values while driving business success.

Embedding Sustainability in Product Marketing

Sustainability is no longer an optional add-on; it is a key factor in decision-making for consumers and businesses alike. Product marketers of the future will need to integrate sustainable practices throughout the product lifecycle, from design and development to packaging and distribution. Highlighting these efforts in marketing campaigns is not only an opportunity to differentiate products but also a way to build trust and loyalty with environmentally conscious customers.

For example, communicating a product's reduced carbon footprint or recyclable packaging can resonate with eco-minded consumers. Companies that transparently share their sustainability journey, including successes and areas for improvement, are more likely to earn credibility and respect in the marketplace.

The Rise of Ethical Marketing

Ethical marketing extends beyond sustainability to encompass fairness, inclusivity, and honesty in branding and messaging. Customers are increasingly scrutinizing how brands represent diversity, treat employees, and source materials. In response, product marketers must ensure campaigns are inclusive and free from misleading claims, such as greenwashing, which can damage reputation and erode trust.

Marketers will also need to collaborate with cross-functional teams to verify that the brand's ethical commitments are upheld across all touchpoints. This includes ensuring supply chains adhere to fair labor practices and product ingredients are responsibly sourced. Such efforts go a long way in fostering brand authenticity and long-term customer loyalty.

Leveraging Technology for Transparency

The future of sustainability and ethical marketing will rely heavily on technology to enhance transparency. Blockchain, for example, is emerging as a tool to verify the origin and sustainability of raw materials. Digital tools that calculate and showcase environmental impact metrics can provide customers with clear, factual insights into a product's eco-friendliness.

In Sum

The future of product marketing demands a commitment to sustainability and ethical practices as core components of business strategy. By embedding sustainable principles, practicing transparency, and embracing technology, marketers can align with evolving consumer values, foster trust, and create a meaningful impact. Brands that champion these efforts will not only differentiate themselves in a competitive market but also contribute to a more sustainable and equitable future.

BY NITIN KARTIK

The Future is Fractional

Fractional product marketing is emerging as a significant trend, offering businesses a flexible, cost-effective way to access senior-level marketing expertise without committing to a full-time hire. As companies navigate rapid market changes, the rise of startups, and budget-conscious strategies, fractional product marketers are becoming an integral part of the modern workforce, shaping the future of product marketing.

What Is Fractional Product Marketing?

Fractional product marketing involves hiring experienced marketing professionals on a part-time or project-based basis. These fractional marketers bring deep expertise, often gained through years of leadership roles, to organizations that need strategic guidance but may not require—or cannot afford—a full-time director or VP of product marketing.

This model is particularly beneficial for startups and small to mid-sized businesses, which often face budget constraints but still require a seasoned professional to lead critical initiatives like product launches, go-to-market strategies, and customer segmentation.

Why Is It on the Rise?

Several factors are driving the rise of fractional product marketing:

- **Economic Uncertainty**: Many companies are seeking to maximize efficiency by focusing on flexible talent acquisition. Fractional marketers provide expert-level services without long-term employment commitments, reducing overhead costs.

- **Access to Specialized Skills**: Fractional marketers often have diverse industry experience, offering specialized skills and insights that can be difficult to find in a single full-time hire.

- **Remote Work Revolution**: The normalization of remote work has broadened access to talent pools globally. Fractional marketers can seamlessly collaborate with companies regardless of geographic location, making this model more viable than ever.

- **Speed and Agility**: Businesses operating in fast-paced markets benefit from fractional marketers' ability to quickly step in, contribute value, and drive results without lengthy onboarding processes.

The Impact on Product Marketing

Fractional marketers are redefining traditional product marketing roles. Their adaptability allows businesses to scale marketing efforts up or down based on demand, whether it's leading a product launch, conducting competitive analysis, or refining messaging for new audiences. Fractional product marketers also serve as mentors, upskilling junior team members and enhancing organizational capabilities long after their tenure.

Challenges and Opportunities

While fractional product marketing offers flexibility, companies must handpick professionals who align with their goals and culture. Clear communication and well-defined objectives are essential for achieving success in this model.

In Sum

As the workforce becomes more dynamic, fractional product marketing is set to play a larger role in shaping business strategies. Offering expertise, adaptability, and cost-effectiveness, it represents a forward-thinking solution for organizations striving to remain competitive in today's evolving market landscape.

BY NITIN KARTIK

The Best is Yet to Come

The future of product marketing is filled with boundless opportunities. As technology continues to advance, markets evolve, and businesses increasingly prioritize customer-centric strategies, product marketers have a wealth of tools and insights at their disposal to drive growth and innovation. The power of data, digital transformation, and deep customer understanding has never been more impactful, providing product marketers with new ways to reach and engage their audiences. For those who embrace these changes, the potential for creating transformative, value-driven marketing is limitless.

However, the landscape is not without its challenges. The rise of AI and automation, while offering efficiencies, also raises concerns about job displacement across various sectors, including product marketing. As these technologies evolve, it is crucial for product marketers to adapt by continuously investing in their professional development. Learning new tools, staying abreast of emerging trends, and enhancing strategic thinking will be essential in navigating these shifts.

Despite these obstacles, the essence of product marketing—delivering value through understanding customers, crafting impactful stories, and creating meaningful experiences—remains unchanged. The future is filled with promise for those who stay agile, open to learning, and proactive in building their skills. By embracing change and continuing to evolve, product marketers can not only weather potential disruptions but also thrive and lead the way in shaping the future of business. The journey ahead is one of growth, resilience, and exciting possibilities. The best is yet to come.

ACKNOWLEDGEMENTS

ACKNOWLEDGEMENTS

This book would not have been possible without the support and inspiration of a great many people, all of whom I would like to express my sincere gratitude for. While the entire list is too long to mention herein, I would like to especially thank the following.

My Parents

For teaching me to erase the word "impossible" from my dictionary.

My Wife Kirtana

For being my pillar of unconditional support through thick and thin.

My Daughter Tara

For helping me realize the transformational power of faith.

My Son Akaash

For always reminding me that all work and no play makes Jack a dull boy.

My Colleagues, Past and Present

For challenging me to become a better version of myself.

My Professional Network

For your encouragement, support, advice, and so much more—you are the wind beneath my wings!

*"Do not wait to strike till the iron is hot;
but make it hot by striking."*
– William Butler Yeats